This informative book provides a detailed account and analysis of the absolute and highly effective control exercised by Hastings Kamuzu Banda over the political, economic, and judicial life of the people of Malawi. The author portrays President Banda as an autocrat, a ruthless man of considerable guile, courage, and political acumen.

T. David Williams explains the background of Dr. Banda's rise to power, illustrating both the similarities and the differences between the policies and performance of the colonial regime and of the independent government. He shows how the protracted struggle over the British attempt to force Nyasaland into the Central African Federation brought otherwise disparate groups together in an effective unified movement and provided the basis of party discipline which Banda subsequently used to prevent discussion of controversial issues. Offering a careful appraisal of Malawi's economic performance since Independence, he explains the factors that have contributed to a high rate of growth since the end of World War II. Finally he examines the relationship between domestic political strategy, economic constraints, and Dr. Banda's "special" foreign policy, and he speculates on the future of Malawi.

Timely and comprehensive, *Malawi: The Politics of Despair* will be of particular value to Africanists, political scientists, development economists, and those concerned with United States and British policy toward Africa.

AFRICA IN THE MODERN WORLD

Edited by GWENDOLEN M. CARTER
Indiana University, Bloomington

The Cameroon Federal Republic
by Victor T. Le Vine

Dahomey: Between Tradition and Modernity
By Dov Ronen

Ethiopia: The Modernization of Autocracy
by Robert L. Hess

Guinea. The Mobilization of a People
*By Claude Rivière; translated by
Virginia Thompson and Richard Adloff*

Liberia: The Evolution of Privilege
by J. Gus Liebenow

Malawi: The Politics of Despair
by T. David Williams

Rhodesia: Racial Conflict or Coexistence?
by Patrick O'Meara

West Africa's Council of the Entente
by Virginia Thompson

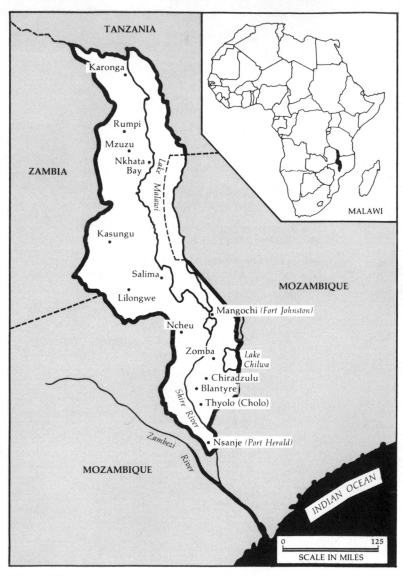

MALAWI

MALAWI

The Politics of Despair

T. DAVID WILLIAMS

Cornell University Press

ITHACA AND LONDON

First published 1978 by Cornell University Press.
Published in the United Kingdom by Cornell University Press Ltd., 2–4 Brook Street, London W1Y 1AA.

International Standard Book Number 0-8014-1149-1
Library of Congress Catalog Card Number 77-90915
Printed in the United States of America
Librarians: Library of Congress cataloging information appears on the last page of the book.

Foreword

President Kamuzu Banda is the maverick among African heads of state. Alone among the African-controlled states in the international subsystem of southern Africa, Malawi under his direction has established formal diplomatic relations with the Republic of South Africa. When other sources of international financing proved unwilling to underwrite the costs of building Lilongwe, a new capital in the center of Malawi where Dr. Banda's own ethnic group is paramount, he willingly accepted South African financing (though on a strictly business basis) and construction. Economic ties then forged have been continued.

Nonetheless, President Banda has also pointedly demonstrated his independence from the white minority regimes of southern Africa. In 1972, Malawi voted at the Organization of African Unity Liberation Committee meeting in Dar es Salaam in support of free transit for men and material to battle zones in contested areas in southern Africa. Although no formal arrangements were ever published, he later permitted unarmed troops of the Front for the Liberation of Mozambique to traverse Malawian territory at a time when such mobility aided their struggle with the Portuguese.

A still more striking evidence of President Banda's independence of action in relation to South Africa, as well as of his absolute control within his own country, was his abrupt ending of the flow of Malawian workers to the Witwatersrand mines after a tragic crash of the recruiting company's plane killed miners returning home at the end of their period of service. Until that point, Malawi had sent a substantial proportion of its labor force to work in the South African gold mines, where their services were greatly prized. Moreover, their remittances had provided a significant source of foreign exchange for the Malawian economy. That Dr. Banda long continued to resist the mineowners' efforts to restore the flow of Malawian labor is even less remarkable than his ability to force the absorption of so many additional males into the subsistence-level Malawian economy.

When Dr. Banda was invited back to his native Nyasaland by the vigorous and imaginative young leaders who were planning to remold an independent Malawi, these men envisaged him as a father figure whose distinguished medical record in Great Britain and abroad would provide an aura of dignity and stability that would underpin their policies. To their chagrin and ultimate disaster, President Banda had no such view of his role. When he spoke of the young leaders as his "children," he meant, indeed, that they were to be subject to his will. When they finally resisted with force, he crushed them.

Malawi's policies since independence—both the repressive measures that have led to much outside criticism and the constructive ones that have resulted in a surprising degree of prosperity within this essentially poor country—have been of his making. Tough minded, arbitrary over even such details as women's dress, decreeing instant expulsion for any foreigner openly critical of his actions, and imprisoning fellow Malawians who he believes, often on very slender evidence, are plotting against him, President Banda is an autocrat who has preserved some of the forms but not the reality of democratic procedures. It is often difficult to discern the rationale of his policies, and he has been known suddenly to change a recently imposed policy. But his hospitality to international finance and multinationals and his protection of their interests, which proved not infrequently to parallel his own and those of his close associates, have provided Malawi with a good credit rating that maintains the inward flow of foreign capital.

What cannot be denied is that Malawi has developed economically to a greater degree than outsiders ever expected. Part of the reason that levels of production rose impressively after independence lies in the fact that the country was just emerging from the exceptionally low levels of a prolonged depression. Partly, good results have come because Dr. Banda, unlike other African leaders, insisted that his country concentrate on agricultural production. Malawi is far from having the character and policies those young leaders of preindependence days would have chosen, but it may be developing a sound enough base to maintain the distinctive—some would say idiosyncratic—international path President Banda has adopted. He still maintains more harmonious relations with white-minority-ruled South Africa, and even with Rhodesia, than with his immediate neighbors, Tanzania and Zambia, and yet also has passable, if not cordial, relations with their leaders. As tensions rise in southern Africa, Dr. Banda continues to hold Malawi aloof from formal commitments to either side. It remains to be seen how long he can continue to do so, and at what price.

GWENDOLEN M. CARTER

Bloomington, Indiana

Contents

Acknowledgments

In 1966 and 1967 I was living in Malawi, working as a lecturer at its university. I had the good fortune to listen to a great many Malawians, in all walks of life—including a number who were political activists—explain their views on the past, present, and future of their country. It was an instructive experience. Many of them were academically unsophisticated, but they had a clear eye for the realities of a situation and, in the company of friends, could face the implications of that situation with honesty, intelligence, and humor. Many of them would, no doubt, disagree with my interpretation of some of the incidents I describe in this book, but I hope they will not feel that I have completely misjudged their nature.

Some of my colleagues at the University of Malawi, without necessarily sharing my views, helped me a great deal by suggesting answers to some questions that had baffled me and by encouraging me to clarify my own ideas. I am particularly indebted to Leslie Corina, and scarcely less so to Nicholas Wincott and Daniel Anderson. Since leaving Malawi for Edinburgh, I have had discussions with a number of people who have been good enough to give me the benefit of their opinions or knowledge about various matters related to my work. I did not always follow the advice I was given, but I am nonetheless most grateful to the Reverend Andrew Ross and Henry Ord (of the University of Edinburgh), Paul Mosley (University of Bath), and Roger Sandilands and Douglas McAllister (University of Strathclyde).

My greatest debt is to Professor Gwendolen Carter, who has been unfailingly generous in encouragement, advice, and comment. An anonymous reader commented on an earlier draft in great detail, with imagination, knowledge, and sympathy. Both Professor Carter and the reader have done a great deal to improve the book, but I did not always follow their suggestions, and the errors and eccentricities that remain are entirely my own responsibility.

Finally, I am most grateful to Alexandra Glogowska and Jane Morrison for the highly efficient way in which they not only typed the manuscript speedily and carefully but brought a number of inconsistencies and inaccuracies to my notice.

T. DAVID WILLIAMS

Edinburgh, Scotland

MALAWI
The Politics of Despair

Introduction

For almost two decades the political life of Malawi has been dominated by the habitually formidable and sometimes sinister personality of Dr. Hastings Kamuzu Banda. When he returned to his homeland on the sixth of July 1958, after more than forty years' absence, the adulation with which he was treated by his countrymen reflected to no small extent the success of a group of dynamic young militants who had played a decisive role in transforming the nationalist party into an effective mass movement, and who had set out, quite deliberately, to present Dr. Banda to the people of Nyasaland as a man of suprahuman qualities, come to lead them out of bondage.

He was then nearing sixty; he had achieved a very considerable degree of professional success and had been actively involved in politics in his spare time, but he had never been a full-time politician, had never depended on politics for his livelihood, and had never borne major responsibility for the organization of a mass campaign. He was encouraged to return to Nyasaland and the way made smooth for him by men who knew that, in spite of their evident capacity to inspire, and even to organize, their countrymen in the ranks of the nationalist movement, it was not yet possible for them to win the wholehearted allegiance of a society still deeply imbued with respect for the wisdom of its elders; they had every reason to expect that Dr. Banda, about whom they knew very little, would serve admirably as a national figurehead during the decisive stages of the struggle for independence and then accept an honorable retirement, leaving younger men, already experienced and astute politicians with an intimate knowledge of Nyasaland politics, to deal with the tedious chores of organizing the new state.

If they did, indeed, believe this, they were to find themselves profoundly mistaken.

Dr. Banda was to prove, in his sixties, an apt student of techniques of political manipulation. Subtle, ruthless, and determined, he was to establish effective control over party organization before independence was achieved, and within a few months after it had been achieved he came into head-on conflict with the same young men who had engineered his return to the country and who were, by this time, the only potential leaders, apart from himself, to have any real base of political support in the country. They were outmaneuvered and outfought; routed, they fled the country. Dr. Banda was left in unrivaled command of parliament and party, with virtually no one holding any position of seniority anywhere in the country which was not owed directly to his patronage; it was soon clear that there were few, if any, limits to his voracious appetite for power. His object was to exercise precise and comprehensive control over the entire political, judicial, and economic life of the nation and its people; in their scale and scope, the legislative measures directed to this end have so matched the president's ambition that the only limits to his power appear to be those imposed by the increasingly feeble state of his physical constitution.

Government policy in Malawi cannot be explained simply by reference to Dr. Banda's idiosyncratic personality, although there are few countries in which there is greater opportunity for a strong man to determine not only the answers that people will be given but the questions they ask—at least in public. There does, however, appear to have been enough public acceptance of many of Dr. Banda's policies to indicate that he has been accorded, if not the active support of, at least tacit acceptance by, a substantial part of the population. The roots of this acceptance lie as much in the historical experience of the people as in the character of the president.

The traditions of Malawi contain few folk memories, far less authentic records, of sustained resistance to invading forces or of the subjugation of neighboring tribes, save among those, like the Ngoni, who invaded Malawi itself in the nineteenth century, scoring their most clearly demonstrable successes against the traditional inhabitants of the country and themselves losing their power, very shortly afterward, to the colonial power that had finally taken a reluctant decision to take charge of the country. With little recollection of martial achievement or of the sagacity of traditional leaders, the traditions are predominantly those of adaptation to a harsh environment and accommodation, sometimes remarkably successful, to the threat imposed by more powerful intruders.

The Maravi (or Malawi) Empire, of which the Chewa were a part, was a very loosely organized society that covered a great expanse of territory. Both the rights and responsibilities of leadership rested on the joint perceptions of mutual advantage held by the leaders and the led rather than on effective central control of monopoly power; the Chikulamayembe dynasty of the Timbuka was established by adventurous outsiders whose principal merit was that they had a more astute sense of trading opportunities than had the great majority of the people in the lands to which they migrated The Chewa and the Timbuka displayed some admirable characteristics, but neither was able, with the exception of a handful of chieftains, to offer any effective resistance against the onslaught to which they were subjected during the nineteenth century.

The simplicity of traditional social and political systems in Malawi, the lack of sophisticated and extended ties of loyalty and obligation, made it more difficult for the people to resist the challenge imposed either by intruders or by determined men or women within the system, but it may have helped them adapt to new rulers and survive under a new system. The Ngoni and the Yao, although more warlike or better armed than the forces they met when they entered Malawi in the nineteenth century, were themselves organized in small units much given to fragmentation. The sense of identity of the Malawi people and of its major subgroups is derived less from common traditional allegiance or from the obligations imposed by a socially cohesive society than from the shared experience of oppression at the hands of a common enemy. Unity has rarely been a spontaneous process but has more frequently been a response to the folly and greed of oppressors.

The impetus to both centralization and modernization was very much stronger during the colonial period than it had been

previously, which is not to say that no significant changes would
have taken place if colonization had not occurred. Insofar as
Malawians hold a strong conviction of national identity, they
have derived it to a large extent from a sense of united purpose
in dealing with the colonial authorities and, more particularly,
from their widespread and deeply felt opposition to the Central African Federation, of which, in spite of their strongly
expressed views, they were forced to become a part. The experiment with federation was the single most powerful stimulus
to the emergence of an effective, broadly based nationalist
movement in Malawi. The experience of what was felt to be
betrayal by the British government of its responsibilities to Malawian Africans was not without significance in shaping the way
that Dr. Banda and other Malawian leaders were subsequently
to think about politics, and the manner in which various British
governments sought to reconcile domestic political advantage
with pursuit of an ostensibly high-minded policy abroad serves
to illustrate the relatively weak bargaining position from which
Malawi operates in international politics.

The economic problems of colonial Malawi serve in like fashion to illustrate the severe limitations imposed on the rulers of
an impoverished landlocked country with few natural resources, but the response of many people in the country to the
very narrowly constrained options in both the economic and
political sphere shows the Malawians' ingenuity and dogged-
ness, together with their capacity to adapt themselves to an
entirely new environment.

The colonial authorities did not always appreciate the efforts
made by their critics to publicize dissenting views. A degree of
censorship was imposed from time to time, but critics were
allowed very much more latitude than was to be the case after
independence was gained in 1964. The authorities themselves
kept records, subsequently made available to the public, illustrating the often different and sometimes conflicting views of
various members of the colonial service. There are important
aspects of political and economic life during the colonial period
about which we know very little because they were matters
about which the authorities had little or no knowledge or interest or because these matters did not attract the attention of

those people outside the administration who committed their views to writing; we may exaggerate the significance of views held by the minority of relatively well-educated men in the political associations and independent churches simply because these men have left a record of their opinions while we have very little direct information about the attitudes of the great majority of the population, but there are many more sources of recorded information than were to become available in the postcolonial period, while the probing of folk memories of events during the colonial period was one of the few modes of political enquiry permitted to research workers during the mid and later 1960s.

Analysis of events during the 1960s and 1970s poses formidable problems. Dr. Banda has maintained a very tight control over both parliament and the party; it has always been clear that where the press was not run directly by the party it was obliged to exercise great discretion in its treatment of news, and powerful informal control has in recent years been supplemented by government decree. Casual rumor, which was for long the only current source of information not self-evidently false, is an offense carrying harsh penalties.

The president has, however, been given to the most remarkably candid exposition of his own behavior, delivered at length to a sycophantic audience. He has, on a number of occasions, explained how and why he outwitted his opponents (including men and women who were at the time elected and widely supported members of the Assembly and senior officials of the party) even though his explanation has made clear that he had previously misled the Assembly; he has not merely justified, but exulted in, policies that can only be explained by reference to problems no one save the president could acknowledge without the most direct threat to the security of themselves and their families. The speeches of Dr. Banda himself were, for many years, a most valuable source, if interpreted with some skepticism, about what was happening in Malawi.

From the early 1970s, however, the president's monologues became less informative. At the very time when penalties were becoming increasingly harsh—carrying life imprisonment for passing "false" information, with the president deciding what was "false"—Dr. Banda himself, for whatever reason, became increasingly immersed in his recollections of what had happened during the brave days of his opposition to Federation.

In the last few years, there has been little detailed information about what is going on in Malawi and virtually no opportunity to question what one does hear. Almost the only thing of which we can be sure is that the people of the country have had need of their capacity for resilience in the most difficult of circumstances.

CHAPTER 1

The Seeds of Change

The boundaries of contemporary Malawi owe less to the influence of ancient tribal loyalties than to the largely fortuitous establishment of British, and especially Scottish, missionaries along the Shire River and the shores of Lake Malawi in the latter half of the nineteenth century.[1] The new nations of Africa often emerge with a geographical shape and ethnic composition that has been profoundly affected by the convenience or interests of a colonizing power, but seldom has the balance of power among tribal groups been as fluid at the time of colonial expansion as it was in Malawi during the second half of the nineteenth century. Whether in spite of this or because of it, the borders of present-day Malawi follow, to a very considerable extent, natural geographic lines dividing it from neighboring countries.

The Western boundary was effectively decided in 1884 as a by-product of the attempt by European powers to define the Congo basin in order to facilitate the determination of agreed spheres of influence. It follows the watershed between the Shire and Zambezi rivers in the south and the watershed between the Zambezi and Congo river systems farther north. The eastern boundary follows the shore line of the great Lake Ma-

1. Dr. Livingstone set out in 1858 on a well-publicized enterprise intended to demonstrate the navigability of the Zambezi and to establish that the Batoka plateau was suitable for white settlement. When he found the way was barred by the Kebrebasa rapids, he sought to salvage the mission by retracing his steps along the Zambezi and moving northward along the Shire River and up to Lake Nyasa. Livingstone was anxious to find territory hospitable to European settlers and, according to Jeal, he had strong reasons for following a river rather than striking out overland. See Tim Jeal, *Livingstone* (New York: Laurel Edition, Dell, 1973), pp. 263–264.

lawi for some two-thirds of its length, extends southward around the fringe of Lake Chilwa and the Mlanje massif, and then along the Shire River, where it forms a narrow corridor thrusting toward the Zambezi.

Malawi is a slender elongated territory that lies in the southern part of the Great Rift Valley. The most accessible routes into the country have traditionally been along the natural divide of the Rift Valley in the north; along the Shire River in the south; across the Luangwa depression in the west and thence into the central plains of the country, and, from the east, across Lake Malawi or around its southern tip.

Both the depth and width of the Shire River, flowing southward from Lake Malawi to join the mighty Zambezi in its eastward passage to the Indian Ocean, have frequently been subject to considerable fluctuations. These have been due in large part to changes in the level of Lake Malawi and to the growth of sandbars around the outlet from the lake. The river level has had an important and sometimes crucial effect on the agricultural prosperity of the Lower Shire basin and for a brief period prospective European colonists were much concerned about whether, or how far, the river was negotiable by ocean-going steamers.[2]

The major lakes, several minor ones, and the rivers that run into or out of them make up a substantial proportion of the total area of Malawi. Together with great differences in altitude throughout the country they are largely responsible for the variety of climatic conditions and ecosystems. The general level of soil fertility is high, and the greater part of the land has enough rainfall for the successful cultivation of a wide range of crops,[3] but some areas face much more severe problems than the rest of the country.

2. See Jeal, p. 294, on Livingstone's reports about the navigability of the lake; John G. Pike comments on the causes and effects of variations in the lake level (*Malawi*, London: Pall Mall Press, 1968, pp. 11–14).
    3. John G. Pike and G. T. Rimmington, *Malawi: A Geographical Study*, (London: Oxford University Press, 1965), p. 17. Swanzie Agnew, "Environment and History: The Malawian Setting," in Bridglal Pachai, ed., *The Early History of Malawi* (London: Longman, 1972). Pike comments on the considerable variation in rainfall from year to year (pp. 16–17).

There is very good farming country in the Central Region, especially in the Lilongwe plains, while the Shire Highlands in the Southern Region, with a climate and altitude suitable for a number of valuable crops, has appeared most conducive to European settlement. The north, characterized by plateaus of rugged beauty but infertile soil and often inhospitable climate, could support only a relatively sparse population, and the low-lying valley of the Lower Shire promontory, though blessed with rich soil, has been so hot and humid that it has severely taxed the health and spirit of its inhabitants.[4]

The earliest race of men known to have occupied Malawi was a pre-Bantu people similar to the Bushmen of South West Africa and Botswana; hunters and food gatherers, these people were either destroyed or assimilated by other peoples moving into or through the country. They left few distinctive traces, their only memorial being a few wall paintings similar to those found at the Bushmen sites spread from the Congo to the Indian Ocean and from Tanzania to the Cape.[5]

By the second or third century after the birth of Christ, an iron-using people had moved into the country, migrating southward from the northern areas close to Lake Malawi.[6] About the ninth century another people, probably coming from around Lake Tanganyika, immigrated. Some of them later moved on toward the Zambezi, but those who settled in the country appear to have blended peacefully with the previous inhabitants, perhaps because population density was relatively sparse.[7]

Among the peoples now living in Malawi those who have the

4. Pike and Rimmington, pp. 64–66.
5. Bridglal Pachai, *Malawi: The History of the Nation* (London: Longman, 1973), p. 2.
6. P. V. Tobias, "The Men Who Came before Malawian History," in B. Pachai, ed., *Early History*, says that "evidence presents itself that Iron Age cultural traits were introduced into Malawi from about 2,000 years ago" (p. 10); J. D. Clark, "Prehistoric Origins," in the same book, writes that "the earliest cultivators who were also metal-workers, occupied the plateau and Rift about the middle of the second century A.D." (p. 25).
7. Clark says, "Only much later, from the sixteenth century onward, did competition for land and other resources lead to major conflict among the tribal populations of Ghana" (p. 25).

longest acknowledged history of residence are the Chewa.
There is some uncertainty about the time of their first appearance in the country and the manner of their coming, but they
probably arrived in present-day Malawi between the thirteenth
and fifteenth centuries, coming from an area around Katanga.
They were a part of the Maravi Empire, a very loosely structured association of people but, at its peak, widely extended,
covering an area ranging from the Congo basin to the Indian
Ocean.[8]

The principal Maravi migration was into the central plain
and the Shire Valley, but a related group, possibly after
wandering in Mozambique, found its way, to the north of Malawi and established settlements that were to form the basis of
the Tonga and Tumbuka peoples, assimilating the previous
inhabitants, who gradually adopted the institutions, language,
and customs of the newcomers.[9]

There seems to have been one acknowledged king or paramount, the *kalonga,* to whom the Maravi acknowledged allegiance until the late sixteenth century. In order to be eligible
for succession, a candidate was required to be a son of the
nyangu (the mother or sister of the *kalonga*) and also to receive
the support of the senior council of chiefs and elders. A dispute over the succession occurred in the late sixteenth century
when Undi, a brother of the deceased *kalonga,* was passed over
by the council in favor of his nephew. The offended brother
migrated with his supporters and set up his own kingdom,
taking with him the *nyangu* and all other female members of
the royal lineage. In spite of this bifurcation, the *kalonga* was
still chosen in the same way as before. On the death of the
ruler the council, now dominated by local Banda clansmen,
chose among the *nyangu*'s sons, now brought up in the Undi

8. See, for example, J. M. Schoffeleers, "The Meaning and Use of the Name
'Malawi' in Oral Traditions and Precolonial Documents," in B. Pachai, ed.,
Early History, pp. 95 ff. According to Clark (p. 23), the Maravi probably arrived
in the late fifteenth or early sixteenth century; Pachai says that settlement took
place between the thirteenth and sixteenth centuries but notes that "some clans
arrived in Malawi before the emergence of a political leader over the Maravi as
a whole" (*Malawi,* pp. 4–5). See also G. T. Nurse, "The People of Bororo," in
Pachai, ed., *Early History.*
9. Pachai, *Malawi,* pp. 5–6.

kingdom. This circumstance probably weakened the personal power of the *kalonga,* who was no longer brought up among the people he was to rule, and the council introduced a new rule that the candidate would not be recognized as *kalonga* unless he married the *mwali,* who was of the Banda clan. The prerogatives of the *kalonga* were diminished, and it is likely that the council played an increasingly significant role in determining effective policy.[10]

The relationship between rulers and subordinates, both in the Kalonga and Undi kingdoms, was apparently a loose one, dependent on a sense of mutual advantage rather than the power to enforce obedience, and the diminished authority of the *kalonga* may have contributed to the high degree of local autonomy enjoyed by the constituent units of the Empire.

In the more cohesive periods of the Empire's history its kings had a monopoly of trade in or through the kingdom, entitling them to tribute from foreign and local traders. They were, in particular, able to obtain revenue from the ivory trade. There is evidence that the network of trade extended over a long distance, from the Congo basin to the Indian Ocean, as early as the eleventh century, but it was probably of a much lower level of intensity than was reached in the eighteenth century.[11] The king, in turn, distributed goods to headmen and, by maintaining large stores of grain, was able to assist stricken areas during times of local famine. Another function of the ruler was to assist in settling disputes among his people, but his role in these matters appears to have been that of a conciliator, or occasion-

10. The account that follows of the history and organization of the Maravi draws heavily on the chapter by H. W. Langworthy, "Chewa or Malawi Political Organisation in the Precolonial Era," in Pachai, ed., *Early History.* See also H. Langworthy and J. Omer Cooper, "The Impact of the Ngoni and the Yao on the Nineteenth-Century History of Malawi," in Pachai, Smith, and Tangri, eds., *Malawi, Past and Present* (Blantyre: University of Malawi, 1968).

11. Pachai says that "there is plenty of evidence of coastal trade in northern Malawi from the eleventh century A.D." (*Malawi,* p. 3). There is some evidence supporting this in Brian Fagan, "Early Trade in Raw Materials in South Central Africa," chapter 2 of Richard Gray and David Birmingham, eds., *Pre-Colonial African Trade* (London: Oxford University Press, 1970), esp. p. 29. There is some very slender evidence cautiously provided by K. R. Robinson, "The Iron Age in Malawi," in Pachai, ed., *Early History,* pp. 56–57, and by Monica Wilson, "Reflections on the Early History of North Malawi," in the same book.

ally an arbitrator, rather than that of lawmaker. The king's power to raise troops was severely constrained. In the view of one of the leading authorities on the period the army "was mainly a popular levy gathered from those areas which were willing to send troops" when the people in those areas felt that there were suitable mutual interests involved.[12]

A third breakaway kingdom was founded at Lundu; it went to war with the *kalonga*, who was at the time in alliance with the Portuguese. The *kalonga* appears to have got the better of the fighting and was able to reassert a measure of dominance over Lundu, but the trend toward decentralization and disintegration continued. By the beginning of the nineteenth century many people with a similar language and similar culture were spread over a wide geographical area, covering large parts of what are now Zambia, Malawi, and Mozambique, but there was very little political or military cohesion among them. With few exceptions they were unable to provide effective resistance to the outsiders who moved into the area in the nineteenth century and quickly achieved dominating positions.

The Maravi had a reputation in some quarters as being rather more prosperous and "advanced" than their neighbors. They built bamboo bridges, albeit of a rather fragile kind; their hoes, knives, arrows, and spears were, according to Gamitto, "as polished as if . . . done by European instruments," and food was, at least in good years, abundant. Gamitto wrote that they possessed "many cattle, sheep and goats," while Livingstone was later to refer enthusiastically to the growing of cotton and to well-provided food markets. There was, perhaps, more controversy about some of their other qualities, and Gamitto reported that the Maravis had a formidable reputation as thieves and liars.[13]

12. Langworthy, p. 114.
13. A. C. P. Gamitto, *King Kazembe*, trans. Ian Cunnison, Estudos de Ciencias Politicas e Sociais No. 42 (Lisbon: Junta de Investigacoes do Ultramar, 1960). There are references to Maravi bridges on pages 20 and 50, to the polishing of hoes (etc.) on page 55, and to their allegedly thievish qualities on page 45. P. A. Cole-King says that all Central African languages have incorporated the Chichewa word for a bridge (*ulalo*), which suggests that the Chewa were the first bridge builders ("Transport and Communication in Malawi to 1891," in Pachai, ed., *Early History*, p. 72).

The Tumbuka, living on the northern shores of Lake Malawi, had a social structure not dissimilar to that of the Chewa with whom they had some linguistic affinities as well as historical links.[14] The leadership of these people had, however, changed significantly in source if not in style during the late eighteenth century when a small party of Balowoka traders crossed the lake from Mozambique in order to take advantage of the largely untapped sources of ivory in Tumbuka country.[15]

The leading figure among these traders, one Mlowoka, was an astute man with a rare skill in diplomacy. He made himself very useful to the Tumbuka by drawing their attention to economic opportunities they had previously ignored, and he showed them how these opportunities might be exploited. His services were appreciated and rewarded, and not long after his arrival he was recognized as a leader among the Tumbuka people. He strengthened his position by a series of judicious marriages and gained the friendship of clans that were strategically placed to dominate the ivory trade. Several of his companions established similar though less extensive claims to power, and the blend of Balowoka enterprise and tact with Tumbuka complaisance produced a new dynasty, that of the Chikulamayembe, based far more on the use of persuasion and the recognition of mutual interest than on military power.

The political structure remained very loose. H. L. Vail, one of the more prominent of younger historians studying the history of the Tumbuka, has had this to say about the strengths and weaknesses of the new dynasty:

In the first place, it was successful because it coupled economic strength through an ivory monopoly with an intelligent programme of amalgamation with, not conquest of, the local Tumbuka. Because the regimes set up by the Balowoka were tolerant of local customs, did not

14. H. L. Vail, "Suggestions towards a Reinterpreted Tumbuka History," in Pachai, ed., *Early History,* points out even closer linguistic ties between the Tumbuka and some tribal groups to the north. He also explains that the Tumbuka-speaking people included many groups and clans with quite different historical origins, traditions, and types of organizations.

15. The account that follows is drawn largely from Vail. Being much briefer it is presented in much simpler form than the complex and subtle delineation by Vail.

try to interfere greatly in the local habits and institutions, accepted the religious cults associated with the area, were generous in their trade dealings, and did not attempt to remake the Tumbuka clan areas into a politically united empire, these regimes were accepted readily by the local Tumbuka. Yet such a system, although earning for itself a good reputation locally and developing the area's prosperity, could not survive indefinitely, given the changes that were taking place throughout East-Central Africa. It had within its structure the reasons for its own eventual easy destruction.[16]

The new rulers did not (at the time) need an effective military force and perhaps for this reason did not seek to establish one, but because their authority was largely derived from their successful manipulation of trading opportunities, they were highly vulnerable to forces that reduced their control of trade. During the early nineteenth century other traders moved into the area and began to undermine the Chikulamayembe's dominance of trade, defying efforts to drive them away. A few years later when the society had to meet armed invasion, it was unable to summon an effective resistance. "Although united in language," said Vail, "and, to a certain degree at least, in culture [the Tumbuka] had no political or religious institutions capable of providing leadership for any resistance."[17]

The peoples of Central Africa were subjected, from the early part of the nineteenth century onward, to the increasingly intense depredations of the expanding coastal slave trade, of which Zanzibar was one of the principal centers together with the Portuguese Mozambique ports of Quelimane and Inhambane.

The institution of slavery had long been recognized in the societies of Central Africa, but domestic slavery was significantly different both in intent and in effect from the long distance commerce in slaves which ravaged Central Africa during the nineteenth century. In traditional practice, people became slaves because they were taken prisoner, were found guilty of criminal conduct or of offending against traditional social codes, or were debtors who were committed to slavery until they had redeemed their obligations.

16. Vail, pp. 161–162.
17. Vail, p. 162.

Without doubt, certain aspects of this system bore with harsh ferocity on those subject to it. In some societies, for example, slaves were buried alive during the funeral of their master, but in most circumstances slaves were accorded a measure of protection from abuse; female slaves were accorded the status of junior wife, their children were free members of the community, and in other respects there was a measure of integration between slaves and freemen.[18] Gamitto thought that the institution of domestic slavery was in decline in the early nineteenth century and he lamented that it should be so because he felt that the effective alternative was much worse. It was his view that those taken prisoner or those who would have been reduced to slavery under "the established laws and customs" were, in the absence of a well-established custom of slavery, "alike cruelly killed in order to be got rid of."[19]

The long-distance commercial trade in slaves began to acquire significance during the eighteenth century. The slaves themselves found conditions much harsher under the new system of slavery than under the earlier form. They lost whatever protection had been afforded by traditional practice, they were driven far from their homes and their kinsmen, and they were more likely than not to die at the hands of traders or from the rigors of the march. The commercial slave trade often proved fatal to the individuals unfortunate enough to become its victims, and its impact on the societies from which they came was hardly less devastating.

There were constraints in the traditional system limiting the number of people who could be made slaves. Except in the event of war or criminal behavior or other unusual circumstances it was not permissible to reduce free citizens to slavery, nor was there much incentive to do so. As soon, however, as it became common practice to sell slaves to strangers, rulers were tempted to increase the number of offenses punishable by slavery, and they were less likely to examine with care any evidence suggesting that an accused person was not guilty. Persons found guilty were tortured to reveal their "accomplices" and

18. See Maliwa, "Customary Law and the Administration of Justice in Malawi, 1890–1933" (M. Phil. thesis, University of London, 1965).
19. Gamitto, pp. 42–43.

thus further augment the supply of slaves. Instead of being a relatively humane way of dealing with the consequences of war, slavery became itself a cause of war, with men prepared to risk their own lives in order to enslave others. Slavery having become an instrument of commerce, the slave who could not be sold was valueless, and traders were reckless about the number that died providing there were sufficient survivors to make a journey profitable.

The greatest commercial demand for slaves came from the Arab enclaves on the east coast and from the European-owned sugar and coffee plantations on the off-coast islands of Mauritius and Reunion. The plantations had been developed on a large scale following the appointment, in 1753, of an enterprising governor of those islands who was on friendly terms with the governor of Mozambique, a man described by Alpers as being "as corrupt an official as ever graced the administration of the Portuguese colonial empire."[20] There had been Arab settlements on the east African coast since the seventeenth century, but Arab control was strengthened after the conclusion of a major civil war in Oman, about 1744. Zanzibar became the major center for the export of slaves to the Arab states and, a little later, to Brazil. The demand for slaves in Brazil was greatly stimulated by what might otherwise be considered a minor effect of the Napoleonic wars. The Portuguese royal family fled to Brazil to escape seizure by the Napoleonic forces and, being satisfied by the apparent warmth of the welcome accorded to them, granted a number of concessions and local monopolies to Brazilians. This made plantation agriculture a more profitable business and consequently increased the demand for slaves. By 1820 the British government had taken steps to halt the flow of slaves to Brazil (and elsewhere) from areas north of the equator so that Zanzibar replaced other sources of supply in what what was, in any event, an expanding market.

The Brazilian trade was halted in 1850 by the decision of the British government to prevent slave traders from transporting

20. Edward A. Alpers, *The East African Slave Trade,* Historical Association of Tanzania, Paper No. 3 (1967), p. 6.

slaves across any part of the sea which could then be controlled by the British navy. While it was very difficult to elude British warships on the long voyage around the Cape and across the Atlantic, there were fewer British ships in the Indian Ocean, the journey to Arabia was shorter, and it was a great deal more familiar to Arab seamen than to the British sailors who were instructed to bring the slave trade to an end. The rate of increase of the trade was probably diminished but the demand for slaves was still high, and Arab leaders along the coast may have had other and perhaps more impelling political reasons in the second half of the century for seeking to dominate routes into the hinterland.[21]

Slave traders followed the routes from the coast to the interior which had been established and used by African traders—among whom the Yao had played an enterprising role—who had been dealing in iron implements, tobacco, animal skins, and later ivory. These established trade routes were expanded and strengthened, and supply camps and trading centers were set up.

Vast areas were devastated and societies terrorized, and most people found themselves in a situation even worse than they had been when the perennial threat of starvation and disease and the erratic, but everpresent, threat of war had put their lives at continual risk. However, some individuals and some groups were able to seize advantage, sometimes very considerable advantage, from the changed situation. Tribes, groups, or individuals who acted as agents of the slave traders or provided them with acommodation or supplies became wealthy and, of even more importance, were able to obtain firearms. These weapons, whether because they really were lethal or because they made enough noise to frighten those without them, proved decisive on most occasions even when their owners

---

21. Andrew Ross says that there is evidence that Arabs were responding to the development of European interest in the coastal areas by seeking to strengthen their links with the interior and find allies against European expansion ("The Origins and Development of the Church of Scotland Mission, Blantyre, Nyasaland, 1875–1926" Ph.D. diss., University of Edinburgh, 1968, p. 165). See also H. W. MacMillan, "Notes on the Origins of the Arab War," in Pachai, ed., *Early History*, p. 270.

were faced with a larger and ostensibly better organized force. The men who controlled the trade routes—for example, Jumbe of Nkota Kota, who was in charge of the principal crossing point on the west bank of Lake Nyasa—acquired the power that was being lost by traditional rulers whose people were devastated by the trade.[22]

The trading routes and stations which supported the slave trade (and the equally savage extension of ivory trading)[23] also secured channels and organizations through which "legitimate" trade could take place. In view of the general disorder prevailing at the time, it is not surprising that evidence about the beneficial effects of trade is rather sketchy, but the subsequent experience of such European trading ventures as the African Lakes Company was to demonstrate that patterns of trade were a good deal more sophisticated and effective than was generally thought to be the case by the first missionaries to travel in Central Africa, including the illustrious David Livingstone.[24]

The Chewa and the Tumbuka had been vulnerable to the depredations of slave traders from the early days of the trade, but the Chewa in particular were to experience the greatest horror and devastation about the middle of the nineteenth century, when their already precariously weak political structure had been shattered by the multiple invasions of the Ngoni and Yao peoples.

There were at least three quite distinct groups among both Ngoni and Yao newcomers. Few of them had demonstrated an overwhelming military prowess before their arrival in Malawi, but they were too formidable for the Chewa.

22. Pachai, *Malawi*, pp. 42ff.
23. H. M. Stanley is reported to have said that "slave raiding becomes innocence when compared with ivory raiding" (Alpers, p. 25).
24. See H. W. Macmillan, "The Origins and Development of the African Lakes Company, 1878–1908" (Ph.D. diss., University of Edinburgh 1970), for example: "The commercial system which [the missions] wished to change, of which the slave trade formed only a part, was a system which worked, which had deep roots, and which involved most of the population. By continuing to function in spite of the far reaching political change of the middle years of the century it had shown considerable strength and resilience. The task which commerce and Christianity were called on to perform was not an easy one" (p. 39).

The Ngoni had fled from Zululand during the reign of Shaka the Terrible. Some of their leaders had been commanders in the army of the Ndwandwe, a tribe whose chief had the temerity to oppose Shaka. "When the fortunes of war began to go against [them]," says Pachai, they fled, taking with them "a motley collection" of fellow warriors, kinsmen, and refugees.[25] There were separate groups of Ngoni led by men who had been associated with other chiefs, but all of them had managed, in one way or another, to arouse the anger of the mighty Zulu leader. They made their way northward in two main groups. The first, led by Zwangendaba, crossed the Zambezi in 1835 and was followed about a year later by the Maseko Ngoni.[26]

They continued to push on, sometimes in search of more hospitable lands, sometimes in search of weaker neighbors.[27] Tribes or groups of people that were conquered were absorbed into the Ngoni social and military system, so that although different groups of Ngoni had some characteristics in common, they were significantly affected by the heterogenous nature of their assimilated subjects. The Ngoni were a military and a pastoral people; the regiment (or *impi*, as it was known among the Ngoni) was a fundamental social unit as well as a weapon of war; Zulu methods of fighting and at least some of their discipline were implanted in youths at an early age, and this pattern of life greatly affected the Ngoni attitudes about appropriate

25. Pachai, *Malawi*, p. 22.

26. The account of the Ngoni in this chapter draws heavily on the work of Ian Linden, particularly his paper "Some Oral Tradition from the Maseko Ngoni," *Society of Malawi Journal*, XXIV July 1971. Linden emphasizes the heterogeneity of the Ngoni and is more skeptical than most writers of "the myth of the all conquering Ngoni."

27. According to Pachai, Zwangendaba "had heard of red cattle further north and it was in search of this that he continued on his march to the chosen land, the land of his dreams" (*Malawi*, p. 23; but Linden, writing of the Maseko Ngoni who were presumably responding to very similar pressures at this time, says, "These great treks of the Maseko Ngoni were not some northwards goldrush for cattle and captives, far less the triumphal march of a victorious army. . . . Their failure to form any permanent settlement before 1870 was not entirely a choice of their own making" ("Some Oral Traditions," pp. 71–72).

standards and codes of behavior.[28] But though bravery and loyalty were paramount virtues, their war machine was rarely, if ever, as effective as had been that of the Zulus which they had taken as a model.

Their standard of life, as well as its style, depended on their being able to raid whatever neighbors they happened to have for cattle and crops. In their best years they appear to have had a relatively high standard of life—in the view of some authorities it was higher during this period than it later was during the colonial period—but a corollary of that style and that standard was that their weaker neighbors lived in constant apprehension that often bordered on terror, their poverty compounded by the tribute that fed the unproductive Ngoni.[29]

The continual absorption of conquered people was counterbalanced by a recurring fractionalization. Groups broke away because aspirants to leadership would either be forced to flee and would take with them kinsmen or members of the regiment or, despairing of ever achieving their ambition in the main body, would set out to establish a breakaway kingdom, which then proceeded to grow in influence as it, in turn, overran and assimilated other peoples.

Zwangendaba had taken his regiments through what is now northern Malawi and into what is presently Tanzania, where he died toward the end of the 1840s. After his death the community broke into four groups. One moved north toward Lake Victoria; another (under Zulu Gama and Mbonani) moved southeast but remained in the area of southern Tanzania and

28. Margaret Read quotes the "famous war leader," Ngonomo, telling missionaries that "the foundation of our kingdom is the spear and shield. God has given you the Book and cloth, and has given us shield and spear, and each must live in his own way" ("The Ngoni and Western Education," in Victor Turner, ed., *Colonialism in Africa, 1870–1964*, Cambridge: Cambridge University Press, 1971, pp. 354–355).

29. Read wrote of a later period that "the cessation of warfare, as it proved, lowered the general level of living in terms of diet and curtailed the lavish hospitality of the chief's household" (p. 356). The effect of the Ngoni on their neighbors is discussed by J. K. Rennie, who points out a marked difference between accounts provided by the Ngoni themselves and those provided by their neighbors ("The Ngoni States and European Intrusion" in Eric Stokes and Richard Brown, *The Zambesian Past*, Manchester: Manchester University Press, 1966, pp. 307ff.).

northern Mozambique; a third moved southwest and settled on the Zambian side of the border near Mchinji, while the fourth group, the Jere Ngoni under Mbelwa, moved back into northern Malawi and settled around the Vipya plateau. Some decades later the Jere Ngoni sent a raiding party, toward Dowa; the raiding *impi* elected not to return to the main body but instead to set up its own kingdom. The leaders of the Jere Ngoni attempted to punish the breakaway group, but in the ensuing fighting the breakaway unit won the day.

The Maseko Ngoni, who had followed Zwangendaba's northern journey from the Zambezi, entered Malawi in the southern central area, near the present site of Dedza. From there they moved eastward into Mozambique, crossed the Rovuma, and about 1850 came up against another group of Ngoni moving south. For a while the two groups lived in peace, but eventually fighting broke out and the Maseko were driven from the land. They made their way back into Malawi, crossed the Shire River, and settled in the Dedza area, through which they had passed several years earlier.

Few of the indigenous peoples were able to put up an effective resistance against the Ngoni, although there were some scattered successes. The Tonga were able to beat back an attack on Chinteche. The Chewa leader, Mwase Kasungu, who repelled a Ngoni attack on his stockade appears to have been treated with considerable respect by Ngoni leaders and was counted as a very useful ally by some of them. These instances of success were, however, more notable for their rarity than for any other reason.

When the Ngoni came against the Yao, they found them an altogether different proposition. Until the early part of the nineteenth century, the Yao had been living in northern Mozambique, where they had achieved an important role in long distance trade between the Indian Ocean and the Congo, and they had, by the end of the eighteenth century, achieved a good deal of success in wresting control of the ivory trade from the Portuguese.[30] They appear to have had good commerical relations with the Chewa, in which the Yao were the more active partners without, so far as is known, seeking to dominate

30. Pike, pp. 58–59.

or impose their will on the Chewa and without engaging in the hideous traffic in human beings with which they later became associated.

In the early part of the nineteenth century, however, the Yao homeland was ravaged by locusts, and they had barely recovered from this disaster when their security was even more gravely threatened by the migration into the area of large numbers of Makalolo and Maconde tribesmen. Unable to cope with the new situation the Yao began, about 1830, to seek out new land to the southwest. Whether it was because they had become more acutely aware that they needed greater strength to repel invaders to their land or whether it was because they had perforce become invaders themselves, seizing from weaker tribes land to compensate for that which they had lost to stronger ones, or whether it was because they perceived for the first time the gains that could be made by intermediaries in the slave trade, the Yao became heavily involved in the commercial slave trade, as agents of the coastal Arabs. They acquired wealth and, of more importance to their neighbors, they acquired the firearms that were to make them considerably more formidable opponents.

They continued their migration southward, moved around the shores of the Great Lake, and entered Malawi. There were three main groups, but most often they operated in small autonomous communities.[31] In many cases they first came to Malawi as small bands of strangers seeking the blessing of local chiefs, and it was only after settling in, and having perhaps lulled the suspicions of local chiefs, that they began to assert themselves, appropriating the lands of their erstwhile hosts and either driving their hosts away or seizing them as slaves. The spectacle of lands being ravaged, people being slaughtered, and societies in confusion and disorder made a most powerful impression on the first Britons who, quite fortuitously, arrived on the scene to witness the slave trade in the flood tide of rapacity.

Some recent commentators, without minimizing the fearful consequences of the slave trade, have suggested that there were more signs of hope in the circumstances of the time than were

31. The account given here is derived to a large extent from three sources: Langworthy and Omer Cooper; Pachai, *Malawi;* and E. A. Alpers, "The Yao in Malawi," in Pachai, ed., *Early History.*

appreciated by missionaries and explorers reaching the area, among whom David Livingstone was preeminent. Several writers have argued, for example, that the Ngoni were a powerful potential stabilizing influence and might well have provided the basis for a new society that would have been much more cohesive and purposeful than the loose aggregation of small communities that made up the Maravi Empire. The Ngoni brought with them a well-regulated system of law and order, wrote Ross, and they played "a protective as well as a destructive role in Zambesian society in the nineteenth century."[32] Margaret Read reported a belief among the Ngoni themselves that "the Europeans spoiled our country, and they came too soon, before we [the Ngoni] had finished our work."[33] The Ngoni were imbued, she continued, with the idea "of a task to be done, a mission to be fulfilled and [that, consequently] the frustration of non-achievement was deeply imbedded in Ngoni attitudes."

Writing about Tanzania, where circumstances might have been a little more favorable but were probably not very different, Roberts has commented that "for the historian it is . . . important to note that this was a time of integration as well as disintegration. People's horizons and ambitions were rapidly expanding; and they were learning, however painfully, to live together in larger units with greater access to the material and intellectual resources of the world outside."[34]

The disruption or overthrow of established order may contain the seeds of a more dynamic, prosperous, or humane social order. Contemporary Europeans often failed to appreciate either the virtues or the strength of African societies, and some among them were predisposed to concentrate on the defects of African economies and societies because they had other reasons for wishing to justify a British presence in Central Africa. But

32. Ross, p. 11.
33. Turner, ed., p. 353. J. K. Rennie supports this view, but Stokes and Brown, in the introduction to *The Zambesian Past*, say that it is "an open question how far the internal strains were caused or heightened to a destructive pitch by European encroachment" (p. xxiv).
34. A. Roberts, "Political Change in the Nineteenth Century," in Isaria N. Kinambo and A. J. Temu, eds., *A History of Tanzania* (Heinemann Educational Books, East African Publishing House, 1969), p. 84.

there is very little positive evidence, as distinct from hopeful surmise, that the new equilibrium that would have been established if there had been no European intervention would have been significantly more dynamic or progressive than the kinds of society that had existed earlier.

A more potent instrument of change was introduced in the early 1860s when David Livingstone, failing to find a passage westward along the Zambezi past the Kebrebasa rapids [now the site of the Cabora Bassa dam], sought to rescue his expedition from total failure by choosing the only alternative available to him in the circumstances. He attempted to save the goals of his expedition by completely changing their geographical provenance: he decided to move northward along the Shire River. When he had left Britain on 10 March 1858, he had persuaded a number of influential people that his original destination, the Batoka plateau along the Zambezi, was a potential "paradise of wealth," was readily accessible to the Indian Ocean, and was suitable not only for an extension of British enterprise but for colonization as well.[35] When Livingstone entered the Shire River on New Year's Day 1859, he was looking for land that could be colonized by British (or, more specifically, Scottish) artisans and farmers and that would be commercially attractive to British merchants.[36]

35. The phrase was that of Sir Roderick Murchison, whose impression of the area had been derived from Livingstone's account (Jeal, p. 241). Several books, written from different perspectives, provide valuable insights into the complexity of Livingstone's motives and the motives of those who supported him. Jeal's book is very good, as is George Seaver, *David Livingstone: His Life and Letters* (London: Lutterworth Press, 1957). George Martelli provides a critical but often sympathetic introduction: *Livingstone's River: The Story of the Zambezi Expedition, 1856–1864* (London: Chatto and Windus, 1970). A useful supplement is R. Foskett, ed., *The Zambezi Doctor: David Livingstone's Letters to John Kirk, 1858–1872* (Edinburgh: Edinburgh University Press, 1964), and some important aspects of the subject are treated in *David Livingstone and Africa*, Proceedings of a Seminar held at the Centre of African Studies, University of Edinburgh, May 1973, and Bridglal Pachai, ed., *Livingstone: Man of Africa* (London: Longman, 1973).

36. In his speech at the Senate House, University of Cambridge, on 4 December 1957, he told his audience, "I go back to Africa to try to make an open path for Commerce and Christianity," quoted in Michael Gelfand, *Lakeside Pioneers*

Livingstone was not, as was commonly supposed in Britain at the time, the first white man to set eyes on what is now Lake Malawi but the popular belief was not entirely misplaced. He was the first to arrive in the country with the firm intention of bringing it to the notice of the most powerful nations in the world. Livingstone believed that he had reached the shores of the Great Lake as an instrument of a Divine Providence whose interests, at least in the short run, were most happily similar to those of British merchants and settlers.

Livingstone not only expected to find a country rich in natural wealth, he was convinced that he had found one. Food was abundant, he wrote, and cotton was already produced on a large scale. He believed that the land could sustain a large white population, which would relieve the pressure on British, and especially Scottish, cities, and the colonists would themselves make a mighty contribution to the social and spiritual change that Livingstone wanted to bring about. 'I think," he had written earlier, "twenty or thirty good Christian Scotch families with their ministers and elders would produce an impression in ten years that would rejoice the hearts of all lovers of our race."[37]

He had long since acquired a horror of the slave trade and was greatly distressed that so much of the cotton and sugar imported into Britain was produced by slave labor in the southern states of America. If land could be found where these products could be cultivated efficiently by free men, it would not only bring commercial benefit to his countrymen but would strike a blow at the very heart of slavery in the Western world.

The spectacle of great areas of apparently good land supporting a meager population was deeply offensive to Living-

---

(Oxford: Basil Blackwell, 1964), p. 2. He frequently insisted on the prospective wealth of the areas he visited and the benefit it would bring to fellow Britons. "We could not only get cotton and sugar in abundance from the region I am opening up but in doing that by our own people we should be conferring incalculable blessings on our own poor toil worn fellow countrymen" (quoted by Seaver, p. 345). Both Seaver and Jeal refer to Livingstone's "secret plans" for the region which attached considerably greater importance to colonization than was clear from his public statements (Seaver, p. 308; Jeal, pp. 232–233).
   37. Seaver, p. 342.

stone. Opportunities were being wasted and the prodigality of
the Lord was being spurned. "How many millions," he insisted,
"might flourish in this Africa, where but hundreds dwell!"[38]
Livingstone's influence on British opinion was considerable
before he embarked on the Zambezi expedition, and it was to
be far greater at the time of his death in 1874. It suffered a
very serious if temporary decline in the 1860s when the great
hopes he had encouraged proved to be far less securely based
than his supporters had been led to believe. In January 1863
The Times of London complained that "we were promised cotton, sugar and indigo . . . and of course we got none. We were promised
trade; and there is no trade . . . We were promised converts and not
one has been made. In a word, the thousands subscribed by the Universities and contributed by the Government have been productive
only of the most fatal results."[39]

From Livingstone's point of view, worse was to come. A series of dramatic speeches appealing for men to join him in
building in Central Africa "a highway for Christianity and
commerce" had led to the formation of the Universities' Mission to Central Africa by Oxford and Cambridge Universities
(with the support of the universities of Dublin and Durham).
Livingstone was asked his advice about the most suitable area
for it to begin its work. He had replied, in October 1859, that
the Shire Highlands would be an ideal location. This was, as
Jeal has pointed out, a gamble on Livingstone's part. A small
group of missionaries, lacking the support of a European flock
and unable to undertake the commercial and trading developments that Livingstone expected of the colonists, would be in a
singularly precarious position; on the other hand if Livingstone
had voiced any doubt about the suitability of the area as a
location for a mission station, it might be apparent to others
that some of his reports had been overly sanguine, and prospective colonists would be discouraged. The mission's advance
party, led by Bishop Mackenzie, reached Nyasaland in 1861.
Livingstone successfully pressed them to establish their headquarters at Magomero, a site that otherwise had little to com-

38. Seaver, p. 89.
39. Jeal, p. 331.

mend it, because their presence there would provide a barrier against the southward sweep of the slave trade. "If you fall back to Mount Soche," he told Mackenzie, "all this densely populated country will go before the Ajawas [the Yao], if you take a stand here it will be saved."[40]

The bishop soon found himself confronted by a terrible dilemma, which had never been appreciated by Livingstone and was not understood, even after Mackenzie's unhappy experience, by more than a handful of those who wished to encourage European settlement or mission stations in Central Africa. The members of the settlement or station would be obliged either to accept the existing patterns of authority and practices with respect to law and order or to attempt to provide an alternative framework, which would upset the local balance of power and bring the missionaries or colonists into direct conflict with their neighbors. Many of the existing practices were unacceptable or even abhorrent to the missionaries—indeed, one of the reasons for setting up the United Mission station was to bring an end to the slave trade, which the Yao had no intention of abandoning. The missionaries were unable to appeal to the moral authority of their calling and life style because these were based on assumptions and perceptions not shared by the people among whom they lived.

In many other areas in Africa and elsewhere, missionaries or settlers had no need to resort to the direct use of force because they were beneficiaries of a fear among their neighbors that any liberties taken against white men would be severely punished by the nearest British authorities, who would be quite capable of sending a military expedition if they felt that to do so would provide a useful example. Any directives issued by missionaries in these happy circumstances were accordingly sanctioned by an implied use of power no less real because seldom invoked. But in Nyasaland in the 1860s few of the most powerful tribal leaders were aware of the consequences that might follow their disregard of white opinion.

The pursuit of European interests and the imposition of European values could be achieved only if Europeans were to

40. Seaver, p. 391.

supplement persuasion with coercion, and in the 1860s the missionaries were obliged themselves to fashion the instruments of chastisement. It is perhaps not altogether surprising that Livingstone failed to appreciate Mackenzie's dilemma because he had never been able to establish a mission station himself and had long since given up the attempt to do so.

The Manganja, victims of the Yao, soon appealed to Mackenzie for protection. It was not enough to fight an occasional defensive action, and his men took part in an attack on a Yao village, ostensibly to rescue Manganja prisoners who would have become slaves. There was later to be some suspicion that the Manganja took advantage of the situation to acquire Yao prisoners as slaves for themselves.[41] British opinion was deeply shocked and Livingstone was concerned lest his own reputation suffer as a consequence of Mackenzie's action, but the incident failed to stimulate much serious thought about the position in which the bishop had been put. A few months later Mackenzie was dead of fever. His successor, Bishop Tozer, decided that it was impracticable to sustain a mission station in Nyasaland, and the United Mission was temporarily withdrawn to the coast. Livingstone was furious; he made some effort to undo the damage he had done to Mackenzie's reputation and severely abused Bishop Tozer, accusing him of cowardice as well as misjudgment, but the decision was a severe blow to Livingstone's plans to induce colonization of the area.

When the Zambezi expedition was recalled in 1864, in circumstances deeply wounding to Livingstone's pride,[42] his reputation stood at its lowest point for many years. Livingstone took his setback with the stubborn courage that was one of his enduring qualities. After a brief sojourn in Britain he returned to Africa alone and set off for the interior with a retinue of African guides and porters to seek the headwaters of the Nile, determined to set such an example by his fortitude, his faith, and his consideration in dealing with Africans that he would achieve through the sheer force of character and capacity for

41. Martelli, pp. 176ff.
42. The dispatch was taken to him by Bishop Tozer, arriving to take up his appointment and knowing that Livingstone's expedition had been judged a failure.

sacrifice what he had failed to do through organization, persuasion, and appeal to objective evidence. Despite the formidable achievements of his earlier years it was to be his experience, or what people heard of his experience, during the years from 1866 until his death in 1873 that would form the basis of the Livingstone mythology.

His indomitable disregard of danger, the triumph of his spirit over the most severe mortification of his flesh, his compassion and humility—so starkly different from his behavior to European subordinates or even to "educated" Africans—and the devotion, bravery, and endurance of the Africans who nursed and protected him in the last days of his martyrdom and who finally, with a disregard for their own safety that matched the extraordinary standard set by Livingstone himself, carried his body from Lake Bangweolo, in what is now northern Zambia, to the Indian Ocean so that he might be taken by sea to rest at the last among his kinsmen; these were the heroic qualities that moved his countrymen to tears and admiration. From pulpit to pulpit throughout the land of his birth the call was sent forth to take up the martyr's crown. When Livingstone was buried in Westminster Abbey, the *Glasgow Herald* spoke for many thousands of people in Britain, recording that "the virtues which distinguished Livingstone are those which our country has always been ready to acknowledge, which our religion has taught us to revere and seek to cultivate and conserve."[43]

The achievements of his last years were almost completely irrelevant to the purposes with which he was most closely identified and which were now urged upon the British people. They provided no evidence that Nyasaland offered viable commercial prospects, that the area was suitable for colonization on terms that would not be oppressive to the native population, that the slave trade could be broken without head-on conflict with some of the most powerful African tribal groups in the area, or that mission societies could establish a significant sphere of influence without becoming deeply involved in a struggle for temporal power.

A lack of clarity about Livingstone's message had always been

43. Jeal, p. 450.

one of its most beguiling features. Delivered in ringing tones that satisfied the listener that he stood firmly with the austere but gallant company of Christian heroes, the message nonetheless appealed to all manner of more worldly impulses among Victorians and led them to contemplate with satisfaction the involvement of their countrymen in the interior of Africa. The extension of commerce, the relief of overcrowding in urban slums, the replacement of the Portuguese and other rivals, the eradication of the slave trade, the provision of cheap raw materials, spreading the gospel, introducing the benefits of liberal industrial civilization, protecting the interests of the natives, exploring a still largely uncharted continent and seeking answers to biblical mysteries were to be found among the reasons why men and women felt drawn to support work in Africa. All drew inspiration from Livingstone's experience and writings, and few were much concerned about possible conflict of interest between the purposes closest to their own hearts and the quite different motives that had drawn others to pursue the goal of imperial expansion.

The revived enthusiasm for Livingstone's work was not entirely due to admiration for the man or his works. By the time of his death, doubts had begun to emerge about the continued expansion of the British economy. These may have been insufficient to undermine the self-confidence of businessmen, but they were enough to suggest that any prospect of viable commercial enterprise in new lands should be taken seriously. Businessmen who had contact with church groups establishing mission stations in Africa were naturally aware of prospective opportunities in the continent and realized that one did not always have to wait until the next world in order to reap the advantages of generosity to a good cause.

The feasibility of extending commercial activity to the east coast of Africa and its hinterland had been materially improved by two recent events, one of which made it a good deal easier to reach the east coast while the other made it more attractive to strike into the hinterland. The Suez Canal had been opened in 1869. This had been followed in 1872 by the establishment of a monthly mail boat service, run by a Scotsman, between Aden and Durban which called at Zanzibar. The interior of Africa had long had the reputation of being both inhospitable and unproductive, but during the latter part of the 1860s diamonds had been discovered north of the Orange River. Men of ambition and resolution began to think of it as a place where an enterprising man might make his fortune.

Both the established Church of Scotland and the Free Church of Scotland were resolved to take up Livingstone's work. Shortly after his death each sent a missionary group to Nyasaland. There were a number of differences between the two groups, and in some important respects the Free Church treated its representatives in the field rather more generously than did the established Church. But the similarities between them were perhaps more important. They were both, in the early years (until about 1900), committed to a Christianity that looked for changes in this world as well as the next. In the words of the Reverend David Scott, one of the great leaders of the mission set up by the established Church at Blantyre, in the Shire Highlands· "Africa for the Africans has been our policy from the first, and we believe that God has given this country into our hands that we may train its people how to develop its marvellous resources for themselves."[44]

They intended to bring about an economic and social revolution in the country that would end the slave trade, eradicate poverty, and enable Africans to claim their rights and duties as, in Scott's phrase, "co-inheritors of civilisation." The sponsors of the missions did not always share the objectives of those who were in charge of operations in Nyasaland. Both missions were to find, albeit in different ways, that their ability to bring about effective change was much more limited than they had anticipated and that the consequences of such changes as they were able to bring about were often different, and sometimes quite contrary, to what had been intended.[45]

44. Ross, p. 204. Scott believed it was their duty to impart the "civilisation one has received to those whose co-inheritance it is"; one of the objectives of the mission should be "to give the native the place in the development of this land to which he is called to prove he is fit for it and to see him through" (Ross, pp. 103ff.).

45. The impact of the Free Church mission at Livingstonia has been capably described by K. J. McCracken. See, for example, his "Livingstonia as an Industrial Mission," in W. Montgomery Watt, ed., *Religion in Africa* (Centre of African Studies, University of Edinburgh, 1964).

The Glasgow businessmen who financed the Free Church mission also set up a trading company, the African Lakes Company, with a capital of about £30,000. The company was intended to provide supplies for the missions and to encourage the development of "legitimate" commerce among Africans, in the expectation that this would reduce dependence on the slave trade. The company was forbidden to trade in either armaments or alcohol, but its sponsors expected it to make a profit and hoped that it would provide a sound base from which to develop a wider range of commercial activities.[46]

The company, like the missions, was worried about the possibility of Portuguese expansion into Nyasaland. A further concern was that goods bound for the company from Britain were obliged to pass through Portuguese territory, since it was not at first known that there was a navigable passage from the sea through the sandbanks in the mouth of the Zambezi River. The company's sponsors, being prudent men of business, were reluctant to risk more money than necessary for the minimal form of shoestring budget, and the company was always struggling to meet its commitments. The African trading network proved to be more effective than had been expected, and the company found considerable difficulty in obtaining adequate supplies of ivory, the most profitable source of trade open to it. The lines of communication upon which all operations depended were long, time-consuming, hazardous, and subject to arbitrary, albeit temporary, closure by all manner of powers from the Portuguese to local tribal rulers, some of whom had only recently seized control from traditional chieftains. The company had difficulty in obtaining a regular supply of African porters, laborers, and storemen. When it did get them, the missions, who were hard pressed to meet their own demands, complained. The quality of the few Europeans available for work was highly variable; the company employed some admirable Europeans (though few, if any had any serious experience of business) but, like the missions, had to take others who were in Nyasaland only because they could not find employment

46. See H. W. Macmillan, esp. pp. 157–160, with discussion of the company accounts. Macmillan says, on p. 172, that after nine years' work "it appeared to be about to enter a new and more successful period."

elsewhere. Among them were thoroughly disreputable and irresponsible men who were to do the company a great deal of harm.

In spite of these difficulties, the company appeared to be establishing a viable basis of operations during the 1880s and by the middle of the decade was making a modest profit. It had begun to obtain an increasing share of the ivory trade and had set up a successful trading station at the north end of the lake, where it apparently had achieved a cordial and mutually beneficial trading relationship with Mlozi, a powerful Arab trader who had established a military as well as commercial presence near Koronga.[47]

Before long, however, the company found itself faced by the problem that had troubled Mackenzie. Mlozi had at first been welcomed by the Ngonde who lived in the area. Living, like most of the tribes that had long been resident in Malawi, in small loosely structured groups, the Ngonde were aware of the benefits of exchange, and Mlozi had, or so they thought, set up base in the area in order to further a mutual interest in trade. It soon became apparent that Mlozi had at his disposal a military force far more formidable than that of the local Ngonde chiefs; disputes originating in commercial transactions and other mutual arrangements as well as those due to Mlozi's involvement in the slave trade led to open conflict, with the Ngonde getting the worst of the fighting. Fugitive Ngonde sought refuge in the company's compound, and when Mlozi demanded that they be turned over to him, the company's representatives refused. They were criticized by the British consul in Mozambique for undue interference in a local dispute which would probably lead to a far more serious involvement than the company (or any other British agency in the area) could afford. In one sense the consul was right. But if the company had not resisted Mlozi's demand, it would have abandoned any claim it might have on the good will of the Ngonde, the achievement of which had been one of the principal reasons for setting up the trading station in the first place.

47. Of the early relationship between the company and Mlozi, Macmillan says it was "not one of commercial rivalry but one of partnership" (p. 252).

Whether or not the company's representatives fully understood this is another matter; there is reason to believe that they misjudged Mlozi's strength and thought that he could have been beaten more easily than proved to be the case.

The war between Mlozi and the company began with an elaborate display of courtesy, but protracted, bitter, and inconclusive fighting absorbed the energies and capital of the company for several years.[48] It was to end the company's rather precarious grip on commercial viability, but it was also, for reasons that were not entirely foreseen by the company's leaders in Nyasaland and that might not have moved them if they had been appreciated, to have a most powerful impact on opinion in Britain. The war was to prove of critical importance among the pressures bearing on the British government when it finally decided to introduce formal British control over the Nyasaland protectorate.

Reports in the British press and in British (and especially Scottish) pulpits of fighting between the small British and Christian band of company men and an Arab slave-trading force, which had arisen because of the company's refusal to hand over Africans who had sought its protection, roused every missionary instinct of the Livingstone lobby. That the commercial interests of a British company were also being threatened did the company's case no harm among businessmen even though some were, perhaps, inclined to think that the company's conduct of its affairs left a good deal to be desired.

The most potent influence on British opinion was the behavior of the Portuguese authorities in Mozambique. The Scottish missions in Nyasaland had been aware from the start that encroachment by the Portuguese presented a more fundamental threat to their long-term objectives than the skepticism or outright hostility of some African leaders. The missions were aware that an official British presence in the area would ensure their capacity to carry out their work (whether, or to what

48. The company became convinced that Mlozi was about to attack them when he carefully settled all outstanding debts due to them. According to Macmillan, the attack came "almost immediately after the settlement of the last account" (p. 267).

extent, they appreciated that a British colonial administration might impose restraints on their activities is not clear), but there was little enthusiasm in Britain for proposals to extend the imperial commitment to a territory that offered so little of material value. The Arab war, however, generated an emotional response, and insular pride was affronted by the failure of the Portuguese to adopt a more sympathetic attitude toward the company. The Portuguese authorities had already irritated the British government when they claimed a monopoly of transport on the Zambezi, in defiance of treaty obligation. But that minor incident did not attract much attention and might soon have been forgotten by members of the cabinet, who were preoccupied with more weighty considerations. It was, in any event, still necessary to pass through Portuguese territory to reach the navigable waters of the Zambezi, and during the war the Portuguese authorities held up the transhipment of arms intended for the company. The balance of the war was delicately poised. To more than a few people in Britain it seemed as though the Portuguese were not only siding with the company's enemies but were behaving in an astonishingly insolent manner to the citizens of a country that, as all Britons knew, was much superior to Portugal.

"It was the Arab war," said Hugh Macmillan, "which created the first awareness of the Company and the missions outside their own immediate circle and prepared a wider public to take an interest in their future welfare."[49]

The political impact in Britain of this interest was enhanced by two quite fortuitous events. A navigable channel from the sea into the mouth of the Zambezi was discovered in 1889 with the consequence that men and supplies could reach Nyasaland without being obliged to pass through Portuguese territory; it would still be difficult to sustain a formal British presence in Nyasaland, but it was no longer completely impracticable. The other important factor was the close balance of political forces in Britain. Lord Salisbury was prime minister, but his own party could not, alone, command a majority in Parliament, and political tacticians were more than usually sensitive to the opin-

---

49. Macmillan, p. 297.

ions of well-organized pressure groups; in circumstances like
these the united voice of church activists was not to be treated
lightly.

The government was not yet persuaded, however, that it
should commit itself to accepting formal responsibility for Nyasaland. To do so would offend the Portuguese who were in a
position to embarrass the British settlements lying along the
Zambezi and would entail a financial burden on the Exchequer
that did not sit well with an influential chancellor who had set
his mind on a policy of retrenchment.

Salisbury sent an emissary to Portugal to explore the possibility of a settlement which would concede that substantial parts
of Nyasaland lay in the Portuguese sphere of influence in return for Portuguese recognition of a British sphere of
influence along the Zambezi. The area Salisbury was prepared
to abandon included territory in which the Scottish missions
had been working and in which they felt that they had already
achieved a considerable degree of influence. The Scots,
inflamed by the "Arab War," were outraged, and it was made
clear to Salisbury that any such deal would have significant
political consequences in constituencies where either of the major Scottish churches had any influence.[50] The pressure for
annexation was stimulated by the maladroit performance of the
Portuguese, who chose this time to assert their claim to land
lying along the Shire River. The authorities in Mozambique
had been provoked by the behavior of some Africans living in
Nyasaland, particularly the Makalolo of the lower Shire, but
their attempt to deal with them was badly timed. The British
government was being forced into a position in which a decision not to annex Nyasaland might be interpreted as weakness
in its dealing with a far from formidable foreign power.

In May 1899, Cecil Rhodes made it known that he would be
prepared to provide money for a treaty-making voyage and
may also have indicated at this time that he would subsequently
be prepared to meet the costs of administering the area. He
shared with Harry Johnston (who was to become the first commissioner of the area when it was declared a protectorate) the

50. Ross, p. 174; Macmillan, p. 295.

vision of a British-controlled area extending unbroken from the Cape of Good Hope to the shores of the Mediterranean. No doubt he deeply loved his country and believed that it would be greatly to the advantage of less fortunate people to become subjects of a still mightier British Empire, but he was also, and perhaps preeminently, a shrewd man of business. It was not lost on him that the territories he would help to administer might contain valuable mineral resources and, although the understanding that was reached between Rhodes and Johnston has not been fully revealed, he would at the least have had first claim on mineral rights over a vast expanse of territory. In any event, little was found in Nyasaland, and during Rhodes's lifetime there was little awareness of the mineral wealth of Zambezi, but if strikes had been made and Rhodes's companies had had first claim to exploit them, the pay-off on a relatively modest outlay would have been great indeed.[51]

Rhodes provided £2,000 for the treaty-making expedition; during 1890 and the first half of 1891, he had paid some £13,500 as a subsidy to the African Lakes Company so that it might maintain law and order in the area. But this arrangement was unsatisfactory both because Rhodes and Johnston had a poor opinion of the company's personnel and because, as the British government pointed out, the company had no authority to administer the area. An agreement was reached that Johnston, on behalf of the British government, should receive a subsidy of £10,000 a year, which would provide the bare bones of administration and policing in Nyasaland, and that he would also keep a watching brief on the area to the west, now Zambia, which had been granted to Rhodes's South Africa Company. Sundry other expenses were met by Rhodes, but Johnston was obliged to run into debt, and in 1894 this fact, together with mounting suspicion in Scotland of Rhodes's ultimate intentions, persuaded the British government that it should take direct responsibility for administration of the protectorate.

51. At one time, Rhodes believed, or affected to believe, that the chartered company had sole rights to mining privileges throughout the entire area of the protectorate (Roland Oliver, *Sir Harry Johnston and the Scramble for Africa*, London: Chatto and Windus, 1959, p. 226).

During 1890 and 1891 agreements were reached with the Portuguese and German governments and with the British South Africa Company to determine the boundaries of the British Central Africa Protectorate, as it was to be known until 1907. Treaties with the Portuguese fixed the eastern and southern boundaries of the new territory (as well as making some other adjustments both north and south of the Zambezi), those with the Germans provided the demarcation between Nyasaland and what is now Tanzania, while the western boundaries with what is now Zambia were set out in the agreement with the British South Africa Company.

A British protectorate was declared in May 1891, and Johnston, who had been British consul in Mozambique since 1889, was appointed commissioner and consul general. In addition to being responsible to the British government for Nyasaland, he acted until 1894 on behalf of Rhodes's British South Africa Company in the territory to the west, where it had been granted the status of a chartered company. This was, in itself, an anomalous situation, with a person carrying the authority of the British government in one territory and acting as the agent of a private commercial enterprise in the next. Johnston himself may have been quite aware of the significance of changing hats, but it is unlikely that the chiefs with whom he was dealing were aware of the distinction, and Rhodes had great difficulty in appreciating it.[52]

The problem was compounded by the fact that Rhodes was buying up the African Lakes Company, which had very large landholdings in Nyasaland. The Blantyre missionaries were profoundly suspicious of Johnston's motives and felt that his policies left a great deal to be desired. He in his turn considered them narrow-minded bigots who had no idea of the way in which government or business should be run and who were jealous of him personally because he had superseded

52. Dr. David Scott and his colleagues at Blantyre had serious doubts as to whether Johnston himself always understood the distinction; they felt that there was evidence that he had seriously contemplated an arrangement that would have granted Rhodes much more power than was publicly acknowledged (Ross, pp. 198–200).

Scott, the leader of the Church of Scotland mission at Blantyre, as the "British authority" in the Shire Highlands.[53]

Scott and his colleagues had rather wanted to have the best of two quite different worlds. Worried about the possibility of Portuguese expansion and concerned about the broader problem of conflict in the Shire Highlands, they had favored a formal British presence in the area. But they were most unhappy when the new administration took steps to make its presence effective, asserted its authority, and insisted that Africans pay taxes in order to meet the costs of administration. The British government provided a meager grant to cover the minimal costs of administration, but its members would have been either amused or indignant had anyone suggested that colonies were acquired for the benefit of the colonized, except in the indirect sense that they derived benefit from more competent and honest administration. The costs of suppressing the slave trade and maintaining law and order were considered to be a proper charge to levy on the African population. The churches were scarcely able to provide funds to meet the minimal needs of the missions and were in no position to meet the costs of administering the country. Business organizations willing to put up money, such as the British South Africa Company, did so in the expectation of substantial concessions, and members of the Scottish mission viewed any concessions with the greatest suspicion. That Scott should have wanted the advantages of colonial rule without the disadvantages is natural enough; that he should actually have expected to get them suggests that he was quite unable to grasp the mechanics of power. It is not surprising that a master practitioner such as Johnston should have been more aware of Scott's failure to grasp political realities than he was of Scott's ability to understand and sympathize with powerless and illiterate Africans. Scott did have a clear idea of the purpose a British administration in Nyasaland

53. This view is endorsed by Oliver, whose account is very hostile to the Blantyre Mission. An entirely different view is taken by Ross, both in the work already cited and in "The African—'A Child or a Man'—the Quarrel between the Blantyre Mission of the Church of Scotland and the British Central Africa Administration, 1890–1905," in Stokes and Brown.

should serve and, if he sometimes failed to appreciate the necessity of compromise in order to meet an immediate practical
problem, he did see that an endless series of compromises
would first jeopardize and ultimately defeat the purpose of
being there at all. If on every important issue the interests of
Africans were to be subordinated to those of Europeans; if for
administrative convenience the traditional structure of African
society was to be destroyed; and if for the forseeable future it
was to be assumed that Africans would be unable to achieve
positions of leadership in the new society being formed on
their land, then the noble objective set by Scott and his colleagues of bringing about a social and economic (as well as
spiritual) transformation that would bring the African to his
rightful place as "co-inheritor" of a common civilization would
be lost. Scott was acutely aware of the danger of company rule
and settler rule, and he was suspicious that Johnston was more
concerned about the extension of imperial power than with the
future welfare of the protectorate's African subjects. The stubborn and sometimes abrasive pressure brought to bear by Scott
and his colleagues on the administration made them unpopular
in the protectorate's seat of government, but their fears about
Johnston's proclivities were not without justification.[54]

Meanwhile Johnston had set about the task of establishing
British sovereignty over the area, of laying the framework of
administrative control, of exacting revenue, and of attempting
to provide some measure of justice in determining the legitimacy of settler claims to land obtained in the short period of
European penetration.

He carried out a series of campaigns against the Yao chiefs,
who were not disposed —for a variety of reasons— to recognize
the virtue of accepting British rule. With the small force at his
disposal, despite the remarkable energy and endurance displayed by his colleagues and himself, it took several years before the power of the Yao was finally broken. A number of the
more recalcitrant chiefs had part of their land taken over as
crown property, and they ceased to be an effective focus of
opposition to the colonial administration. Elsewhere the control

54. Ross, "Origins and Development," pp. 198–200.

of the administration was expanded either by punitive expeditions, which included the burning of villages whose inhabitants had been reluctant to pay taxes, or by treaties with chiefs. Several of the chiefs appeared subsequently to have had an interpretation of what was being agreed to different from that of the British authorities. By the time that they had doubts about the matter, it was too late for them to do anything about it. In some cases chiefs thought they were entering into an alliance only to learn that they had surrendered their independence.

The opposition proved to be halfhearted (except among the Yao) or else Johnston's small force would not have accomplished as much as quickly as they did. In some instances British overlordship provided protection against stronger neighbors and afforded some relief from the often extensive and sometimes arbitrary power exercised by local chiefs over their subjects.

The difficulty of providing a set of laws that would express the sense of justice of the colonial authorities and would carry some of the moral sanction of traditional custom as well was considerable. It was not only the fact that, on some points at least, notions of justice and equity differed between the new rulers and their subjects nor even the fact that some of the new laws were primarily designed to entrench the power of the new rulers and the small white-settler population. There were, in addition, considerable differences among the customs of different tribal groups, and a rule that seemed reasonable to one might be offensive to another.[55] The administration sought to make allowance for a dual system of law under which a large number of offenses, including most of those involving relationship exclusively among Africans, were judged according to customary law (though with provision for appeal to the colonial authorities). But the overriding consideration remained the establishment and maintenance of undisputed colonial rule, and there were times when principles of jurisprudence played a distinctly secondary role to administrative expediency.

An attempt was made, both in the administration of justice and the implementation of policy, to work through the tradi-

55. See, for example, Maliwa, *passim.*

tional leaders, but the government was aware that this procedure might give Africans the impression that the colonial authorities lacked substantive power. In the view of Scott and others this would not have been altogether a bad thing, but the authorities were perhaps more aware than he was of the slender resources at their command in the event of a real challenge to their control. A chief who was believed to have substantial independent power might become the focus of discontent or a source of inspiration; Johnston and his immediate successors were scarcely in a position to take chances, even had they been more sympathetic to Scott and his aspirations than they were.

The first priority of the administration was, and perhaps had to be, the achievement of authority in the area that it was to govern. Next it set its mind to the establishing of a viable economy that would provide the financial resources needed to continue its work.

CHAPTER 2

The Pursuit of
Economic Viability

From its inception, one of the most pressing objectives of the
colonial administration was the establishment of conditions that
would enable the handful of British settlers in the colony to
achieve commercial success, a success sufficient to allow them to
maintain a satisfactory standard of life and, in turn, provide
the foundations of a viable monetized economy to which the
local exchequer could look for a substantial part of its revenue.
In the words of a senior official of the time: "[Our] first and
most natural care was to protect the interests of the British
settlers there."[1]

Most Britons then in Nyasaland shared the conviction that
members of their race had not only the right but the obligation
to exercise authority over the primitive people of the newly
acquired territory. No doubt, a few missionaries and colonial
officials felt that these rights should be circumscribed and
looked forward to a day when Africans themselves would take
up the heritage of civilized, Christian and industrial society, but
few of them visualized, at least in the short run, any fundamental challenge to the right of Europeans to shape and control the
economic and political life of the community. The points at
issue between planters and the more radical missionaries usually concerned the limits of power rather than the right to

---

1. Chief Secretary H. L. Duff, in his book *Nyasaland under the Foreign Office*
(Bell, 1903). The quotation goes on, "The natives of the country thus taken
over are to enjoy the benefits of a strong and humane government, and are to
participate in all such advantages of modern civilisation as, from time to time,
may be safely extended to them." The quotation is taken from Griff Jones,
Britain and Nyasaland, p. 68.

power, and there were many members of the missionary community for whom even that debate suggested an unwarranted
meddling with the natural order.[2]

Even had the administration not accorded so closely with the
mood of the time, it would have been powerfully tempted to
cultivate the interests and goodwill of the small community of
British planters. Colonies were acquired for the benefit of the
parent state, and unless they were needed for strategic reasons
they were expected to pay for themselves. Financial support
from the British government was insufficient in the long run to
sustain anything beyond the barest form of administration, and
the tax revenue that would accrue from taxes on Africans was
severely constrained by the meager income-earning possibilities
open to them, which were largely determined in the short run
by the demand of European-run estates and trading companies
for wage labor.

To the colonial authorities at the turn of the century it
seemed unlikely that either African agriculture or trade would
develop in any form that could lead to a substantial increase in
government revenues. There were, on the other hand, hopes—
perhaps unduly sanguine—that British settlers, adequately supported by the government, would be able to establish enterprises sufficiently profitable to provide both a good living for
themselves and ample tax revenue for the government. These
enterprises, which would offer employment, would enable Africans to pay the poll tax and would provide a practical demonstration to them of the virtues of advanced agricultural and
commercial practices. It was, in short, expected that estate agriculture under British direction, supported by other British
commercial and industrial activities, would provide the means
for transforming the economic life of the territory. Some of the

2. It may be that the influence of politically conservative evangelical views
was a good deal weaker in Nyasaland than in either of the Rhodesias. See, for
example, Robert Rotberg, *Christian Missionaries and the Creation of Northern Rhodesia, 1880–1924* (Princeton: Princeton University Press, 1965). Nonetheless,
few European missionaries were advocates of revolutionary political change.
One was Joseph Booth, whose work in Nyasaland has been described by
George Shepperson and Thomas Price, in their monumental work, *Independent
African* (Edinburgh: Edinburgh University Press, 1958).

European population expected that this in turn would bring such great advantages to the entire community that it would amply compensate Africans for any hardship suffered during the transitional period.

Perhaps not many people were as optimistic as was Harry Johnston, Her Majesty's commissioner and consul general, but even the most skeptical could think of few alternatives once it had become clear that the mineral wealth at first anticipated either did not exist at all or would be difficult to find. If the planters offered the best hope of administrative solvency, it was quite evident that a great deal of help would be needed before the establishment and maintenance of plantations and other commercial activities in Nyasaland could be made attractive to Europeans.[3]

The planters brought with them some knowledge of modern agricultural practices (or the ability to acquire it), some understanding of the foreign markets in which they expected to sell their products, and perhaps some useful connections among potential buyers, together with some organizing ability and enough capital to enable them to live for a few years until the farm or estate began to provide them with an adequate income. They found themselves at a considerable disadvantage compared with their compatriots in Southern Rhodesia and in the Union of South Africa. The means of communication were primitive, slow, and expensive and the wastage rate, both in lives and in goods, was substantial; they were dependent on workers who had little or no previous experience of wage employment, many of whom were required on their family holdings at the very time when their services were most urgently needed on the European farms.

Three basic requirements had to be met if European planters were to establish viable economic institutions in Nyasaland. These were adequate communications (especially transport), a sufficient and reliable supply of cheap labor, and abundant cheap land. The attempt to meet these requirements was to

3. Pachai reviews some of the evidence on coffee output during this period (*Malawi*, pp. 153ff.). A much more pessimistic estimate of what a planter might reasonably expect is cited by B.S. Krishnamurty, "Land and Labour in Nyasaland, 1891–1914" (Ph.D. diss. University of London, 1964), p. 141.

dominate the political and economic agenda of the colonial administration throughout most of its effective existence. There were, of course, other objectives which it sought to achieve, some of which were intended to bring substantial benefits to the African population. These included the development of African administrative control of some matters of local interest; the gradual introduction of "responsible" political representation of African opinion; the encouragement of, and assistance to, African farmers engaged in improved agricultural practices and the spread of cash-crop agriculture; the development of a sound educational system; the provision of basic health facilities, and other similar matters. But these were peripheral rather than fundamental objectives, by-products rather than the main focus of activity, which was the establishment of an effective economic base for the maintenance of colonial rule.

The transport constraint was perhaps the most intractable during the first years of the colony and was exacerbated by the fall in the level of Lake Nyasa during the 1890s, which led to a reduction of the flow along the Shire River and made it more difficult for oceangoing vessels to negotiate its lower reaches. The building of roads was not considered to be a means of providing an adequate alternative, according to a report that Johnston sent to the Foreign Office in 1894, "because of the presence in various tracts of the tsetse fly, which would render the passage of horses or oxen too risky for them to become constantly used as a means of transport." He then went on to say, "I fear the only certain and practical way of opening up communications with this country will be by a railway running between the lower and the upper Shire."[4]

There was general recognition among the planter community that substantial commercial advantages would be derived from the construction of a railway, but Europeans in Nyasaland were either unwilling or unable to raise the money to pay for it. The administration, which had its headquarters at Zomba, was extremely hard pressed to cover its own basic expenses and the imperial government did not feel obliged to provide or subsi-

4. Pachai, *Malawi*, p. 142.

dize a railway line in Central Africa, even for the benefit of its own citizens.

There was still, however, a demand for land in Nyasaland, since the hope that it might contain mineral wealth had not entirely faded, and a considerable amount of land still appeared to be unoccupied. Practical men soon appreciated that Nyasaland had assets that might be acceptable to men who could build the railway line; less attention was paid to the question of who properly had a claim on these assets.

Two companies offered to build a railway in return for a number of concessions, mainly with respect to the acquisition of land, and in 1897 a departmental committee of the Foreign Office recommended that some such arrangement be made. The principal features of the first set of concessions proposed by the Foreign Office were that 1,000 acres of land should be granted, including mineral rights, for every mile of railway constructed and that the company be guaranteed a monopoly of rail transport in Nyasaland for some time in the future.[5]

Negotiations with actual or prospective railway companies were held up by bureaucratic inertia, but in 1901 the Shire Highlands Railway Company contracted to undertake the work on a line of a little more than thirty miles between Chiromo and Blantyre. There was further delay as it apparently proved impossible to raise money overseas on the terms arranged, and in the following year the government agreed to grant the company 6,400 acres of land for each completed mile of rail.

Work began in 1903, making substantial demands on the limited labor supply and obliging the company to double the wages of African labor. The company soon asserted that, because of the continually falling level of the Shire River, it would not be possible to get the construction materials up to Chiromo unless an additional length of line was built from Chiromo to Port Herald at the southern tip of the territory. After a good deal of discussion this was eventually conceded by the government, and the company undertook to build another forty-two miles, for which it would receive 3,200 acres of land per mile of railway.

5. This account draws heavily on Pachai, *Malawi*, pp. 143ff.

The line between Blantyre and Port Herald was opened on 1 January 1908. The company, which had acquired over 360,000 acres of land, was to have a monopoly position for twenty-five years, after which the Nyasaland government would have the right to purchase the railway at a cost of £4,750 a mile. Meanwhile, however, members of the Lomwe tribe had migrated in large numbers from Portuguese Africa, and many of them had settled on land that was being granted to the railway company, greatly increasing the density of African population in the area. It became clear that handing over the land would be more complicated than initially expected. A new agreement was negotiated; as a result the company acquired some of the land promised to it, was given compensation for the remainder, and the government agreed to underwrite the interest (at 4 per cent) on the company's capital investment (of £300,000) for a ten-year period.

In 1912, the government undertook support of a project to build a railway line that would join Blantyre to the Mozambique port of Beira on the Indian Ocean. The Shire Highlands Railway Company had acquired a concession from the Portuguese to construct a railway line in Mozambique, and the Nyasaland government agreed to grant a subsidy of £7,500 a year for twenty years on the condition that it would extend its line from the south of Nyasaland passing across Portuguese territory to the Zambezi, while the Mozambique Company, whose director and general manager was Sir Alfred Sharpe, formerly governor of Nyasaland, was to be responsible for a line from the Zambezi to Beira. Both lines were intended to be operational by 1915, and it was expected that a bridge across the Zambezi would also be built by then. In fact, the line from Port Herald to the Zambezi opened in May 1915, but the other section was not completed until 1922. The bridge at Sena was not built until the 1930s because until then it had proved impossible to obtain the massive loans required for building what was, at the time, the longest bridge in the world, some two and a half miles long.

During the thirties, Nyasaland received loans of approximately £3.5 million in order to build the Zambezi bridge and undertake other improvements in the transport system, most notably the construction of a northern extension of the railway to Salima, on the shores of Lake Nyasa. Loan receipts and repayments in connection with the railway extension dominated the revenue and expenditure accounts of the colony during the 1930s. Although the onset of World War II prevented the colony from gaining an immediate and significant commercial advantage from this relatively massive investment in infrastructure, the opening of a direct line to Beira did much to reduce the competitive disadvantage from which Nyasaland exporters had previously suffered.

There were still complaints about the length of time the journey took on the narrow gauge railway to Beira, but the barriers to world markets were substantially reduced. The export of cash crops became much more attractive; with underemployment in agriculture and surplus land there were no other immediate bottlenecks preventing the expansion of cash crop agriculture for export. This, by raising the average level of incomes in the country, was to make feasible the establishment within the country of a number of small industries which it had previously been impracticable to set up because of insufficient local demand. At the same time imported components needed by these industries would be both cheaper and more readily available as a result of the completion of the Zambezi bridge.

The economic benefits did not materialize immediately. The world economic depression had scarcely lifted before World War II broke out. Nonetheless, with the completion of the Zambezi bridge and the establishment of a direct rail link between Blantyre and Beira, the fundamental problem of transportation had largely been resolved, albeit at a high cost. Many other critical problems remained. The most contentious of them was the vexing question of land tenure.

The circumstances under which Europeans had acquired land in Nyasaland were such that, even had there been no instances of bad faith, there would have been ample occasion for subsequent question about the validity of titles to land. The colonial administration had been established during a period of intense tribal and intratribal conflict, when control over land

(and the people on it) was changing hands time and again. There had from the outset been room for uncertainty about which chief or headman, from whichever tribe or group, had legitimate claim to the land, and in what respects his rights to dispose of land were circumscribed. The colonial administration had been far from consistent in its own interpretation of the conflicting claims of present and traditional rulers and, not surprisingly, was inclined to adopt whatever position suited its interests at the time. Individual Europeans buying land were not always scrupulous in their concern for the legitimacy of these transactions and were not always given a clear idea of the government's views.[6]

The crux of the matter was that European settlement, even on a small scale, was viable only if Europeans were able to obtain, in substantial amount, the best land in the protectorate at a very low price. However much the administration wished to be fair to Africans, it could not fully protect their rights to own or live on the land in terms of traditional practices in the country without at the same time jeopardizing the entire position of the European community in Nyasaland.

Not long after the colonial administration was established, Sir Harry Johnston (as he soon became), already burdened with an enormous range of responsibilities undertaken almost single-handedly, attempted to weed out the most blatant forms of malpractice in the acquisition of land, but he had little opportunity to undertake a detailed and impartial inquiry. The landlords whose claims he accepted as valid were granted "certificates of claim," but little more could be said of some of them than that there was no conclusive evidence that the claims were invalid; in view of the uncertainty about the relative value of conflicting traditional claims, the absence of written documentary evidence, and the circumstance that agreements between Europeans and Africans were almost always conducted between parties who both literally and metaphorically spoke a different language, it would have been difficult to achieve more without much greater resources than were available to Johnston. In only a few cases could it have been conclusively proved

6. See, for example, Krishnamurty, "Land and Labour," pp. 73ff.

that the owners had an incontestable right to the land, and sometimes the benefit of doubt may have been extended to Europeans whose claim to the land was almost entirely fraudulent. Johnston asserted that land acquired by Europeans should be put to productive use as a condition of ownership, but this proved to be little more than a pious hope. A great deal of the land for which certificates had been issued was lying idle several decades later.

In an attempt to limit the hardship of Africans whose rights to land on which they had been living had been severely curtailed by the recent agreements, the certificates of claim contained a "nondisturbance" clause, which began with a firm statement and went on rather more ambiguously:

No native village or plantation existing at the date of the certificate on the said estate shall be disturbed or removed without the consent in writing of Her Majesty's Commissioner and Consul General . . . but when such consent shall have been given the sites of such villages or plantations shall revert to the proprietor of the said estate. No natives can make other and new villages or plantations on a said estate without the prior consent of the proprietor.[7]

The normal agricultural practice among Africans at the time involved shifting cultivation, and for this reason an African community was not likely to remain in precisely the same location for very long. It may have been Johnston's intention to provide nothing more than some temporary protection for African residents, which would have shielded them from the harshest effects of immediate loss of their land and homes but which offered them no security in the long run. If so, Johnston was less than candid about the probable effects of his policy, and its significance appears to have escaped the attention of his principal biographer.[8] The organization of European estate

7. Quoted in the *Land Commission Report*, 1946 (Zomba: Government Printer) presented by Sidney S. Abrahams to the governor of Nyasaland (subsequently to be cited as *Abrahams Report*), par. 28.

8. Roland Oliver says simply that "it was an invariable condition that all land occupied by native villages or plantations was excluded from the claims, and when he thought it necessary Johnston took pains to inform the inhabitants of such villages that they were under no obligation to pay rent or render service to the adjacent landlord." Nothing is mentioned in Oliver's account of the matter of reversion (*Sir Harry Johnson*, p. 220).

owners was, however, later to assert that this was exactly what the clause meant:

This clause simply meant that natives originally on the land at the time of the purchase were not to be disturbed (except by Government permission) *as in the natural cause of events they would move, and leave the land* [italics in original] when they had exhausted its fertility. It secured to the native the usufruct of the land so long as he remained on it, which is the universal condition of native tenure. A native who has a garden claims, under native custom, the right to the produce of the garden so long as he cultivates it, *but he claims no right to the land itself* [italics in original] as, when he abandons it, the land reverts to the Chief and the Chief may allot it to others if there are applicants. This clause crystallises this native custom and says in effect that the original natives may remain as long as they use the land, but when they vacate it the land reverts to the Chief, i.e. in this case the landlord. This is actually what has happened. It is significant that no applications were made to Government to disturb these original settlers. They were allowed to remain until they vacated the sites *of their own accord as contemplated by the above clause* [emphasis added].[9]

The analogy between chiefs and landlords was disingenuous. Traditional practice allowed for villagers moving from one plot to obtain rights to another, but while some landlords might have been prepared to supply other land, they recognized no judicial or moral obligation to do so. If they followed the practice, it was regarded by them only as a matter of personal generosity which created no precedent. The estate owners were, in effect, claiming that they should be granted the rights of traditional chiefs with none of their traditional obligations.

In any event the clause soon became a matter of dispute for another reason. At the time when the land was acquired by the British, the African population was unusually sparse, largely because of the slave trade. As the area became more settled, the population level would be expected to rise to its former density, and since there was also migration from Portuguese East Africa, the overall rate of increase of population was substantial. It has been estimated that on the 160 thousand acres of the Bruce Livingstone estates there were no more than 350 people in 1895, but by 1920 there were about 15,000, and at the end

9. *Abrahams Report*, Appendix VI, par. 6.

of World War II the number had risen to more than 30,000. This cannot, it would appear, be attributed to any particularly attractive features offered to Africans by terms of service on the private estates of Nyasaland because the density of population on native trust land was even greater.[10] Whatever the deficiences of the colonial administration in Nyasaland and of the conditions of work on the principal estates, the country was very attractive to Africans who would otherwise have been living under Portuguese rule.

Africans known to be protected by the "no disturbance" clause could not be deprived of their land and were not required to pay rent, but clearly there was a great deal of room for dispute about which Africans were protected. Those Africans who were, for any reason, living on the estates at a later period had an incentive to claim original resident status regardless of whether or not their forebears really did live on the land, while landowners had a very powerful incentive to deny that any of their tenants had "natural claim" to rights to the land and to insist that those people now on the land were migrants from elsewhere. There were few records that could accurately identify the original tenants and far too much depended, in the phrase used by Griff Jones, "on the accuracy and honesty of human memories."[11] Not surprisingly the question arose whether the onus should be on the tenant to prove that he held land by right of the original residence of himself or his family or on the landowner to prove that the tenant was not protected.

In 1903 J. J. Nunan (later knighted), presiding judge of the Protectorate High Court, ruled that except in the case of Anguru tenants (who were clearly migrants from Portuguese East Africa and not original tenants) the onus of proof was on the landlord to establish that someone was not an original tenant before claiming rent from him. Following this decision a commission, under the chairmanship of Justice Nunan, was named to indicate ways in which the law might be amended to cover the matters dealt with in the 1903 judgment and, as a result of its recommendations, the Lands Ordinance (Native Locations) was enacted.

10. *Abrahams Report,* par. 11 and 12.
11. Griff Jones, p. 107.

This ordinance provided that Africans resident on private estates should be treated as original residents and that in certain scheduled districts landlords should set aside a portion of their land on which squatters would be accommodated, at eight acres per hut, with a liability to an annual rent of four shillings. The commission also proposed a tax of one penny or more on each acre of all underdeveloped land in excess of ten times the landlord's developed acreage. The ordinance was never put into effect. When much later S. S. Abrahams was appointed to examine the land question, he remarked that he had been "unable to discover" why this was so.[12]

The planters took a very different view, insisting that Africans should hold land on the estates only if they were willing to provide labor services for the estate owner. Some evidence suggests that they were prepared to accept a compromise, according to which 20 per cent of the Africans on the estates would be able to maintain their homes on payment of rent while the other 80 per cent would be obliged to provide labor services. The issue was not resolved, and it continued to be a source of bitterness and misunderstanding. Shortly before World War I, when the matter was again being debated, the journal of the Blantyre Mission had this to say:

At present with the exception of a few—a very few—natives who have got grants of land from the Government or have secured them by purchase or lease, no native has any security of tenure for himself or his crops. If he has a house or garden on an estate owned by a European, he may be moved any day after certain notice, or he may have to make such arrangements as regards rent or services to make it suitable for him to move elsewhere. If he is on Government land he may have the land he has settled or transferred to some private purchaser; and though the deed of transfer secures his rights, yet the new conditions are such as he will no doubt prefer to move elsewhere. In neither case is there permanency of occupation guaranteed him which alone can induce him to put his surroundings on a permanent basis. He will not build a permanent house nor will he care to plant and cultivate slow maturing plants, crops or trees.[13]

The Commission of Inquiry into the Chilembwe Rising of

12. *Abrahams Report*, par. 29.
13. Shepperson and Price, p. 199.

1915 again drew attention to African grievances over security of tenure, which were felt to have been one of the causes of the rising. Scottish missionaries at Blantyre, following the line of argument earlier presented by the Nunan Commission, proposed that the government should purchase "undeveloped land in European hands" for the benefit of African tenants.[14]

The Native Rent (Private Estates) Ordinance, passed in 1917, sought to prohibit the exaction of involuntary labor service in lieu of rent, but it made no mention of the rights of original tenants, and it empowered estate owners to charge rent to all Africans with homes on the estate and to evict any African on six months' notice. Although this may have been an improvement for the majority who had no claim as original settlers, it was gained at the expense of the original tenants. Three years later an attempt was made to revive the cause of the original tenants. The Lands Commission of 1920-21 expressed the view that if Africans were able to establish "that they had remained on the sites of their original settlements on estates granted under certificates of claim" they should not be evicted.[15]

A lucid analysis of the situation prevailing in the early 1920s was presented by the Ormsby-Gore Commission, which had been appointed by the United Kingdom government in 1924 to visit and report on Northern Rhodesia, Nyasaland, Tanganyika Territory, Uganda and Kenya. In the commission's view two questions were critical: whether or not the demands for rent from "resident natives" were sound in law, and, whether land held by Europeans had been adequately developed. The way to deal with the problem, they suggested, was for the government to purchase land from Europeans and make it available for African settlement. The necessary revenue should, they suggested, be financed by a graduated tax on land and differential rates on developed and undeveloped land. Rebates would be granted to those estates that had undertaken substantial capital expenditure and development, so that most of the cost would be borne by estate owners who held large tracts of idle land. Whatever the objective merits of this scheme, its lack of appeal

14. Ibid., p. 393.
15. *Abrahams Report,* par. 31.

to landowners is hardly surprising, and since the landowners had influence with the administration, there was never much chance that the proposal would be adopted.

In 1928 the Natives on Private Estates Ordinance was passed. No distinction was made between original settlers and others, but security of tenure for the majority was improved. In each subsequent five-year period, the landowner would have the right to evict no more than 10 per cent of Africans resident on the estate and then only on giving six months' notice prior to the end of the quinquennium, except for non-payment of rent. Subsequently, in 1938, an amendment to this ordinance made the government responsible for people evicted under the ordinance by providing for settlement on native trust land.[16]

There were no evictions during the quinquennium following the enactment of the 1928 ordinance. The landlords claimed that this was because they did not wish to embarrass the government, but it should be borne in mind that the planters had been severely affected by the depression and that land was not in demand.

By the end of the 1930s the questions to be answered about European landholdings were much the same as they had been at the beginning of the century. Three principle issues were still unresolved: how much security should tenants be granted, what obligations rested on the landowner to develop the land, and to what extent were landlords entitled to demand labor services in lieu of rent.

Attempts had been made, as we have seen, to protect the right of original residents, but it had proven to be virtually impossible to establish who were the original residents and who, among present tenants, were qualified to be treated as members of the family of an original resident. Moreover, once it was recognized that shifting cultivation was widely practiced, the moral validity of distinguishing between someone who happened to be "on" the land in a particular year and someone else who might well have moved to it a few years later became questionable. On the other hand, if no distinctions were made, it would be difficult for the landowner to prevent a steady

16. On African trust land, see Pachai, *Malawi*, pp. 104ff.

stream of squatters from claiming the right to settle on his land.

If the land occupied by the squatters would otherwise have been unproductive, no economic loss would have been suffered as a consequence of their arrival. But it was almost invariably claimed by landlords, sometimes no doubt with justice, that the land would shortly be brought into productive use and that it would be a serious economic blow to the country as well as to themselves if they were inhibited from making effective use of it. In this view African occupation would reduce the amount of land that could be brought into cultivation and African methods of cultivation would significantly reduce the fertility of the soil.[17]

Serious disturbances in both 1943 and 1945 arose out of attempts to evict Africans alleged to be in arrears with their rent, and in 1946 there was yet another report, this time by Sir Sidney Abrahams. Sir Sidney undertook a clear and detailed survey of the historical position before putting forward his own suggestions for dealing with the problem. In some respects the situation was less intractable than it had been before the war. The colonial administration was by this time receiving substantial assistance from the British government, and had, in any event, more substantial resources available to it within Nyasaland as a result of rising export earnings.

The Land Commission Report, containing the "findings, opinions and recommendations" of Sir Sidney, proposed that undeveloped but potentially cultivable land should be subject to compulsory purchase by the government and should be administered as native trust land. The officials entrusted with responsibility for these lands had always been specifically instructed to attach high priority to the interests of resident Africans, although Africans had no legal right to prevent their alienation. It was further recommended that Africans living on estates which had been developed should be given a choice among three options. First, a tenant could leave the private estate and establish a home on native trust land; second, leave the private estate and receive compensation for his home and garden from

17. Griff Jones, pp. 106ff.

the government; and third, he might enter into a labor contract with the estate owner which would enable him to maintain his home on the estate as long as he was working for the owner, and at such time as that arrangement was no longer satisfactory to the tenant and the contractual period had expired, the tenant would leave his home on the estate and receive compensation from the government.[18]

The former tenants would gain some advantage from these proposals: they would henceforth have much more adequate security of tenure, albeit on different land. The estate owners also stood to gain several advantages if the proposals were adopted. African tenants on developed land would no longer have any permanent claim on part of the estate, and squatters would have no opportunity to encroach on the estates, claiming that they were descendants of the original residents; while the land which the government acquired was of little immediate value to the owners, who would now be able to gain some immediate advantage in selling it to the government.

There were, however, some important problems left unresolved. The estate owners had always wanted to make residence on an estate contingent on working for the owner, mainly because this would provide them with a secure supply of labor; it would, of course, do so only if Africans were unable to make homes elsewhere or found the effective alternatives unsatisfactory for one reason or another. Here lies the rub, for if the Abrahams proposals were successful in dealing with the principal African grievances over the land issue, then Africans would have little incentive to seek temporary homes on the estates; in that case the estates would (if previous assessments had been correct) face a shortage of labor; if labor was still attracted by the accommodation on the estates, it would mean that African land hunger remained unsatisfied. Perhaps what was intended was that in the future estates would be expected to pay more attractive wages than they had needed to do in the past, but if this was so, the intention appears to have passed unnoticed at the time.

The government accepted the proposals. In the next few

18. *Abrahams Report,* esp. part iv, pars. 76–81.

years a substantial amount of land was purchased, and the number of Africans dependent on private estate owners for their homes was greatly reduced. Whether or not this would, in the absence of other irritating factors, have significantly improved relations on the estates was never to be clearly established because within a few years the country was torn by the bitter dispute over federation, in which Europeans, who were the landowners and employers, were ranged on one side while Africans, whether workers or tenants, were almost unanimously on the other.

The provision of an adequate supply of labor for the development activities of the settler population had been one of the principal concerns of colonial administration in Nyasaland since its inception. Inextricably bound, as it was, to the land question, some aspects of this other great demand of Europeans seeking to establish commercial and farming enterprises (and sometimes even missions) have already been touched upon, but it deserves, and indeed requires, more systematic discussion.

The introduction of hut and poll taxes in 1881 and their maintenance have been primarily intended to raise revenue for the conduct of the colonial administration, but it was widely understood from the outset that the demand for cash payment would oblige Africans to seek wage employment which, with few exceptions, meant working for European employers.[19]

In 1901 the revision of tax regulations could leave no doubt that, whatever the original intention, tax policy was now to be used directly as a means of increasing the supply of labor to European employers. The rate of tax on Africans was to be doubled, but those who worked for a European for at least one month during the year were granted exemption from half the tax. The pressure on Africans to work for a European employer was compounded when it became accepted practice for a landowner to pay the taxes of his tenants and then demand

19. There were, however, other views. Griff Jones says that some employers feared that the tax would increase the cost of labor, but he goes on: "The settlers' fear of native taxation [did not] materialise; the cost of labour did not materially rise. Indeed, taxation encouraged men to seek employment to find the necessary cash" (p. 72).

that they provide labor services at a time suitable to himself in order to make up the value of the tax payment. The effect was described succinctly by Krishnamurty: "A European, by paying in cash the taxes of a whole village, could claim a month's work from the owners of huts and if they refused to turn out he could call on the strong arm of the administration."[20]

European employers were legally obliged to issue labor certificates to Africans but, as Shepperson put it: "Often more than the statutory minimum was taken from the African by unscrupulous employers. The perplexity of the continuing series of regulations did not make it easier for the African to defend himself against this, and as most of the regulations were in English, not in the native vernacular, confusion and resentment were natural."[21]

These regulations, apart from their direct effect on the welfare of Africans, gave rise to an unforeseen but nonetheless significant effect on African food supplies. Workers were obliged to seek wage employment even when it could only be obtained at the cost of reduced food production in the subsistence sector. When the country was faced by a long period of intermittent drought, as it was from 1911 to 1913, there were severe and prolonged food shortages.[22] With many workers obliged to earn wages during the period when the demands of their own farms were greatest, there was heavy dependence on the prodigality of nature (which in most years did not fail them). Wages, designed primarily to pay taxes, provided little margin for the purchase of food.

Local conditions of employment were not, in any event, very attractive. Africans seeking employment, whether in order to pay the poll tax or to acquire goods previously unavailable to them, soon found it sometimes necessary and often advantageous to go outside of the country, to Rhodesia or South Africa, to find work.

Wages in Nyasaland were lower, work was of a highly specific kind and concentrated in a short period—the very time, indeed, when the Africans were wanted on their own farms—and

20. Krishnamurty, p. 160.
21. Shepperson and Price, pp. 189ff.
22. Ibid., p. 189.

some of the estates had a reputation for treating African workers harshly and unfairly. Particularly for Africans from the northern part of Nyasaland (the area which provided the largest proportional outflow of migrants) who would have to undertake a substantial journey to reach the Shire Highlands, it seemed more sensible to continue the journey further, to stay longer and make considerably more money.

European attitudes toward the migration of African labor reflected a diverse assortment of interests and ideals. Most planters were in favor of allowing migrants from Portuguese East Africa to enter Nyasaland, where many of them worked on the estates, but objected strongly to Nyasaland Africans being allowed to move south, where employers were offering more attractive conditions than those in Nyasaland were willing or able to do. Colonial officials were perhaps more impressed by the fact that opportunities for wage employment within Nyasaland were insufficient to enable all Africans to meet their hut tax obligations and were very much aware of the difficulty of enforcing a ban on labor migration.

The mission communities were subject to conflicting impulses. There was widespread belief in the virtue of disciplined work, and many missionaries, for moral as well as economic reasons, favored measures that obliged Africans to become wage laborers or cash-crop farmers. Some of the same people were keenly aware that large scale migration, even of a temporary kind, imposed hardship on communities deprived of a substantial proportion of their adult male workers and that social problems could arise for both the migrants and their families when many vigorous young men were away from the families for long intervals. Some missionaries feared that the migrants would be badly treated in areas where white settlers were a more potent political force than they were in Nyasaland and that some migrants would be corrupted by the style of life they would find in the relatively sophisticated urban centers in southern Africa. Among those missionaries most committed to belief in African development, there must have been some unease that men of enterprise and determination, often the products of mission schools, should be denied an opportunity to gain the rewards available in neighboring territories: these missionaries would have preferred to see more opportunities created in Nyasaland, and they pressed for the encouragement of African cash-crop production. In the absence of governmental encouragement for domestic African enterprise, a ban on migration would have made it even harder for Africans to temper the poverty of their environment.

In spite of some opposition within Britain, the Witwatersrand Native Labour Association (WNLA), the recruiting agency for the Chamber of Mines of Johannesburg, was allowed by the colonial administration to establish facilities for direct recruiting of labor for the mines in Nyasaland. In a number of cases colonial officials, such as district commissioners, acted as intermediaries between the recruiting agents and Nyasaland Africans, and the officials believed that they protected Africans from unscrupulous employers. Their presence, however, together with some of the methods used in recruiting workers for service on the estates, sometimes gave rise to serious doubts about the extent to which labor migration was a spontaneous response by Africans to their own assessment of the opportunities available to them and to what extent they believed that the involvement of colonial officials meant that sanctions might be invoked against tribes or individuals who did not respond with some appearance of enthusiasm to the overtures of the recruiting agents.

WNLA was allowed to recruit one thousand workers in 1903. This was raised to five thousand the following year, but the high mortality rate in the mines stimulated concern in Britain, and in 1907 facilities for recruitment were withdrawn. This did not greatly diminish the flow of migrants because WNLA had been responsible for a relatively small proportion of the total. In 1909 an attempt was made to prohibit any outward migration by Africans unless they had been provided with an official pass (that was issued only to those who had paid their taxes, made provision for their families, and agreed that half their wages would not be paid until after their return to Nyasaland). In 1911 the administration imposed harsh punishment on unauthorized migrants: of 1,535 men known to have returned that year, fines were imposed on 1,368, and the other 167 were imprisoned for periods of between two and six weeks.

The government's action proved ineffective. "In spite of [these] measures," wrote Krishnamurty, "unauthorised migration went on unabated," although it was not until several years later that the government was prepared to grant official sanction to labor recruiters.[23]

The outbreak of World War I, and in particular the prolonged campaign against the German forces commanded by Von Lettow in Tanganyika, made very heavy demands on the labor resources of the protectorate. Almost 10 per cent of the potential male labor force enrolled in the King's African Rifles, and a high proportion of the remainder were employed at some time or other on the hard and dangerous *tengatenga* (porterage) work.

General Northey, the commander of the Nyasaland-Rhodesia field force, told the men of his command that he deeply appreciated the tenacity and courage shown by all men and women in his command, but that he "would award the palm of merit to the *tengatenga*." Murray, quoting Northey, commented: "They suffered all the hardships of unusual exposure to wind and rain, cold and heat, mountain heights and low lying swamps, and they had none of the compensating excitement of active warfare, although often exposed to the fire of the enemy."[24]

More than 17,000 soldiers were killed or died as a result of the campaign and almost twice that number of carriers and other "noncombatants" lost their lives. Some of the carriers were probably volunteers in the generally accepted sense of the term, but the British in Nyasaland, including many missionaries, brought a good deal of pressure to bear on Africans to encourage them to volunteer. Missionaries drew on the prestige and goodwill that they had acquired as a result of their efforts to provide educational and health facilities; the administration made it clear that they expected full cooperation from chiefs, who were in turn expected to make it clear to their people that there was a duty to contribute to the British war effort. Not all chiefs were prepared to do this, and Cimtunga,

23. B. S. Krishnamurty, "Economic Policy: Land and Labour in Nyasaland, 1890–1914" in Pachai, ed., *Early History* p. 398.

24. S. S. Murray, *A Handbook of Nyasaland* (London: Crown Agents for the Colony, 1922), pp. 271–272.

chief of the northern Ngoni, was banished to Zomba for his refusal to recruit carriers.

Once the war had ended, however, the critical labor problem in Nyasaland was again that of an excess supply of unskilled labor. In several districts in Nyasaland, most notably some of those in the Northern Province, more than a third of the male labor force was obliged to seek work in Rhodesia or the Union of South Africa. The economic, as distinct from the social, effects of this massive drain of labor are subject to a great deal of controversy. In the short run, there were few opportunities for productive work in the areas from which the migrants came, and the remittances that the migrants sent home or brought with them on their return may well have contributed more to local income than anything they could have produced had they stayed home. It is, however, quite possible that in the long run the departure of so large a proportion of the able-bodied men, if only as temporary migrants, materially reduced the likelihood of an effective response to changing conditions within Nyasaland. In particular, it may have inhibited the development of cash-crop agriculture in the north. That undeveloped area, which was pitifully short of natural resources and infrastructure, was further handicapped as a consequence of migration by the stagnation of traditional agriculture, with small farms tended by a labor force that was often insufficient to improve the quality of either crops or soil. This, in turn, meant that there was little effective pressure to improve the grossly inadequate communications between the sparsely populated lands of the north and the more prosperous parts of the country in the Lilongwe plain and the Shire Highlands.

The quality of the labor force available to European employers was, of course, significantly influenced by the type of educational system prevailing in the country. In several important respects the planters and the missionaries had very different views about the sort of education that was most appropriate in Nyasaland, but before World War I the opinions of planters about appropriate educational policies did not carry much weight at either Livingstonia or Blantyre.

The Scottish missions were eager to produce Christians who were at the same time literate and skilled artisans, capable of assisting in the transformation which they hoped, and initially expected, would be brought about in the material environment. But it soon became apparent that both the missionaries and their sponsors had underestimated the obstacles to such transformation.

Although there had been some initial skepticism about the virtues of European education among many Africans, and severe resistance to it in some areas,[25] a few groups had proved highly responsive to its apparent opportunities. The Tonga of the northern districts were perhaps more disposed than other Africans of the protectorate to seek positions of influence through independent achievement, but their experience in the period immediately preceding the assumption of British rule had, in any event, borne in on them, in a harsh and not infrequently humiliating manner, the realization that traditional modes of life left a good deal to be desired. They quickly appreciated the merits of a scheme which, with some adaptability and hard work on their part, would give them access to favored positions in the social order introduced by colonial rule.

It was not long before others realized that some familiarity with the new style of formal education held out an opportunity to do well for themselves and their kinsfolk. As a result, there were, especially in the north, a relatively large number of young men (and some young women) who were literate, spoke English, and who had some industrial training, but there were very few opportunities for them locally to make productive use of the skills they had acquired.

This dearth of opportunity had several consequences, which had been unforeseen by the missions and would have been regarded by most of them as highly undesirable. There was very heavy demand for the few jobs that the missions themselves were able to offer to people with the qualifications achieved by the ablest and most ambitious students within their own system. The almost limitless opportunities that had seemed within the grasp of a young man while he was struggling to secure his education turned out to be far more re-

25. Margaret Read, "The Ngoni and Western Education," in V. Turner, ed., *Colonisation in Africa, 1870–1964* (Cambridge: Cambridge University Press 1971), p. 355.

stricted than he had supposed and often required a long additional period of apprenticeship. Some of the more promising students to pass through the mission schools became frustrated and embittered; more than a few blamed the missions that had nurtured and encouraged them but that had also, as they saw it, lured them with false promises.

The second unforeseen consequence was the incentive to migration provided by education. Some movement away from the north was inevitable, because of the need to earn money to pay the poll tax coupled with the limitation on income earning in the Northern Province, but the education that was provided, especially at Livingstonia, was typically a great deal better than that available to Africans in the more prosperous territories to the south. Nyasaland workers soon acquired an enviable reputation for their skill and literacy, and many of them were able to reach the highest positions open to African workers in neighboring countries. Thus the education that it had been hoped would help transform the north instead encouraged many of the ablest young men there to leave, even if only for a couple of years, and deprived the area of one of the few significant sources of dynamism that it possessed.

Most employers appreciated the advantages in having a labor force with a rudimentary grasp of literacy and numeracy and which had become accustomed in the classroom to regular habits of attendance. They felt, however, that little benefit was to be gained from providing Africans with a more advanced education and that any serious attempt to go beyond elementary education would encourage the spread of impractical and dangerous ideas. The educational structure favored by this type of employer was one in which a relatively large proportion of the population had some exposure to education but in which very few, or better still none at all, had more than was necessary to implant a few basic skills and some degree of discipline.

The missionary community was itself divided in its attitude toward the most appropriate form of educational structure. Scott and Laws, and others like them, believed that an important (and in some instances, central) purpose of the missionary presence was to create conditions that would eventually lead to a large or even complete measure of African control over the resources and the political life of the community. They were committed to the development, at as rapid a rate as feasible, of good quality postprimary (and eventually higher) education. Those men who thought that the most important, and in some cases exclusive, objective of the missions was to implant the seeds of the gospel in as many minds as possible, did not think it appropriate to devote resources to the expensive process of upper and postprimary education. They believed that priority should be given to reaching as many people as possible even if it meant that the resources devoted to each person would be very meager.

In the period up to World War I the powerful Scottish missions at Blantyre and Livingstonia pursued the first approach and were not much swayed by the opposition of the planter community. By the 1920s, however, the missions had drawn back from their commitment to the immediate provision of postprimary education, and in the view of many observers the standards achieved in the upper classes of Livingstonia during the first decade of the century were not again approached until the inauguration of formal secondary school education during World War II.

In a community as small as that of the European missions in Nyasaland at the turn of the century, it would be unwise to discount the influence of a handful of strong men. One reason for the change in mission policy may have been the change in the composition of the Scottish missions. This would be particularly likely at Blantyre where the Reverend David Scott had been a dominating figure during the 1880s and had attracted a group of able and like-minded men who had, indeed, been drawn to Nyasaland largely because of Scott's personality and aspirations. As they were replaced by men less sympathetic to the cause of racial equality, the early educational policy found more critics than advocates; and as the missions changed their views about the prospective role of Africans, they became more sympathetic to the concerns of the settler community.

The relatively large European immigration during the immediate postwar period, perhaps in response to the attractiveness of tobacco and cotton farming, made it seem unlikely that there would be an opportunity in the near future for substantial

African advance toward positions of authority in either the business or the political life of Nyasaland.

The flow of funds from Britain to the Scottish missions, which had never been ample, and which had always depended heavily on the generosity of a few men who had been successful businessmen as well as devout members of the church, became distinctly meager; when the early benefactors died, there were few to succeed them, and dependence on their benevolence was not relieved by a significant increase in the numbers of people making contributions. The financial difficulties faced by the missions during the 1920s and 1930s would, in any event, have led to reexamination of educational priorities, but the decision which was reached, to cut back drastically on postprimary facilities, was not only a fundamental reversal of the missions' earlier objectives but ran counter to the policies being pursued by both religious and secular bodies in most of British-ruled Africa.

A relatively large proportion of the population had some limited contact with formal education, but it was not until 1941 that the territory acquired its first secondary school, long after many parts of British Africa had established schools of very high quality, and it was not until several years later that the administration was prepared to accept Nyasaland Africans as teachers in the senior primary schools. In other parts of the continent, British officials had been pleased to appoint Africans to senior positions in secondary schools as early as the 1920s but, in spite of the devoted work of Laws and Scott and the early educational promise of Livingstonia and Blantyre, the educational system in Nyasaland at the end of World War II was one of the least developed in British-ruled Africa.[26]

The conversion of the missions to an educational policy favored by the planters meant that by the 1920s the economic and social program being pursued in Nyasaland was similar on all matters closely affecting settler interests to that which might have been carried out by a government which explicitly endorsed the primacy of those interests. The arguments usually presented in support of these policies turned, instead, on the

26. A relatively large proportion of the school-age population had attended the first classes of primary school but few had any experience of secondary education. See T. D. Williams, "The Ashby Report in Retrospect," *The Economic Bulletin of Ghana,* 2d ser., vol. 1, no.3.

supposed benefits that accrued to the African population as a consequence of the superior farming and trading practices that had been introduced. This proposition cannot easily be judged, but some information about the economic record of the colonial period should help to place it in perspective.

Before the arrival of the British, the Africans in Nyasaland were growing some crops that could have been exported. Livingstone had probably exaggerated the abundance of cotton growing, but the area did produce and export some cotton—a crude type, perhaps, but nonetheless useful—and there were sources of wild rubber which the first European settlers attempted to supplement with an imported variety that enjoyed a brief success, although the climate and rainfall were not conducive to its continuing exploitation on a systematic basis. In the middle of the nineteenth century the most valuable resource was ivory, but by the 1890s there had been a sharp fall in trade because the introduction of modern weapons had led to decimation of the elephant population.

Coffee was introduced by the first European farmers and for a brief period looked as though it would be a profitable plantation crop. Johnston was enthusiastic about its prospects, but his estimates of the costs involved in establishing a plantation and the return that could be reasonably expected by a capable and hardworking farmer appear to have been optimistic, even in terms of the evidence available during the most favorable period, and during the first decade of the new century it became apparent that there was much less scope than had been imagined for any major expansion of coffee production. To some extent, this was due to the development of the coffee industry in Brazil which affected world prices, but other factors may have been more important. Few areas in the country had the climate and rainfall appropriate for successful coffee production; coffee leaf disease was brought in with imported seedlings; a variety of local pests ate the flour and the berries; and in a number of cases the agricultural practices of the European plantation owners left a good deal to be desired, so that a combination of overcropping and failure to maintain soil fertility contributed to a sharp fall in output per acre.

Cotton production was stimulated by the formation of the British Cotton Growing Association in 1902. Its object was to reduce British dependency on American cotton, and one of the ways of doing this was to promote cotton production in the Empire. Capital was advanced to settlers in Nyasaland to enable them to invest in the cultivation of cotton and to import seedlings which, it was hoped, would produce a crop able to compete with American and Egyptian cotton on the world market. This program did not prove to be an unqualified success. Acreage devoted to cotton increased rapidly during the early years of the century, but many planters soon learned that tobacco was a better investment from their point of view. The association lost a good deal of the money that it had advanced and eventually decided that it would do better by trying to provide facilities for African cash-crop farmers rather than European plantation owners. In 1910 it set up the first of its ginning factories in Nyasaland and distributed seed to African growers, in spite of the protests of European planters that they were being faced with "unfair competition" from Africans.[27]

Cotton grown by Africans could be sold only to licensed buyers at specified auctions, but the government agent was empowered to raise the price if he felt that the bids were unfairly low. The government had a rather ambivalent attitute toward African production. On the one hand, it felt that African farmers would be easily discouraged by the formidable difficulties which they would face but, partly because plantation agriculture was not proving as successful as had been hoped, it did seek to encourage African production by exempting growers from part of their tax requirements and by providing various forms of technical assistance.[28]

Tobacco was another product that had been grown and consumed locally before Europeans settled in Nyasaland, but the domestic variety was not readily salable on the world market. Just before 1890, Virginia tobacco was introduced, and was grown both on estates and by African farmers who sold their output to European planters or traders. Improved techniques were introduced, and in 1908 the Imperial Tobacco Company

27. On the development of cotton growing, see Pachai, *Malawi*, pp. 163ff., and Murray. especially pp. 157–158 and pp. 171–172.

28. On skepticism about the potential of African farmers, see Murray, for example, on p. 158.

of Bristol opened a buying and packing station in Limbe, near the recently opened railway line between Blantyre and the south.

On the eve of World War I the economic position in Nyasaland was roughly as follows. The exportable products that had been readily available when Europeans first came to the country had soon been exhausted and were replaced by imported varieties that were, for the most part, intended to be developed as plantation crops. The two most successful exports in the period before World War I were tobacco and cotton but, although these were predominently estate crops, there was already a substantial output (about 10 to 15 per cent of the total) being produced by African small farmers in spite of considerable disadvantages with respect to transport, credit facilities, information, and distribution. The quality of the product, whether grown under European or African management, had improved significantly by the outbreak of World War I, and was to do so even more during the decade following its conclusion. This improvement came in large measure from the superior quality of imported seed and from improvements in equipment, technical knowledge, and the means of distribution.[29]

The administration was evidently satisfied that African money incomes were increasing, and in 1912 the annual hut tax was raised to eight shillings, of which half was waived providing that the person on whom it was levied spent some minimum period in the employ of a European or (after 1911) if he produced and sold to authorized purchasers (who were Europeans) a specified minimum quantity of rice, tobacco, or cotton.

In 1913, Acting Governor Pearce estimated that 70 per cent of the Protectorate's annual revenue came from taxes paid by Africans.[30] The proportion of expenditure devoted directly to African interests was much smaller than this, but colonial officials took the view that substantial benefits were derived by Africans from the establishment of stable rule and the maintenance of law and order and that a large proportion of the

29. On tobacco cultivation, see Pachai, *Malawi*, pp. 160ff., and Edwin Dean, *The Supply Response of African Farmers* (Amsterdam: North Holland Press, 1966).

30. Robert I. Rotberg, *The Rise of Nationalism in Central Africa* (Cambridge, Mass.: Harvard University Press, 1965), p. 44.

administration's expenditures were devoted to these ends. This line of argument was not without substance, but the principal direct beneficiaries of the administration's rule were the small number of Europeans in the protectorate. They were paying no direct taxes at all.

The most striking feature of the 1920s was the upsurge of African cotton production which took place at a time when there was a sharp fall in European production. Between 1922 and 1932, village production increased almost sevenfold in absolute terms and as a percentage of total output in the protectorate rose from 14 to almost 100 per cent.[31] It thus became a significant currency earner and one for which the spread effects to the broader African economy were probably a good deal more significant than earnings which accrued to European planters.

In the 1930s there was a substantial fall in recorded cotton exports originating in the African sector. This fall came in part because Africans could obtain better prices for their cotton in Portuguese East Africa than they could get from the licensed buyers in Nyasaland, and a good deal of illicit trading took place, but aggregate production in the villages dropped sharply toward the end of the 1930s when a periodic upsurge of waters leaving Lake Nyasa and pouring into the Shire River brought flooding in the principal cotton-growing areas of the lower Shire.

Before African incomes from cotton growing fell off there had been a remarkable shift from European toward African-directed production in significant sectors of the export crop economy. The cultivation of tobacco by African small farmers spread rapidly during the early 1920s, especially in the Central Province around Lilongwe where there were 13,000 registered growers in 1926.[32] The onset of the Great Depression, bringing about a severe decline in tobacco prices, was to have yet more dramatic results.

The European plantation owners, who had prided themselves on the efficiency of their operation, were unable to meet the challenge of the depression and European production of

31. See, for example, Baker, "Malawi's Exports: An Economic History," in Pachai, Smith, and Tangri, eds. Dean explains some of the factors affecting African output (*The Supply Response*).
32. Dean.

tobacco fell sharply. The effects on the economy might have been catastrophic were it not for the fact that the African small farmers, about whose industry and determination the government had expressed so many reservations, were able to greatly increase their own production of tobacco. The increased output of African cash-crop production was not, however, matched by an equivalent increase in cash-crop income or in the numbers of Africans directly involved in cash-crop production. There was probably some increase in both income and numbers, but prices were low, and the dependence of Nyasaland communities on the earnings that could only be achieved by migrant labor was not significantly diminished.

The ability of Africans to increase both output and sales in circumstances that had caused a collapse in European plantation production should, one might feel, have raised some question among colonial officials about the supposedly more efficient methods employed on the estates, but there appears to be no evidence that it did so. African small farmers were, it is true, producing a different kind of tobacco, a type that was cheaper to produce and that sold at a lower price, but they were able, in these very difficult circumstances, to provide the drive and the income which offered some chance that the economy could be put on a sound basis.

The failure of European tobacco production at this time might, one would have thought, have prompted someone in authority to wonder whether or not Africans could have done a satisfactory job with the higher quality and more expensive product if they had been granted some of the advantages so long conferred on the European producers, but there appears to be no evidence that it did. Many Africans were most unhappy that, unless they were to cross either geographical or legal frontiers, the tobacco they produced could be sold only on the auction floor at Limbe. Here both the grading and the buying was done by Europeans who were often suspected, whether or not rightly, of conspiring to reduce the price to Africans. As will be shown in the next chapter, the Native Associations which were the only representative bodies of African opinion sought to correct this situation.

There was one product that European planters in Nyasaland were able to produce with considerable profit during the 1930s.

Tea seedlings had been introduced into Nyasaland in the late 1870s, but growth of the industry was slow, and by the end of World War I the value of tea exports was less than one-tenth that of either cotton or tobacco.[33] Output increased during the 1920s, and a further stimulus was provided by the establishment of the Tea Research Foundation in 1929, but the major boost to European tea growers was a by-product of the very depression which had so badly hit the tobacco estates. The International Tea Agreement stabilized prices by limiting sales from all major producing areas, but Nyasaland's output which had been an insignificant proportion of world tea production was not given a restrictive quota. As a result, Nyasaland tea growers enjoyed the advantages of an artificially high price for their product and were also able to increase production. During this period tea became one of the two leading exports of the protectorate.

If one turns from production for the export market, for which the figures are available in some detail and with a reasonably high degree of accuracy, to the production of subsistence on locally traded goods, one finds little precise information though it is possible to say something about the general picture that emerges from the fragmentary and rather crude evidence available. The principal foodstuff in most parts of the country was maize, but this was supplemented by other vegetables and, from time to time, by meat or fish. The cattle population was sparse, but the proximity of so great an area of water gave access to a rich source of fish; enterprising small traders, using cheap bicycles that were being imported in rapidly increasing quantities during the 1930s, could easily take the fish inland, albeit in small quantities. Groundnuts were grown in many parts of the protectorate and had been exported at the turn of the century but were at this time principally a subsistence crop or were sold at small local markets, providing a nutritious addition to the main subsistence crop. Rice was grown near the lakes and in the lower Shire, while soya and velvet beans were useful rotation crops.

33. On tea production, see Pachai, *Malawi,* pp. 158ff., and Murray.

It seems likely, though on the face of it rather paradoxical, that the years of the depression were relatively good ones for several quite substantial groups of Africans in Nyasaland, particularly those who were most assiduously engaged in commercial agriculture. African incomes were much lower than those of Europeans and Asians, but African cash-crop production had proved able to survive in conditions that had been too rigorous for European producers, and local tobacco buyers had been forced into greater reliance on African produce. African farmers were obliged to sell their cash crops to licensed European buyers, and there was a widespread belief that the buyers took advantage of their monopoly position and political power to pay less for African produce than it was worth. Whether or not there was a sound basis for this view, the income of cash-crop farmers, especially those producing tobacco, improved during the 1930s. At the same time African consumers were able to take advantage of inexpensive Japanese products which were becoming available as imports, and a number of articles in great local demand—for example, cotton textiles and bicycles—were being imported in much greater quantities during the thirties. There were, of course, many able and enterprizing Africans who could not find a satisfactory outlet for their aspirations within Nyasaland and were obliged to migrate to Rhodesia or the Union of South Africa.

Between 1933 and 1935, imports from Japan rose from 13 to 30 per cent of total imports, and in the latter year Japanese goods accounted for more than 90 per cent of all cotton piece goods.[34] The advantage that Africans derived from this, however, was rarely appreciated by colonial officials, who were much given to derogatory references to "cheaper and less reliable" products. These officials began to canvass the merits of restricting the importation of foreign products in order to protect the employment of British artisans who were producing

34. *Colonial Report for Nyasaland, 1937* (London: H.M.S.O.), p. 28. Two years earlier, the *Colonial Report for Nyasaland, 1935* insisted (p. 26) that the rapidly increasing demand for imported bicycles was mainly for British products rather than "cheaper and less reliable" foreign manufactures.

the articles which, in the absence of foreign competition, would have been sold in Rhodesia and Nyasaland.[35]

A large proportion of the domestic revenue of the government continued to come from the hut tax. Income tax was eventually imposed on Europeans, but as late as 1935 this provided little more than 10 per cent of the amount raised by hut tax. Customs duties had become the largest single item in the internal revenue account, and although there is no readily available estimate of the extent to which Africans bore the cost of this item, the increase in imported consumer goods for the African market suggests that they were making substantial indirect, as well as direct, contributions to the exchequer.

Government budgets and the territorial accounts were dominated throughout the thirties by the financing and building of the Zambezi Bridge. It was a bold venture. The capital cost was much greater than the annual domestic revenue of the government and, even with generous repayment terms, the burden on the protectorate's resources would be considerable. The bridge would make little direct addition to government revenue, but by improving export prospects it could, in time, make possible a vigorous expansion of cash-crop agriculture. Such an expansion would make it practicable to import the intermediate products required if there was to be any domestic manufacturing industry in Nyasaland.

There was, as it turned out, little chance to take advantage of the improved facilities before the outbreak of World War II radically altered the government's priorities and the state of international markets. Nyasaland producers were able to greatly increase their output of some products, notably tung oil, for which the previous sources of supply had been cut off, but the full impact of more effective communications was postponed for several years. In the five years immediately following the end of the war the value of Nyasaland exports increased rapidly, and the larger volumes of imports that became possible included an increasingly high proportion of investment goods. Development in Nyasaland was starting from a very low base

35. Lewis H. Gann, *A History of Northern Rhodesia* (London: Chatto and Windus, 1964), p. 271.

and, under even the most favorable circumstances, the country would have been hard put to meet its debt obligations. It was most difficult to provide anything more than the most rudimentary stock of social overhead capital and to find the savings necessary to maintain an export drive that would not be perilously dependent on the vagaries of overseas markets for two or three primary products. The task before the government was a formidable one, but the economic prospects for Nyasaland in 1950 were far more favorable than they had been at any time since British rule had first been established.

Under these circumstances the British government decided that Nyasaland Africans should be forced, against their frequently and forcefully expressed oppostion, to become members of the newly established Central African Federation. Before we pursue the story at that point, we must examine the political response of Nyasaland Africans to the imposition and maintenance of colonial rule.

CHAPTER 3

The African Response to Colonial Rule

African reaction to the arrival of Europeans in the country and to the eventual imposition of British rule was far from uniform. As might be expected, the most powerful tribal groups were unenthusiastic about the intrusion of a force more powerful than themselves into the territory which they had hitherto controlled.

Of these groups, the Yao, in spite of their lack of a central authority, wielded the most effective military force, and several of their leaders put up a spirited armed resistance to the invading British. The Yao lived in small autonomous communities and each chief had few warriors at his command, but the resources at Johnston's disposal were also meager; the ensuing conflict, although keen, was on a much smaller scale than those conflicts that had taken place during the occupation of many other countries in Africa. The Yao were deeply involved in the slave trade and saw few, if any, good reasons for offering allegiance to the British, who were officially committed to its suppression. It took five years of sporadic fighting before Johnston finally subdued them, whereupon he set about punishing them for their temerity in resisting him.

Those Yao chiefs who held power in areas bordering on missionary settlements did not, as a rule, show much appreciation of the spiritual benefits offered to them. We have already seen that the unfortunate Bishop Mackenzie became involved in open conflict with the Yao; some years later the Free Church of Scotland mission attempted to establish a base at Cape Maclear, on Lake Nyasa in Yao-controlled territory. Although there was not at that time any resort to arms, the relationship was neither fruitful nor cordial. Scott, of the Blantyre mission of the Church of Scotland, was apparently more successful in establishing friendly terms with the Yao in the Shire Highlands, but it is not clear how much of this was due to his own patient and sympathetic endeavor to understand and respect African customs and how much to the circumstance that Yao strength was less formidable in the Shire Highlands than along the lake shore.[1]

The Tonga, on the other hand, not only welcomed the Free Church missionaries but from an early period sought active involvement in missionary enterprises. They responded enthusiastically to educational opportunities, became members of the church and sought ordination. They worked for the African Lakes Company and moved in large numbers, as migrant workers, to the Shire Highlands and south across the Zambezi. Some aspects of traditional culture may have encouraged greater scope for individual achievement among the Tonga than among their neighbors, and it is quite possible that they were more inclined to respond to the achievement-oriented culture represented by the Scottish missionaries. At the same time their recent experience had left them disinclined to perpetuate those aspects of their tradition that would accord least well with change toward a "modern" society. The Tonga had taken a severe beating at the hands of the Ngoni, had been humiliated by them for more than a generation, and seemed unlikely to be able to reverse the balance in the foreseeable future. The introduction of a new power into the area could scarcely make matters worse and might make them considerably better. New means of defining wealth and power, most notably through the education provided at mission schools, were the more eagerly seized upon because there was little

1. Andrew Ross emphasizes the great importance attached by David Scott of the Blantyre Mission to establishing close and sympathetic relations with neighboring chiefs ("The Origins and Development of the Church of Scotland Mission, Blantyre, Nyasaland, 1875–1926." Ph.D. diss., University of Edinburgh, 1968). It was not entirely coincidental that Sir Harry Johnston's relations with the Blantyre mission were much more strained than those with other missions since one of the things that most annoyed him was Scott's insistence on speaking "on behalf of" the neighboring African populations.

reason to revere the past and to cling to institutions and attitudes associated with it.

The Ngoni, by contrast, did revere their traditions, and they feared that missionaries would seduce their young men from the ancient path of virtue. An elder of the Ngoni told the missionaries: "If we give you our children to teach, your words will steal their hearts; they will grow up cowards, and refuse to fight for us when we are old; and knowing more than we do, they will despise us."[2]

For a number of years members of the Free Church Mission at Livingstonia sought to persuade the northern Ngoni leaders that it would be in Ngoni interests to allow the Free Church to establish churches and schools in Ngoni villages, during which time the Ngoni leaders, politely but firmly holding the church at arm's length, carefully weighed the benefits and costs of alien infusion. Eventually they agreed to allow the missionaries to move in among their people and, when they did so, the manner in which the Ngoni sought to accommodate themselves to the British presence differed from that of both Yao and Tonga.

In the north, a rather loose arrangement was worked out with Johnston. He agreed that there would be no annexation by the British if the Ngoni were prepared to stay within the area they were occupying at the time of the understanding. This suited the British, who would have been very hard pressed to undertake a campaign against the Ngoni, but it is not so clear that the agreement was a great success from the Ngoni point of view. Their neighbors, whom they had been accustomed to raid and from whom they plundered the resources that sustained the Ngoni way of life, were now protected; the Ngoni were unable to move to new land when it was needed, and they were obliged, however reluctantly, to change their way of life.

Their relationship with the Scottish missionaries—the Ngoni had been in much closer contact with them than with any other Britons—was one of mutual respect, and perhaps for this rea-

2. Margaret Read, "The Ngoni and Western Education," in Victor Turner, ed., *Colonialism in Africa, 1870–1964* (Cambridge: Cambridge University Press, 1971), p. 355.

son they were prepared to enter into a new and more formal agreement with the colonial administration.[3] In 1904 the Ngoni accepted British rule, agreed to pay taxes and to observe the laws promulgated by the British resident, while the British for their part promised to respect the authority of traditional rulers, to allow a wide range of internal disputes to be settled according to customary law, and to pay the chiefs a subsidy in return for the acquisition of taxing authority by the colonial government. The terms of the agreement, however, appear to have been imprecise, and there was no thorough examination of its implication; it later became evident that quite different interpretations could be put on what had been agreed, and at least some Ngoni leaders were to feel that the interpretation upheld by the colonial authorities meant that the Ngoni had yielded a much greater portion of their autonomy than they had supposed when the agreement was made. But by that time the balance of power had swung so far away from the Ngoni that there was little they could do about it. Many Ngoni believed that the tax in question was a once-for-all levy, and when they realized, in 1906, that it was being imposed for a second year running, there were demonstrations against the resident. These were contained but resentment and frustration remained, to become manifest again in the resistance to the drafting of labor in 1915.[4]

3. Read refers to Laws, in charge of the Livingstonia mission, and Mbelwa, leader of the Northern Ngoni, as two strong men who each respected the other's force of character. Michael Gelfand says that in the early days Laws made very careful use of his medical knowledge: "In order to win their confidence in the white man's 'magic,' Laws confined his surgery to minor procedures which were likely to be successful" (*Lakeside Pioneers*, Oxford: Basil Blackwell, 1964, p. 40). Elmslie, another medical man, was fortunate in having produced even more striking evidence of supernatural powers: on one occasion, after the Ngoni rain doctor had failed to end a drought, Elmslie and his African assistant, Koyi, prayed for rain the day before the first downpour marked the end of the drought. "From then onwards," says Gelfand, "the future of the mission was assured" (p. 43).

4. K. J. McCracken, "African Politics in Twentieth Century Malawi," in T. O. Ranger, ed., *Aspects of Central African History* (London: Heinemann, 1968), p. 201. See also R. K. Tangri, "The Development of Modern African Politics and the Emergence of a Nationalist Movement in Colonial Malawi, 1891–1958" (Ph.D. diss., University of Edinburgh, 1970), p. 189.

In the south central area, Paramount Chief Gomani, who had emerged as the leader of the Maseko Ngoni following a civil war in the early 1890s, had been unhappy about the government's claim to levy taxes on his people, and he bitterly resented the activities of labor recruiters. It is evident that Africans were often unsure whether they were being offered a chance to work for wages or being ordered to do so by their new rulers, and it is probable that some recruits would have preferred to stay and work on their own farms. Gomani himself had another reason for objecting to the recruiting agents, one that reflected less concern for the welfare of the individual recruits than for the threat to his own prerogatives. Until the British arrived, his predecessors had been able to demand labor services from their subject peoples, but if these now were given a choice of working elsewhere, and for wages Gomani would not have been able to offer, even had he been disposed to do so, his authority would be flouted and the resources at his disposal diminished.

To indicate his displeasure, he burned down a number of villages whose members had entered the employment of Europeans. He was promptly arrested and ordered to be marched to Blantyre. On the way, under rather obscure circumstances, he was shot and killed.

In short, the situation in the early days of British rule was that, except among the Yao, direct military resistance was slight, but the acceptance of, or even apparent welcome to, colonial administration rarely, if ever, reflected an unqualified endorsement of the values and objectives that the new rulers were set upon pursuing. It was, rather, a matter of choosing which of several not altogether agreeable options offered the best terms, and in many cases there was only a very rudimentary idea of what was being offered.

The very enthusiasm with which some of the most dedicated missionaries espoused the cause of progressive social change and African advancement sometimes led to misunderstandings. The Bible and its message was sometimes presented, even if inadvertently, as the key to the acquisition of wealth and influence. Africans who were told that the search for the Kingdom of Heaven would add to them much else besides, were perhaps inclined to interpret this pronouncement more literally than would the British working-class congregation which might, in other circumstances, have made up the audience of some of the ablest and most idealistic men who became missionaries in Nyasaland.

It is quite possible that the missionaries who were most sympathetic to African aspiration and least affected by a belief in any intrinsic racial superiority may, in some respects, have misled Africans more than other, less sympathetic Europeans did. Africans who had received their pastoral care and education from men or women who treated them as though they were, potentially if not immediately, near equals, were likely to have a rude shock when they encountered white employers or officials (or other missionaries, sometimes belonging to the same church) who treated them as though they were barely distinguishable from beasts of burden; sometimes Africans who had been subject to experiences of this kind felt that they had been the victims of a cynical confidence trick; their sense of frustration and betrayal being the greater the more complete had been their faith in their masters.

The Scottish Mission Church at Livingstonia did more than any other to find and develop the talent of young Africans in the villages around the mission and bring them, through a succession of tests and examinations that demanded high qualities of intelligence and determination, to a level of achievement that made its graduates a legend in Central Africa. Few of them were, however, immediately qualified, either by educational attainment or by experience, to take over senior positions in the mission, and even fewer were actually taken onto the Livingstonia staff. Those who were, found that promotion came very slowly. There were probably occasions when their failure to gain advancement was due in some measure to prejudice, but it was inevitable that some Africans who had been singled out for rapid advancement through the educational system and who had achieved a level of education beyond the dreams of their parents should have failed to appreciate that they were a good deal less well qualified than their mentors, and that a further period of apprenticeship was quite properly required of them.

There were, nonetheless, relatively substantial advantages

that accrued to educated Africans, and it was widely believed that church membership was a prerequisite for access to the schools.[5] Partly for this reason, there was great demand, especially among the Tonga, for church membership, and the church authorities felt obliged to resist a widespread desire for instant conversion. A period of apprenticeship was considered necessary before full church membership was granted, but many Africans felt that such precautions were simply a reflection of prejudice and an abuse of power.

A number of educated Africans who left the established missions, either because they were dissatisfied with the way in which they had been treated or because they disagreed with mission policy, set up Independent African Churches. These churches attracted supporters who felt rejected by the missions or objected to the apparent identification of the missions with white supremacy. There has been a good deal of controversy about the role of Independent Churches and in particular their relationship both to earlier forms of resistance to the colonial power and to the later development of national movements. According to Rotberg, "the conquered people cloaked their rejection of colonialism in religious garb," but the more skeptical Shepperson has warned against the "conditioned sociological reflex" of assuming that the Independent Churches were primarily agents of political activity.[6] The religious impulse may have played a very important or even dominant role in the formulation and sustenance of the Independent Churches, but these churches undoubtedly did provide a potent institutional base for the ventilation of political and social grievances.

5. Rotberg insists that this was one of the strongest weapons in the missionary armory (see his *Christian Missionaries and the Creation of Northern Rhodesia, passim*) but Ross denies that church membership was a prerequisite for attendance at Blantyre mission schools (p. 136). In a more general sense Channock was right to say that "education was a part of the missionaries' package" (M. L. Channock, "Development and Change in the History of Malawi," in Pachai, ed., *Early History,* p. 437).

6. Rotberg, *The Rise of Nationalism,* p. 56; G. Shepperson, "Introductory Comments: Religion in British Central Africa," in W. Montgomery Watt, ed., *Religion in Africa* (Centre of African Studies, University of Edinburgh, 1964); the phrase "conditioned sociological reflex" is quoted by T. Ranger in the same symposium, p. 52.

In 1907, a Chikunda prophetess appeared on the border betwen Mozambique and Ngoniland, announcing that Europeans would leave the country by the end of the year and that there would be an end to taxation. The authorities had cause to worry: tax collections for the year dropped substantially, and several chiefs refused to act as tax collectors. In the previous year, Elliot Kamwana, formerly a Livingstonia student and a medical aide in a Rhodesian hospital, had returned to Nyasaland to set up a branch of the Watch Tower movement. This organization, established by Jehovah's Witnesses, combined fundamentalist religious beliefs with a radical, in some ways anarchic, attitude to the role of government—any government, or at least any feasible one—since its members believed that no existing government understood, far less offered allegiance to, the Kingdom of God which was about to become manifest in the temporal as well as the spiritual realm. This doctrine was frequently interpreted by its African adherents in a manner quite different from that intended by its European (or more particularly, American) protagonists: it was not *all* earthly government that was corrupt, but *white* government; the day of salvation might be the one on which the pure would reverse the domination of the impure, but for many of its African adherents this meant the time when Africans would replace Europeans as effective leaders of the temporal world. The movement quickly attracted many recruits and, according to some accounts, Kamwana baptized almost ten thousand people during a few months in 1908.[7]

The messianic Watch Tower literature encouraged a belief that the crises and tribulation through which the world was passing were about to reach a grand climacteric; the Day of Judgment, about to dawn, would search out the wicked and bring the righteous to the seats of the mighty. The authors of

7. Tangri (p. 153) says Kamwana had baptized over 9,000 before his arrest in March 1909; Pachai (*Malawi,* p. 135), says that "by 1908 Kamwana had over 10,000 adherents"; Shepperson and Price refer to a Livingstonia witness who claimed that Kamwana had "baptised as many as ten thousand Africans in a few months" (p. 155). Apart from these sources, there is a useful account of independent church leaders in J. Macdonald, "History of African Education in Nyasaland, 1875–1945" (Ph.D. diss., University of Edinburgh, 1969), pp. 190ff.

these tracts were rarely, if ever, concerned with their political implications, but many of their African disciples believed that they were proclaiming the imminent collapse of white rule and the rise to power of the African elect (that is, themselves). The Second Coming of Christ, which was expected in 1914, would mean, said Kamwana, the end of colonial rule, the revival of African customs, immediate baptism, the end of the hut tax, and free education for all who wanted it. Africans would henceforth acquire and control not only their traditional resources but the benefits of modern technology. "We shall build our own ships," he said, "make our own powder, and make or import our own guns."[8]

In view of Kamwana's utopian prospectus, offering a free shortcut to the benefits of modern society together with instant salvation, it is perhaps surprising that there were not even more recruits for the Independent Churches. Watch Tower had another more prosaic but possibly even more potent source of appeal. It was known to have well-to-do European associates both in South Africa and in the United States who were prepared to spend a good deal of money to further the cause that they so devoutly embraced, and this knowledge may well have aroused hopes in some of its adherents than an appropriate display of zeal would be suitably rewarded.[9]

The colonial authorities were worried that the situation would get out of control, and in 1909 Kamwana was deported from the protectorate. In spite of its more obvious, if less substantial, attractions the organization was not strong enough to survive the loss of its leader and the movement ceased for some time to be a major force in the colony.

Another important figure in the development of the Independent Churches was Charles Domingo. He was born in Mozambique but brought to British Central Africa as a young boy

8. Shepperson and Price, p. 156.

9. Shepperson and Price refer to the experience of William Johnston, a Glasgow man who was sent by the American Watch Tower movement to report on the situation in Nyasaland. "There is manifest," he reported, "a spirit of cupidity and self-seeking [among Watch Tower pastors]. . . . I regret to say that in almost every case . . . their interviews ended with an appeal for financial assistance in some shape or form" (p. 157).

in 1881 by William Koyi, an African preacher from Lovedale in South Africa, who had been transferred to Livingstonia. Domingo became a house-boy to Dr. Laws, who was in charge of the Free Church Mission at Livingstonia, and Laws, a man of great ability and perception—although in many respects a hard taskmaster—recognized that the young man in his charge was a person of remarkable natural talent, and encouraged and assisted him in his studies. In 1897, Domingo became the first African to complete Livingstonia's teacher training course, and three years later he had completed his theological training. Within another two years he received a license to preach (but not to serve as a full minister), and in 1907 he was appointed to take charge of a congregation in the Loudon area. It was, however, made clear, and publicly so, that he would continue for some time to be "under the care and supervision" of the European missionaries in the district.[10]

Domingo was not merely a capable man but was one of markedly independent views. He disagreed strongly with the interpretation that the Scots put on a number of African customs, and it is unlikely that he took kindly to their insistence that he remain in tutelage. During the following year he broke with Livingstonia and set himself up as a Seventh-Day Baptist preacher. He continued to be held in high regard at Livingstonia but was very bitter about the racial attitudes of Europeans. No white man, he wrote, "sees a native as his Brother, but as his boy."[11]

Domingo was a serious protagonist of what was probably a widespread view among Africans, and he appears to have argued his case with a considerable degree of political skill. He favored a radical (social) interpretation of the Bible, but it is not clear whether this reflected a significant interest in, and attitude about, social issues or whether it was due to his hostility to Europeans. The spectacle of landowners withholding wages may, for example, have been offensive to him because he believed that it was an immoral social act (and one which would have been so even had both landowners and laborers been of

10. Pachai, quoting the minutes of the Livingstonia Presbytery (*Malawi*, p. 205).
11. Letters, quoted by Tangri, p. 161.

the same race) or it may have offended him primarily because he saw it as yet another example of white racial arrogance and alien domination. He favored the representation of educated Africans in government councils and was briefly deported in 1916 for his advocacy of equal rights for Africans and Europeans. The financial base on which the church rested had, however, already been eroded when the American Seventh-Day Baptists had decided to withdraw their support, for reasons which had little to do with Domingo.[12] When his period of deportation came to an end, he returned to the protectorate, became a civil servant, and took no further part in political activity.

In 1911, Levi Mumba, who was to play an important role in the development of native associations, was asked to leave the Church of Scotland—he had been an elder—because he had married a second wife. He had already been at odds with the church about the value of many African customs of which the missionaries disapproved, and he made it known that he felt that the criteria of good character "according to native traditions" were often superior to those of the Europeans and that these traditions, moreover, accorded more closely with the law and customs outlined in the first five books of the bible than did the practices being upheld by the Free Church.[13]

At about this time there was a change in the colonial pattern of administration which was to have a substantial effect on the development of political consciousness among Africans in the protectorate. The early period of colonial rule had been characterized by uncertainty about the power and responsibility of chiefs under the colonial administration. In a few cases formal agreements had been reached between the colonial authorities and particular chiefs, but even in these cases there had been, as we have seen, a good deal of misunderstanding, and in the more usual case there was nothing other than an *ad hoc* arrangement. European officials were few, and typically arrived in the country without any experience directly relevant to the duties they were to undertake. Effective control of the protec-

---

12. Shepperson and Price, p. 164.
13. Tangri, p. 151.

torate required, at the very least, passive acceptance of colonial rule on the part of the majority of the people, and the cooperation required if anything constructive was to be achieved could be elicited only if the officials worked through a form of organization with some local support. As it was, the authority of traditional rulers had been undermined in most areas without anything having been put in its place.

To cope with this situation the District Ordinance was enacted in 1912, and the country was divided into a number of administrative units, each with a principal headman. Principal headmen were selected by the colonial authorities—many of them having been traditional rulers, although this was not a prerequisite for the job—and they were placed in charge of the village headmen in their area, while being themselves subordinate to a colonial official, the district resident. The responsibilities of the headmen included the maintenance of order and discipline in their areas, although they were not empowered to deal with major offenses, which were handled by the colonial police and judiciary, and they undertook the local supervision of certain sanitation and health measures. Perhaps their most important role was, as Pachai puts it, that of "government agents who carried information to the people and organized the required responses from the people."[14]

The new system of administration was introduced on a piecemeal basis. The authorities felt that special problems might be raised if an attempt were made to introduce the system into areas such as the Shire Highlands, where many villages were located on European-owned land and where many plantation owners would be loath to accord any formal power to African headmen. Some caution in introducing a new system would, in any event, have been sensible, so the government decided that the system should be tested in a few areas before being generally adopted. It was politically convenient to make the test in the north.

The ordinance turned out to be far from an unqualified success from the British point of view and caused a good deal of unhappiness to educated Africans. It became clear that the

14. Pachai, *Malawi*, p. 183.

authority wielded by headmen was derived not from the support of their own people but was merely a reflection of the power of the colonial rulers, who had introduced the measure precisely because they did not think that their power alone was enough. Instead of absorbing a strengthened traditional structure into the framework of colonial authority, the ordinance still further weakened the power of chiefs and headmen because it gave the impression to many Africans that the price a man paid for maintaining such a position was subservience to the colonial ruler. The consequence of the new legislation, said Levi Mumba, was that headmen were no longer able to act as the representatives of their people: "For fear of offending the Resident . . . it is now a custom to say 'yes' when they mean 'no' and vice-versa."[15]

But if one source of dissatisfaction among Africans was the fear that the proper sanction of traditional authority was being jeopardized through misuse, other Africans were unhappy for the contrary reason that the colonial government was bolstering a form of authority which had outlived its usefulness. A number of educated Africans felt that they themselves were better qualified to represent their people than the men actually chosen and that they were, moreover, entitled by their exertions to some recognition of status and achievement, which the government was continuing to deny them.

Dissatisfaction with the ordinance, particularly in the north where Africans had firsthand experience of its effects, provided a powerful stimulus to the emergence of organizations which would be able to express African grievances and seek to bring some pressure to bear on the colonial authorities. At the same time, many able and articulate Africans were aware that there would be no place of prominence for them in traditional bodies, even if these bodies could be revitalized. The time was ripe for the emergence of new forms and modes of the power struggle; political expression would henceforth be channeled in large measure through "modern" agencies adapted from the institutions of the colonial rulers.

The impetus to a new style of political activity and to a more

15. Tangri, p. 85.

sophisticated response to colonial rule was reinforced by the experience of the many Nyasaland Africans, a high proportion of them from the north, who had spent some years as wage earners in Southern Rhodesia or the Union of South Africa. These men had acquired a good reputation for ability and hard work, and Nyasaland Africans were well represented among the small cadre of African clerical and supervisory workers. Some of them had settled in the areas where they had found work and had become leading figures in the Independent Churches and workers' organizations of their new homes.[16] The great majority, however, returned to Nyasaland and brought back an experience both of the racial policies pursued in countries where there were relatively large numbers of white settlers and more sophisticated political organization among Africans than was then to be found in Nyasaland.

In 1912 and 1914, respectively, Native Associations were established in North Nyasa and West Nyasa. These represented the first attempts by Africans to set up political organizations that rested not on appeals to traditional authority or to mystical or religious sanction but on the ability and right of members to contribute to discussion about the terms on which their institutional, social, and economic activities should be organized. The membership was predominantly one of relatively well-educated Africans. They conducted their meetings according to written rules of order, held elections, and kept regular accounts and minutes; they made recommendations—often considered radical, sometimes dangerous, and not infrequently impertinent by the colonial authorities—that were set in a "realistic" context, in which they sought to distinguish between vague aspirations and what they might reasonably be expected to achieve.

In the years immediately preceding the outbreak of World War I, opposition to many aspects of British rule became widespread and took many forms, but the colonial authorities appear to have been quite confident that by 1914 the most significant manifestations of hostility had been effectively contained. When Sir George Smith was appointed governor in

16. See, for example, Terence Ranger, "The Early History of Independency in Southern Rhodesia," in W. Montgomery Watt, ed.

1913, he was assured, at a reception organized in his honor by the mayor of Blantyre, that "in Nyasaland we are all optimistic," and the mayor spoke about "the harmonious relations that have always existed between the European settlers and the natives of the Province."[17]

There were, however, many Africans in a condition of great distress not many miles from Blantyre itself. The Southern Province had been afflicted by severe drought between 1911 and 1913, and there had been famine in several areas. The export of maize was forbidden, and producers of cash crops were encouraged to increase their output and sales by a grant of exemption from tax payment similar to that previously granted to wage earners on European plantations, but the resources of the African agrarian economy had been seriously weakened by the outflow of men seeking wage emloyment in order to pay their taxes. In good years, when men left their farms to seek employment elsewhere or devoted their energies to the production of cash crops needed by Europeans, the fertility of the land was such that adequate subsistence crops were produced even though the land was not fully exploited, but when the climate turned against the people and every hand was needed to take the last advantage that nature might afford, the shortage of labor may well have been a critical and tragic handicap.

There was bitterness in the southern region about the seizure of good land; some of the most prominent landlords, so far from attempting to soften the bitterness, had earned a reputation as insensitive, avaricious, and not infrequently brutal employers. Nyasaland Africans were reluctant to seek work on the estates, but labor was available because Africans from Mozambique, who fled from the even harsher rule to which they were subjected by Portuguese authorities, were entering the protectorate in large numbers.

Among the European plantations in the protectorate few had as poor a reputation among Africans as the Bruce estates, which were owned at the outbreak of World War I by Alexander Livingstone Bruce, a grandson of David Livingstone,

17. Shepperson and Price, p. 189.

and managed by W. J. Livingstone, a more distant relative of the great missionary. Conditions of labor on the estates were hard, no facilities were granted for African schools or churches on the estates and Africans were forbidden to wear either hats or shoes, since these garments were considered suitable only for Europeans. A. L. Bruce, a prominent member of the Legislative Council, left no room for doubt that he believed Africans in Nyasaland were pampered by missionaries who filled their heads with completely unrealistic expectations.[18] He was outspoken in his view that Africans should not be allowed to establish homes on any part of a European-owned plantation unless they were willing to provide labor services when the owner required them.

In 1911 the Bruce estates had been extended by taking over a substantial amount of crown territory and Bruce made it clear that his African tenants should either be prepared to work for him or face eviction.

When war broke out between Britain and Germany in August 1914, it may well have caused more than a little excitement among those Africans who had been members of the watch tower movement or had belonged to the much larger group which, without being committed adherents, were familiar with watch tower literature. They had been told, time and time again, that their white rulers would be engulfed by catastrophe in October 1914. Nyasaland Africans were of course aware that the colonial authorities in neighboring Tanganyika were German, but in the experience of Africans white people did not attack each other; the mobilization of the white powers to fight among themselves must have seemed impressive confirmation of the prophecy even to many who had been inclined to skepticism.

There were, in addition, many devout members of the established churches who were deeply troubled by the spectacle of two Christian nations going to war with each other, both calling on the same God to sanctify the slaughter of their adversaries. Others, less troubled by metaphysical speculation, were of-

18. The evolution of the Legislative Council is described by Pachai, *Malawi*, pp. 237ff.

fended by the drafting of Africans to serve as troops and porters in a war that did not concern them and from which they could expect no benefit regardless of who won.

In November 1914 the pastor of the Providence Industrial Mission, situated in the densely populated Chiradzulu district and close to the Bruce estates, wrote a letter to the *Nyasaland Times,* the principal European newspaper in the protectorate, which began, "We understand that we have been invited to shed our innocent blood in this World's War which is now in progress throughout the wide world." It went on to say: "A number of our people have already shed their blood, while some are crippled for life. And an open declaration has been issued. A number of Police are marching in various villages and persuading well built natives to join the War." Africans were going to fight, the letter continued, in a quarrel that was not of their making and on behalf of people who treated them with open contempt: "In time of peace everything for Europeans only. And instead of honour we suffer humiliation with names contemptible. But in time of war it has been found that we are needed to share hardships and shed our blood in equality . . . the poor Africans who have nothing to win in this present World, who in death, leave only a long line of widows and orphans in utter want and dire distress, are invited to die for a cause which is not theirs."[19]

The letter was signed "John Chilembwe, In behalf of his countrymen." The writer was already well known among Africans in the Shire Highlands. Many Europeans had heard of him at one time or another, but most of them probably thought of him, in so far as they had paid any attention to him, as a pretentious but ineffective man who did not understand his proper place in society. As a boy he had gone to work for John Booth, a radical and outspoken missionary who believed that no true Christian would claim any comfort for himself while others went hungry. Booth took Chilembwe to America, where he stayed for three years, studying at the Virginia Theological Seminary with the financial and moral support of the National Baptist Convention.

19. The letter is quoted in full by Shepperson and Price, pp. 234–235.

He returned to Malawi in 1900 with the sponsorship of leading black Baptists, who hoped that he would, in Shepperson's words, be "a John the Baptist making in the wilderness of Central Africa a path for American Negro Missionaries." Chilembwe seems to have been in no doubt that he had been led to America as an instrument of Divine Will and that it was his destiny to guide his people to a promised land.[20]

He began his task in modest style, and for ten years or more he gradually built up his congregation, taught school, and attended to his pastoral duties without making any very dramatic impact on the community. It is, nonetheless, probable that many Africans were aware that Chilembwe was the first of his people to become an ordained minister and that he was strongly supported by colleagues in the United States, who provided him with finances and sent their own missionaries to help him with his work. Although his principal concern in the early years was to build a firm base among his congregation, he did not ignore broader issues affecting his countrymen. He was critical of the use of Nyasaland African troops in campaigns against the Ashanti and in the Sudan, and he was a protagonist of racial equality and a critic of European landlords, particularly of A. L. Bruce and his manager W. J. Livingstone. Although most Europeans probably disliked him, he had no serious trouble with the authorities. He apparently put a good deal of emphasis on the ultimately persuasive power of example, and he believed that if Africans were industrious, sober, and respectably dressed, they would eventually acquire the respect they deserved. Indeed, he went so far as to invite Europeans to visit his mission and take photographs of members of his congregation so that their memory of what had been achieved could be perpetually refreshed.

He took part in several business ventures and encouraged his associates to do the same. In July 1911 he was the leading

20. Shepperson and Price recount a dramatic story about Chilembwe apparently on the point of death due to a very severe asthmatic attack while in the United States; surrounded by members of the National Baptist Convention who were expecting his end to be at hand, he raised himself to announce: "Bruddur Jordan, I no going to die. God bring me to this land to get light to take back to me people. He is not going to kill me here" (p. 22).

figure in an attempt to set up the African Industrial Society, a form of producers' and consumers' cooperative. He believed that the inculcation of habits of thrift and the development of institutions to encourage it would enable Africans to acquire the capital necessary for successful commercial enterprise. Shepperson quotes a report that "he appealed to the better educated natives to do something more with their money than to put it into the hands of their Bombay brethren, who do nothing for the country but ship every penny to India."[21] The venture was not a success, perhaps in part because some potential supporters feared that its activities would annoy the authorities, but no clear evidence exists that political considerations were a decisive factor in the failure of the society. The experience may, however, have played a significant role in persuading Chilembwe and his closest associates that a strategy of gradualism was unlikely to be successful and, seemingly, those Africans most openly involved in the attempt to set up the cooperative, nearly all of whom were relatively prosperous storekeepers or cash-crop farmers, were to be heavily involved in the rising that took place in 1915.

After the failure of the venture, Chilembwe became increasingly bitter in his denunciation of Europeans, and his preaching took on more radical and apocalyptic tones. By July 1914 there were widespread rumors in the district that he was involved in a plot to kill a number of Europeans (and some Africans) who were living near his headquarters at the Providence Industrial Mission in the Chiradzulu district. African members of the nearby Catholic mission at Nguludi reported these rumors to their bishop, who passed them on to the civil authorities. The rumors were then treated so casually that one must suppose the authorities shared the mayor of Blantyre's confidence that Africans in the protectorate were either so acquiescent or so cowed that Europeans had no cause for alarm, whatever talk of plots might be circulating at large.

The assistant district resident paid a very brief visit to the area around Chilembwe's mission, but since the inspection lasted only ten minutes, it is difficult to imagine what he

21. Shepperson and Price, p. 167.

thought he was looking for. Not surprisingly, he failed to un-
cover anything but advised his superior that, since there was
unlikely to have been any smoke without fire, Chilembwe
should be arrested and sent to some outstation for the duration
of the war, adding that he would have "much pleasure" in
arresting the man.[22]

The government did not make up its mind about the matter
until the end of the year, and when arrangements for his arrest
were being finalized in early January, word of its intention
reached Chilembwe. No doubt by this time Chilembwe was actively engaged in planning and preparing a revolt against the
colonial authorities, although there is a good deal of uncertainty as to when he first turned decisively to a course of violence and rebellion. The news that the authorities were about
to act against him may have forced his hand and induced him
to launch his revolt before he and his followers were ready to
carry it through with any hope of success. As it happened,
almost everything he had planned went wrong, and the execu-
tion of the rising was marred by confusion of tactics and goals.
It is not clear to what extent this was primarily due to inadequate resources, poor planning, or ineffective leadership and
to what extent it was due to the fact that Chilembwe was
obliged to give the signal before the plans had been properly
worked out; in any event, Chilembwe appears to have had little
idea of the problems that would have had to be overcome if the
revolt was to succeed.

If Chilembwe had begun to plan the rising before 25 November, it is difficult to explain why he was prepared to write to the
Nyasaland Times in terms that would certainly have drawn government attention to himself even if he had not already been
suspected of complicity in a murder plot. Perhaps he so misun-
derstood the nature of the conflict in which he was about to
become involved that he imagined that European power would
collapse like the Walls of Jericho at the sound of the prophet's
trumpet; perhaps he hoped that his letter would open some
fundamental debate about the justice of imperial rule that
would shake the confidence of the colonial authorities, and

22. Pachai, *Malawi*, pp. 215–216.

induce them to make substantial concessions to the views of educated Africans, even if this meant giving up, in the midst of a desperate struggle, the advantages derived from the use of large numbers of Africans as soldiers and porters; he may have imagined that the letter would identify him as the champion of Africans opposed to imperial rule and that thousands of Africans would promptly flock to his standard. Whatever the reason, he jeopardized such chance as he might have had of achieving the surprise that was essential if the revolt was to achieve any measure of military success.

The colonial authorities were quite unprepared to countenance the use of the press at that time for discussion of such fundamental matters, and they seized all available copies of the paper. This action may have been what finally convinced Chilembwe that some far more dramatic demonstration than his letter was necessary and that even a hopeless revolt might eventually bring about some amelioration in the condition of Africans in the protectorate. The Africans' willingness "to strike a blow and die" might impress upon Europeans the despair behind that desperate resolve.[23]

According to the plan, the main thrust was to be from Chilembwe's headquarters at the Providence Industrial Mission, but it was expected that there would be supporting action in other parts of the country. The homes of several Europeans living near Magomero were to be attacked, and the Blantyre warehouse of the African Lakes Company, with its stock of guns and ammunition, was to be seized. These activities in and around the Chiradzulu district were to be supported by risings in Ncheu and Mlanje, and it was hoped that German forces in Tanganyika, who were to be informed of the rising, would attack in the North while British forces were in confusion as a result of the rebellion.

The attack on the houses near Magomero, which took place on 23 January, took the owners completely by surprise. W. J. Livingstone, the manager of the Bruce estates, was killed before he had time to arm himself, and his head was cut off and

23. The phrase was attributed to Chilembwe by George Simeon Mwase, in the account subsequently edited by R. I. Rotberg under the title *Strike a Blow and Die* (Cambridge, Mass.: Harvard University Press, 1967).

carried back on a pole to Chilembwe's base at the Providence Industrial Mission. The attack was carried out so ineptly else-where that most of the intended victims were able to drive off the attackers or to escape from them.[24] The attack on the Lakes Company stores proved to be a fiasco, with Chilembwe's men fleeing from the scene as soon as the alarm was raised.[25]

There was very little open support for the rebellion in other districts. One of the Mlanje chiefs on whom Chilembwe had pinned great hopes reported the matter to the authorities; there was a minor skirmish in the Zomba district involving a small group of Chilembwe supporters who fired a few arrows before making their escape, and in Ncheu there was an ineffective dem-onstration by several hundred Africans who surrounded the government office but were unwilling to risk an attack on the small force inside. Once the authorities had recovered from their surprise, they were able to disperse the demonstrators and arrest the leaders, with the assistance of spearmen provided by some of the principal chiefs of the district.

Chilembwe's own forces retreated to the headquarters at

24. The rebels attacked several houses, achieving complete surprise. Living-stone was able to seize an unloaded rifle and apparently made a good fight of it despite the very heavy odds against him; according to Shepperson and Price (p. 270) he fought his way through three rooms before having his head split open with an ax. There, in the presence of his wife and children, his head was cut off. One of his neighbors had arrived on the scene unarmed—telling his ser-vant that he could attend to any difficulties with his fists—and was killed. At another house the owner, taken by surprise, was speared before he could fight back; even so, he was able to escape, although he died later as a result of the attack. One house was sacked in the owner's absence, and at the other house which was attacked the owner was speared on his doorstep but managed to stagger back in the house, where his wife removed the spear and handed him a gun. It was the only instance in which any of the attacked people was able to get hold of a weapon. The attackers set fire to the house; the Robertsons were able to escape, but their house servant, who had behaved with great courage during the attack, was killed.

25. Complete surprise was again achieved because most Europeans in Blan-tyre were occupied at the annual festivities of the Blantyre Sports Club, but when the attackers thought that the alarm had been given, they fled in dis-order, leaving behind them many of the weapons they had seized. They appear to have panicked before a shot was fired against them, and when a detachment of police eventually arrived and set off in pursuit, many members of the rebel force gave themselves up without a struggle.

Magomero, where there were some rudimentary fortifications. They were able to hold off a small party of the King's African Rifles, which may not have been expecting any resistance after the ease with which the first prisoners had been taken. By the time a larger force was brought up, Chilembwe and his followers had abandoned the defenses and fled toward the Mozambique border. A few days later Chilembwe and a few companions ran into a British patrol; there was a brief skirmish, and Chilembwe was shot dead while trying to escape.[26]

The rising had never presented a serious threat to the local colonial forces, even though most troops were on active service against the German forces in Tanganyika, but it occasioned some alarm among British settlers in the country, since many of them lived in isolated conditions and knew that they would be vulnerable to surprise attacks if ever Africans were to believe it appropriate to carry them out.

The significance that has been widely accorded to the rising, at least since the appearance of the major work on the subject by Shepperson and Price, had perhaps owed less to what happened at the time than to the effect of the events on the subsequent history of the country. One of the most confident verdicts on this interpretation of the country's recent history is that of Pachai:

Chilembwe died a martyr but not in vain. Governor Smith admitted that the rising introduced a new phase in the history of Nyasaland. After 1915 the Shadow of Chilembwe was cast on the private estates, in the missions, in the Legislative Council chambers, in the relations between white and black. Though independence was yet a long way off, 1915 marked the end of the old era. What happened in 1953 and 1959 was a lengthening of this shadow and a reinforcement of all it stood for. Chilembwe's rebellion was not a mere symbolic blow. It was a real instrument of change, even if it was fifty years ahead of its time.[27]

26. Pachai says that Chilembwe was betrayed by "a Judas Iscariot from Kaduya's village near the Portuguese East African border" (*Malawi*, p. 224). But even Pachai's very sympathetic account describes the rising as "a series of panic moves" explained by the authorities' having moved against him before he was ready (p. 223).

27. Pachai, *Malawi*, p. 224.

This interpretation is consistent with the assertion of Governor Sir George Smith, that the rising "opened a new phase in the existence of Nyasaland," but Alexander Hetherwick, who was in charge of the Church of Scotland's Blantyre mission at the time of the rising, later commented that "nothing came of the commission [which was appointed to enquire into the rising] and the whole matter was speedily forgotten."[28]

Several more cautious writers have argued that the rising had a salutary effect on social relations because Europeans became more aware of the offense given to Africans by the behavior of men like Bruce. This is a difficult matter about which to pass judgment: the only open recognition at the time of the need for change in social behavior came from missionaries, who had believed the change was necessary before the rising occurred; there were to be many occasions in the future when Europeans in Nyasaland were insensitive, patronizing, or condescending to Africans, and not a few occasions when they were to seem totally careless of African opinion in the protectorate. Some Africans have said that they felt there was after the rising, improvement and the well-informed and judicious Shepperson finds this plausible, though he feels "the point should not be pressed too far."[29]

The most critical problems in the Shire Highlands had been those related to European ownership of land, the system of land tenure, and the exaction of labor services in lieu of rent. In the few years after the rising several attempts were made to deal with the problem, but they led to no clear improvement in the welfare of Africans on European land. The gains by some groups were balanced by a deterioration in the condition of others. Proposals that would have improved the position of African tenants had been put forward by Justice Nunan more than ten years before Chilembwe's abortive revolt, but they were never implemented. Nothing that was done in the thirty years following the rising was as favorable to African interests as the Nunan report had been. There was, it turned out, no effective policy for redistributing land until after the end of

28. Shepperson and Price quote Smith on p. 396 and Hetherwick on p. 388.
29. Shepperson and Price, p. 392.

World War II, and that could scarcely be considered a consequence of the rising.

Some of the leading authorities on the period believe that the rising had a significant and beneficial effect on educational policy in the protectorate. The point was made, albeit cautiously, by Shepperson and Price, who wrote that "the rising, though it appears to have been rarely mentioned in open discussion of educational problems in the protectorate between 1916 and 1919, had nevertheless a very definite place in the history of educational extension amongst Africans in Nyasaland."[30] In support of this view they referred to the substantial increase in government involvement in education during the 1920s, including greatly increased financial assistance to mission schools, and the establishment of a Department of Education.

The government did become more actively engaged in promoting education after the war, but it is, to say the least, questionable whether this can be ascribed to the effect of the rising. There had been a gradual trend in Nyasaland, as in other British colonial territories in Africa, starting before World War I, toward increased government participation in education and, indeed, toward a general extension of government activities. This trend was strongly reinforced by the visit of the Phelps-Stokes Commission to many African territories, and by the commission's subsequent reports which provided a powerful stimulus to educational development throughout Africa. The reports were well received by the British colonial authorities, and the postwar period saw a great increase in governmental contributions to educational expenditure in all British-ruled territories in Africa.[31]

It would, in these circumstances, have been strange if the government's contribution to education in Nyasaland had not increased, and no evidence exists of any special concern about educational improvement in Nyasaland that could be attributed to the effect of the rising. There was one important respect in which the educational situation deteriorated in Nyasaland (while it was improving in most parts of British Africa) during the

30. Shepperson and Price, p. 391.
31. The reports were published under the authorship of T. J. Jones: *Education in Africa, 1922* and *Education in East Africa, 1925.*

postwar period. The attempt by some missions, particularly the Free Church Mission at Livingstonia, to provide serious post-primary education was virtually abandoned about the time of the Chilembwe Rising, and it was to be more than twenty years before the elements of secondary education were once again available in Nyasaland.[32] This had been the aspect of mission-education policy that had most offended European planters, who had claimed that its main effect was to produce ambitious dissidents. The rising powerfully reinforced criticism of all plans to provide any form of advanced education for Africans in Nyasaland. No doubt a number of considerations influenced the decision of the Scottish missions to give up, at least for the moment, their ambition to produce the African leaders of a new society, but the effect of the rising was to discourage those individuals within the missions who had been most committed to the provision of higher education for Africans.

There is little reliable evidence that Chilembwe had been able to enlist the support of many Africans apart from those who were members of his own church in Chiradzulu or of Chinyama's African Baptist Church in Ncheu. There may well have been some who adopted a wait-and-see policy, but few of them were openly sympathetic; the movement was shunned by the majority of educated Africans, who belonged to the established churches; it received no support from any major chief and it was subsequently condemned by the native associations, which were the principal political voice of educated Africans during the 1920s and 1930s.

The North Nyasa Native Association, of which Levi Mumba was one of the founding members, was very critical of Chilembwe's action: "The Association regretted exceedingly the rising of John Chilembwe and others inasmuch as they knew that a High Court exists to which appeal could have been made . . . the rising being a black mark on the natives of the Protectorate."[33]

The other associations were similarly anxious to disassociate

32. The first secondary school was established in 1941 at Blantyre, but it was widely believed that the education provided in the senior forms of Livingstonia before World War I was of good secondary standard.

33. Pachai, *Malawi*, p. 228.

themselves from any suggestion of revolutionary intent. In the words of the Momberra Native Association, they would do nothing "directly [or] indirectly to subvert the authority of the Government, or of any lawful establishments, [or] to induce the community to do so."[34]

The Chilembwe Rising and the manner in which its supporters had been punished may, indeed, have discouraged political activity by Africans in the Shire Highlands, where they had in any event been relatively slow in setting up native associations despite the fact that it was the only part of the protectorate where educational facilities were anything like as good as those in the North. In 1920 the North Nyasa Association attempted unsuccessfully to contact Africans working in Zomba and Blantyre and encourage them to start an association. Four years later, however, Levi Mumba, who had been secretary of the North Nyasa Native Association for twelve years before moving to Zomba and was at this time employed as a storekeeper in the Public Works Department of Zomba, helped organize a "representative committee for Northern Province Native Associations" in that town to represent the views of northerners working for the government. Shortly afterward, an association was established in Blantyre.

Mumba was anxious to encourage the development of some form of national or regional amalgamation among associations, but there was not yet much general enthusiasm for this idea. He kept up a prolific correspondence with the other associations but was unable to persuade them that any great advantage was to be derived from a national association.

All the associations held their meetings in public and agreed to send typewritten copies of their minutes to the government as well as to all paid up members, but this did not prevent serious discussion of a wide range of issues of both local and national interest. The scope of their proceedings has been described by Pachai:

The native associations did not function purely as instruments of protest. They looked at divorce laws, adultery, cleanliness of the villages, evils of migrant labour, housing conditions for village teachers, im-

34. Ibid., p. 227.

provements to roads and marketing facilities. They discussed price control as well as national political issues. They prepared memoranda for land commissions as well as for commissions enquiring into the feasibility of amalgamating the Central African territories. In all these issues they served the important function of acting as the African voice. They initiated many discussions but equally were invited by the Government to investigate certain matters and act as a forum for collecting public opinion. On many issues of local or national import the Government took serious note of the representations made.[35]

The conditions of membership had been suggested by Dr. Laws of the Livingstonia mission, whose support had been most valuable in gaining governmental approval, and these were subsequently accepted by both the government and the associations. Members should be, it was agreed, "educated, of good character, loyal to the Government and approved by the Government."[36]

The associations were forums for the educated elite, and although they included a number of traditional rulers, these were members by virtue of their education rather than their heritage. The limited nature of the membership did not prevent the associations from making well-considered representations on matters of general importance, but it did mean that there was little direct contact between the associations and the majority of the people.

The style of the association was very much that of men with a sense of dignity and self-confidence, who expected that they would be able to bring about significant social change by the power of argument. They were not revolutionaries but neither were they abject. In a statement to the Hilton Young Commission in 1928, Levi Mumba described their attitude:

We natives of Nyasaland are men of ambition, capable of development and enterprise . . . [but] even in our own country we are merely used as labour for the whiteman. . . . We want to be given facilities for development near our own homes, given markets with good prices for crops grown by ourselves. . . . For those who . . . have to work for others we demand good wages and good treatment . . . as is found in other Colonies and Protectorates.[37]

35. Ibid., p. 229.
36. Ibid., p. 229.
37. Tangri, pp. 208–209.

By the late twenties the members of the associations must have felt that they had firmly established themselves as the representatives of responsible African opinion, but their position was soon to deteriorate.

A step that had, indeed, already been taken would undermine the associations. In 1926 the governor had remarked that "it is certain that the large native population of Nyasaland must be administered to a large extent through the natives themselves."[38] This view was in part a reflection of the growing popularity in British colonial circles of Lugard's views about indirect rule, even where, as in Nyasaland, conditions were different from those from which Lugard had derived his prescription, but it was also a result of the increasing scope of government operations. The colonial authorities were becoming heavily committed to agricultural improvement, public works, education, and other activities, and the heavy demands on the government's limited manpower resources, it was felt, could be relieved by making more effective use of traditional authorities. At the same time, the success of many of these enterprises depended on the informed cooperation of the rural population, which could perhaps be most easily obtained by working through institutions already long a part of the rural communities.

A good deal had been done in some territories in East and Central Africa to increase the functions of local African authorities and to make them responsible for certain types of judicial and executive work, with provision being made for some limited powers of taxation to be transferred to the native authorities. In 1933 two measures were introduced in Nyasaland. These were the Native Authority Ordinance and the Native Courts Ordinance. The first recognized certain traditional rulers as having some limited but not insignificant powers as local authorities and gave them the power to appoint subordinate native authorities and to levy local rates and dues. Many of the rules that came into effect, which affected matters of local interest, were in practice suggested by the district commissioners, but the members of the native authorities were in a

38. Griff Jones, p. 76.

much stronger position than most chiefs and headmen had previously been, both to initiate measures that might be of considerable local importance and to make clear, where appropriate, their doubts about the wisdom of measures suggested by colonial officials. The other ordinance established native courts, which were empowered to apply customary law for a wide range of offenses, excluding those that attracted major penalties, where all the parties involved were African. There were three categories of native court: Grade A courts, under the charge of a senior chief, were able to impose prison sentences of up to six months or a fine up to a maximum of five pounds; Grade B courts were limited to three months or three pounds, and the maximum punishment that could be laid down by a Grade C court was one month in prison or a one-pound fine. Appeals were allowed from lower to higher native courts, then to the district commissioner, the provincial commissioner, and, finally, to the High Court.[39]

The decision of the government to give a great deal more authority to traditional leaders (or, at least, to those traditional leaders acceptable to the colonial authority) was a blow to the native associations. Some of their members were upset that increased power had been granted to traditional leaders whose capacity they doubted. Of greater importance for the future of the associations was the fact that the administration's decision to work through leaders whose authority was derived from their traditional position inevitably meant that less attention would be paid to representation from Africans whose claim to authority rested on the quite different criterion that they were relatively well-educated men pursuing careers in the "modern world." Moreover, the native authorities provided, in addition to their executive functions, a means by which the administration could learn something about African opinion. This reduced the likelihood that colonial officials would pay much attention to the views of the associations since, in the view of many officials, the associations represented a very much smaller constituency than did the native authorities.

The government's decision to revive the prestige of tradi-

39. Pachai, *Malawi*, pp. 188–189.

tional authorities would probably have seen the eclipse, if only temporarily, of the associations even if there had been no other reason for a change in government attitude toward them. A minute to the governor in January 1930 noted: "If we are to lean in the direction of restoring the prestige and authority of the tribal chiefs, it may be preferable not to give any unnecessary recognition or compliments to Associations composed rather of the other type of 'influential person' —i.e. clerks whose influence is new, rather than chiefs whose influence is old."[40]

The change in attitude of the authorities was, however, encouraged by a feeling that the associations were, at that very time, seking to achieve greater influence and status than it had been intended to give them. When the chief secretary said in 1930 that it would be "highly undesirable [that the] clamorous educated natives should in any way displace the District Council as the vehicle of public opinion in the District," he was not merely expressing a theoretical point but reacting to an apparent growth of radical feeling within the associations.[41] This in turn may have been due in part to the influence of the Reverend Yesaya Mwase, and one or two other powerful figures like him, who were becoming increasingly dissatisfied with the previously "moderating" influences of the Livingstonia mission. It was also a reaction to the fact that the government was contemplating, or was believed to be contemplating, several highly contentious measures that profoundly affected African interests, and the associations had little choice, even had they had the inclination to tread warily, but to express the deep concern of their members.

There had been growing fears during the 1920s that large tracts of land in northern Nyasaland would be handed over to Europeans, and it was in the north that the associations had their greatest vitality. In 1929 the West Nyasa Association, which had been involved in a sharp dispute with the district commissioner the previous year, resolved that all land in the district belonged by right to Africans and was inalienable. The chairman of the association also made clear his view that the time was drawing near when a national meeting of the associa-

40. Tangri, p. 241.
41. Ibid.

tions should be established in order to strengthen and coordinate African representation. The provincial commissioner responded by warning the association that unless it expressed itself in more moderate tones, "its existence as a recognized institution may be imperilled."[42]

The major source of trouble, however, was a section of the Penal Code introduced in 1929 that provided punishment for sexual relations between black men and white women while saying nothing about similar contact between white men and black women. It was blatantly racist legislation, and since Europeans had a virtual monopoly of wealth and power and were consequently in a much better position than Africans to persuade, seduce, or threaten, Africans had reason to be acutely aware of, and bitter about, the real problems involved in interracial sexual liasons. Protests were made by almost every association and by the representative committee in Zomba. In responding to one of these protests, the district commissioner at Karonga unwittingly demonstrated the validity of their complaint, for after attributing the complaint to the racism of Africans who had been miseducated at Livingstonia, he went on to describe the legislation as "lamentable" on the grounds that it was "an insult to European women." He added: "The bare fact that the morals of white women are discussed by Native Associations is deplorable."[43]

In 1930 the government decided that the associations would have to work through the district councils, which were dominated by colonial officials who were assisted by representatives of the traditional rulers, and that minutes and resolutions would be ignored unless they were submitted through, and adopted by, the councils. This meant that the district commissioner and the chiefs had a right of veto on all association proposals.

The government did not completely ignore the views of the association leaders, although it dealt with the leaders as individuals rather than as representatives. In 1933 Levi Mumba became the first African to be appointed to the Advisory Committee on Education, where he was to play an active and valu-

---

42. Ibid., p. 217.
43. Quoted by Pachai, *Malawi*, p. 229.

able role. The associations did, however, lose much of the support they had gained among Africans who had cause to feel that they were ineffective, and they were overshadowed in the early thirties by Independent Churches such as Mwasi's "Blackman's Church of God"—"I wish to naturalise and nationalise God," said Mwasi.[44] The Reverend Charles Chinula established a new church, Eklesia Lanangwa (The Christianity of Freedom), the Reverend Y. M. Mkandawire founded the African Reformed Presbyterian Church, and an African National Church established congregations at Mzimba, Lilongwe, and Ncheu. These were not apocalyptic churches and did not anticipate revolutionary social changes in the near future but reflected a more sophisticated approach in seeking some form of national or regional identity. Many of the men most prominently involved in them had already been active members of the associations or were to become so when the associations revived.

The associations most affected by the new regulations were those in the central and northern provinces (except for Tongaland) because these were the homelands of the most important paramount chiefs, whereas the associations in the south, which had previously been relatively weak (apart from the representative committee in Zomba), were less seriously hindered in their development because the native authorities in these areas were much less effective and were, indeed, constrained by the presence of European landowners whose interests would not have been advanced by the strengthening of traditional African authorities in their neighborhood.

The situation was, however, a fluid one. In 1935 the new governor, Sir Harold Kittermaster, turned out to be a good deal more sympathetic to the associations than his predecessor had been. He invited Levi Mumba to discuss matters with him and later noted that it would be "highly impolitic to act in such a way as to force these associations into an attitude of opposition as has happened in Kenya particularly among the Kikuyu. We should try to use them by encouraging their activity if possible on useful lines."[45]

44. Tangri, p. 227.
45. Ibid., p. 246.

The associations were, in any event, soon to receive an incalculable but undoubtedly powerful stimulus as the African population of Nyasaland became aware that there was an upsurge of support among whites in the protectorate in favor of amalgamation with Rhodesia. The recent failure of the associations to evoke a sympathetic response in administration circles had engendered a degree of apathy among their former members, but they were now presented with a threat of so clear and fundamental a kind that few Nyasaland Africans doubted the need to defend their interests. Many of them had been temporary migrant workers in Rhodesia or South Africa and had no need to be told what it would be like to live in a country run without let or hindrance by white settlers.

The Blantyre Native Association invited other associations in the Southern Province, together with representatives of the native authorities and village headmen, to meet with them in order to discuss ways of expressing their joint views on the question of amalgamation. A petition was sent to the Colonial Office expressing complete opposition to any move toward closer union. The associations, along with many individuals, submitted evidence of African opposition to the Bledisloe Commission, which had been set up by the British government to examine proposals for amalgamation in Central Africa. In due course the commission reported on the widespread objection in Nyasaland among Nyasaland Africans to any such move.

The impetus gained by the associations when they took a prominent part in organizing opposition to amalgamation was reflected in the renewed vigor with which they approached many other matters of policy. The Blantyre association circulated its minutes to other associations in the south; its members debated the regulations governing the growing of cotton and tobacco and the recruitment of labor for work in South Africa and Rhodesia; in 1937 they petitioned for the establishment of a secondary school; a submission was presented urging direct political representation for Africans in the Legislative Council and suggesting that educated Africans be entitled to elect half its members; it was pointed out, quite correctly, that the Tobacco Board, which was concerned with setting the price paid to African growers, was composed entirely of Europeans and

particularly of "those who buy our tobacco," and it was urged
that Africans should be given power to elect members of the
board.[46]

The move toward some form of national coordination of
associations was further stimulated when James Frederick Sangala moved from Zomba to Blantyre in 1938 and became assistant secretary of the Blantyre Native Association. Sangala was
sympathetic to Levi Mumba's efforts to set up a national body
and, like Mumba, was also keenly interested in educational
matters. In 1943 the colored community was successful in
achieving separate educational facilities for coloreds, which still
further fragmented the already diverse educational structure.
Sangala, together with Lewis Bandawe (his senior in the Civil
Service), Levi Mumba, and a number of other Africans who
had been active in the associations decided that a national campaign for the improvement of African education was necessary,
and in August 1943 the Nyasaland Educated African Council
was established. The title was soon changed. The term "educated" was dropped because it would unduly restrict potential
support and gave a misleading impression of the organization's
range of interests, which went well beyond the immediate cause
of its formation. Sangala wrote an open letter, which was published in the press, suggesting that the council should meet
once or twice each year.

There was a lively response to Sangala's letter. Nyasaland
Africans were still much concerned about the prospect of some
form of amalgamation, and there was a growing belief that
national unity was essential to deal with this threat as well as
other matters. The Nyasaland African Association, as it was
known for a while (until the name was changed once again, to
Nyasaland African Congress), pursued as wide a range of objectives as had interested the native associations and pressed
vigorously for direct representation in the Legislative Council
and for majority African membership on all advisory boards.

The first annual conference of Congress was held in Blantyre
in October 1944, when Levi Mumba was elected president-general. Sangala was unable to be present at the meeting but was

46. Ibid., p. 274.

made a committee member. Dr. Hastings Kamuzu Banda, who was then practicing medicine in Britain, having been away from Nyasaland for almost thirty years, became a life member of the Congress and supported it with financial contributions and advice. In a letter written in April 1946, he said that "if we organize a strong congress, the Government will allow us to rule ourselves much more than it is allowing us now: We shall have Africans to represent us in the Legislative Council at Zomba and on Government Boards and Commissions . . . we shall then control our schools, hospitals, internal trade and commerce and shall do many other things that we do not do now."[47] Other prominent members at the time were Charles Matinga, Charles Wesley Mlanga, and Isaac Macdonald Lawrence, all of whom were elected officers of Congress. There were several Europeans in the country, among whom W H. Timcke was one of the most enthusiastic and articulate, who were active sympathizers of Congress.

In December 1944 Congress was recognized by the government as "representing the various African asssociations in Nyasaland."[48] Levi Mumba had died shortly after Congress had been established, and it had proved most difficult to find another leader who could successfully balance the need to exert pressure on the government with a realistic sense of what might be achieved, or one who had the ability and standing to contain the rivalries of individuals and groups within the organization.

Dr. Banda proposed that Congress should employ a full-time organizing secretary, and offered to put up the funds for this himself. The proposal was supported by a subcommittee that included Sangala and the Reverend Charles Chinula, who was by this time vice-president, but it was turned down by President-General Charles Matinga, who later said that he was becoming concerned about what he felt to be Dr. Banda's interference in the affairs of Congress. He may have been jealous of the tributes that had been paid to Dr. Banda at the previous national conference; he feared that someone being paid by Dr. Banda would feel that his first loyalty was to the doctor rather

47. Philip Short, *Banda* (London: Routledge & Kegan Paul, 1974), pp. 42–43.
48. Quoted by Short, p. 45.

than to Congress or to Matinga himself. He was not alone in his reservations about Dr. Banda's intentions, and the national conference rejected the subcommittee's recommendation.

With the apparent diminution of the threat of amalgamation, which had been a major preoccupation at the second annual meeting, in 1945 Congress once again concentrated on education and put forward a proposal that the government should take responsibility for all education. It was arranged in 1945 that a deputation from Congress should be sent to Britain, where the colonial secretary had agreed to grant an interview, but what should have been a testament to the increasing maturity of Congress turned out, instead, to demonstrate how feeble was the slender fabric of unity. Congress selected as its representatives Matinga and Chinula, but, before they were due to leave, Matinga departed with a colleague of his own choosing one Andrew Mponda, a fellow Yao. Chinula pursued them to Cape Town but arrived too late to prevent their embarking for Britain and, but for the help of Nyasaland Africans living in South Africa, would have found himself destitute.[49]

Shortly after Matinga's return he was accused of embezzling Congress funds and was dismissed from office. Sangala and a few other devoted men managed to keep Congress in existence, but within a few years of its establishment it was weak, divided, and on the verge of bankruptcy. The Native Associations had, for different reasons, been on the point of collapse during the 1930s, only to be revived by threat of amalgamation; as that threat appeared to be diminishing, the Congress began to lose its momentum and to become obsessed with divisions, rivalries, and antagonisms among its members, who were out of touch, or at least out of sympathy, with the majority of their countrymen. Amalgamation had not, however, been forgotten. While Matinga and Chinula were locked in their unhappy and unseemly struggle, the Europeans of Central Africa were planning the emergence of a new white dominion, and Nyasaland Africans were about to find that they were much more vulnerable than they had begun to suppose.

49. The incident is briefly mentioned by Pachai, *Malawi*, pp. 233–234, and Short, pp. 53–54. Chinula still shook with emotion when recounting the events nearly twenty years later in a talk given at the University of Malawi.

CHAPTER 4

Federation:
Mirage or Catalyst?

The remoteness of Nyasaland, its lack of mineral resources, the sparseness of its revenue, and the presence there of a small but relatively powerful and articulate European community had all contributed in their various ways to a belief among Europeans that considerable advantages would be gained from association with other territories either more fortunately endowed by nature, better placed geographically, or with larger European populations.

Most members of the European community in Nyasaland were agreed that there were certain benefits to be derived from membership in a larger unit. The prospect of economic viability would be better if the burden of government overhead could be reduced and the chances of developing an adequate system of communications with the outside world (either through the Rhodesias of southern Africa or through Tanganyika to the Indian Ocean) improved. A minority of Europeans, including senior members of the Scottish missions, were, however, apprehensive that any form of closer association with the settler societies to the south would seriously diminish the likelihood that there would be effective development by, and on behalf of, the African population.

When Tanganyika was occupied by British forces during and after World War I, some form of union with territories to the north of Nyasaland became feasible. Alexander Hetherwick of the Blantyre Mission, among others, had argued in favor of closer association with the East African Territories.[1] It is possible that such a move would have gained some of the benefits of a larger union—an outlet to the coast, for example, might have been built—and it would have precluded the possibility that the white settlers in Nyasaland might link up with, and come under the influence of, their more dominating counterparts in Southern Rhodesia. Tanganyika was if anything even less well endowed in obviously exploitable resources than Nyasaland and, with a greater area and sparser population, would have been even more difficult to govern and develop with limited resources. Both Kenya and Uganda were relatively prosperous but were so far away that it is unlikely that much direct benefit from association with them would have been felt in Nyasaland. To most Europeans in Nyasaland, in any case, association with the European communities of Rhodesia seemed much more natural. Indeed, at the very time that Scottish missionaries were seeking other forms of association, their own experience was being cited by Governor Sir Charles Bowring as an illustration of the value of the Southern Link. Speaking to the Conference of Governors of the East African Dependencies in 1926 about the natural roots that the Nyasaland churches had in southern Africa, he referred to the many examples of missionary bodies which had come from or through South Africa and noted that the Scottish missions, though with a different provenance, had recently entered into a federated presbytery with the Dutch Reformed Church.[2]

In 1927 the Hilton Young Commission was set up to look into the question of closer union for the territories of East and Central Africa. The chairman favored a division of Northern

1. According to Rotberg there was, for a short period, some "settler" interest in an association between Nyasaland and the territories to the north. It was felt that while the British government would not countenance home rule for either Northern Rhodesia or Nyasaland, it might be prepared to allow a good deal more autonomy to an East African federation. The sentiment was short-lived. R. I. Rotberg, *The Rise of Nationalism in Central Africa* (Cambridge, Mass.: Harvard University Press, 1965), pp. 98–99.

2. Conference of Governors of the East African Dependencies, 1926, *Summary of Proceedings,* London: Waterlow and Sons. Similar evidence was presented in 1925 by the governor of Nyasaland and Northern Rhodesia to the Ormsby-Gore Commission, which was set up to investigate the possibilities of closer union between the East and Central African territories (Rotberg, p. 97).

Rhodesia, with that part of it which was along the railway line, containing the recently discovered copper belt, being amalgamated with Southern Rhodesia, while the much poorer north east would be added to Nyasaland, with which it had a great deal in common in terms of tradition, tribal institutions, and people, and Barotseland in the west would become a separate native reserve. There should, he felt, be a central authority for major policy in the two Rhodesias and Nyasaland, with the governor of Southern Rhodesia as high commissioner, having the duty both to coordinate policies on matters such as customs, communications, and defense and to take over the supervisory powers of the secretary of state with respect to the safeguard of native interests. The chairman was not, however, supported by the other members of the commission, who felt that the future of the mining industry in Northern Rhodesia was still too uncertain to justify a major change in existing arrangements and that Southern Rhodesia had still to demonstrate that it could deal successfully with its own native problems. The report suggested that closer association, perhaps with the East African territories, might be desirable in the long run, even if not practicable at the time, but it took a stand against the desirability of self-government "until the natives themselves can share in the responsibility," and it upheld the virtues of imperial trusteeship, commenting that "experience has taught mankind that a man, however just and honourable, ought not to be made judge in his own cause."[3]

The cause of amalgamation and independence, was soon, however, to attract very much more support than hitherto as a result of three quite separate events. In 1933 the government of Southern Rhodesia resolved an outstanding dispute with the British South Africa Company, over the latter's claim to mineral rights, by paying the company a sum of £2 million. Before this, the company's representatives and friends, who were not without influence in Britain, had opposed any moves that might lead to a diminution of control by Westminster, but in 1934 the company was actively supporting moves for some form of federal arrangement in Central Africa.[4]

3. Quoted in Griff Jones, *Britain and Nyasaland*, p. 130.
4. L. H. Gann, *A History of Northern Rhodesia* (London: Chatto and Windus, 1964), p. 247, and pp. 267–268.

Within Central Africa itself European opinion had been aroused when Lord Passfield, the former Sidney Webb, secretary of state for the colonies in the second Labour government, reasserted in 1930 the doctrine of the paramountcy of native interests. This doctrine had never in fact had a great deal of effect, and it soon became apparent that Passfield's memorandum would be interpreted, both in Britain by his successors and in Central Africa by their principal agents, in a way that would provide little inconvenience to settlers, but the memorandum served to remind the settlers that as long as ultimate power lay in Britain, it was always possible that such a doctrine would not only be propounded but enforced as well.

The onset of the economic depression had a substantial influence on the attitude of the European community in Nyasaland. To the Europeans, the advantages of amalgamation had previously been counterbalanced to some extent by the feeling that as a small and isolated community their regional interests would not be given much weight by the much larger European community in Southern Rhodesia. The depression led some who had before been skeptical to feel that radical measures, of a sort that would never come from the Colonial Office, were necessary and that risks would be justified. The *Nyasaland Times* supported amalgamation on grounds of administrative economy, a possible reduction of taxes, and that closer association with Southern Rhodesia would make it practicable to introduce European development schemes and encourage European immigration.[5]

Southern Rhodesians had, in their turn, become more interested in the idea of including Nyasaland in a scheme of closer association with both Rhodesias. There were indications that Nyasaland labor might be recruited in large numbers for the South African minefields along the Rand and that the supply of Nyasaland migrant labor to Southern Rhodesia would be severely affected unless steps were taken to establish constitutional links between the two countries.[6] In 1933 the British

5. See Rotberg, p. 106; Gann, p. 268; Pachai, *Malawi,* p.258. Tangri says that the Nyasaland *Times* was sometimes skeptical about the issue ("The Development of Modern African Politics," p. 267).

6. Gann, p. 269.

Empire Producers' Organisation (BEPO) decided to back amalgamation of the Central African territories and a delegation, including Lieutenant Colonel Ponsonby, the London representative of the Nyasaland European Unofficial Bodies, called on the colonial secretary. The tobacco buyers, they said, already treated Central Africa as a single economic system, and 80 per cent of the laborers on Southern Rhodesian farms came from Nyasaland. The BEPO suggested that research, customs, communications, mining, nonnative education, and defense should be unified and that there should be a common Court of Appeal. To the economic arguments in favor of their proposals they added a statement that was to become one of the most frequent, if not the most cogent, of arguments put forward by the protagonists of the settler interest: a stable and powerful community led by British Europeans in Central Africa was necessary in order to prevent the spread of Afrikaner attitudes and influence across the Limpopo.[7]

The governors of Nyasaland and Northern Rhodesia were sympathetic toward some form of closer association. Sir Hubert Young, the governor of Northern Rhodesia, favored a customs union to keep out the cheap Asian products that were beginning to enter the area in substantial quantities. He seems not to have understood that cheap imports were a great benefit to the African population, and he was mainly concerned with the prospect of producing goods locally, behind a tariff barrier, and "thus [affording] employment not only to Africans, but also to unemployed supervisors and skilled men from home."[8] The Asian goods that were to be excluded from the Nyasaland market included bicycles as well as textiles; bicycles in the thirties not only contributed to a rising standard of living but, by providing a form of transportation in areas where the only alternative was to go on foot, encouraged the spread of trading and acted as a stimulus to growth of the domestic economy; their exclusion would have obliged Africans to pay far more for

7. Ibid., p. 268. The argument was at odds with the view that there was a natural link with southern Africa. It may be that for some of those who pursued it, the objectionable thing about Afrikaner attitudes was in their attitude toward Britons rather than toward Africans.

8. Gann, p. 271.

these useful and highly desired products or do without them altogether.

In April 1935 a formal conference took place among the Central African governors which furthered the cordial but informal discussions that had previously been concluded. They agreed that closer association was needed with respect to a wide range of subjects, including customs, communications, education, defense, publicity and trade representation in England, and research. Meanwhile, the governors adopted the practice of regular consultation.

During the same year Europeans in Nyasaland formed a Greater Rhodesia League to support closer association with Southern Rhodesia, and in the following year they were represented by seven unofficial members of the Legislative Council at the Victoria Falls Conference of white parliamentarians and unofficials, where a motion was passed in favor of amalgamation.

There does not appear to have been any systematic and clearly articulated African viewpoint on the question of association or amalgamation during the 1920s, and when the Native Associations gave evidence to the Hilton Young Commission, they had taken a rather ambiguous position.[9] By the early 1930s, however, opposition was both widespread and emphatic, and the realization that European pressure for amalgamation was mounting led to a resurgence of African political activity. The native associations, most of which had been inactive in the early thirties, became centers of revived interest as educated Africans sought to rouse their fellows and to establish a forum for the expression of their views.

In 1935 the Blantyre Native Association invited members of other associations in the Southern province, together with representatives of the native authorities and village headmen, to a meeting to discuss European plans for closer association, and drafted a petition to the Colonial Office expressing their complete opposition to any such schemes. The threat of amalgamation had stimulated African political development in at least

9. Tangri, p. 268.

two important respects. First, it made Nyasaland Africans deeply conscious of an overriding mutual interest that would be best protected by some form of national organization, and thus it contributed to the emergence of the African National Congress. Second, it raised doubts about the value of indirect representation, which depended almost entirely on private discussions with government officials, and suggested the importance of much more direct access to all major sources of power. A majority of the Blantyre Native Association supported a proposal that there should be African representation on the Legislative Council—indeed, they felt that half the representation should be African and should be elected by Africans who met some minimum educational qualification—but because of a factional dispute within the association the proposal was not effectively presented to a wider audience.

Attention was not confined to the obviously "political" centers of power. Africans began to feel that they should have some say in the election of members of the Tobacco Board which was manned exclusively by Europeans, and African political leaders began thinking seriously of a gradual but ultimately comprehensive Africanization of all positions of power, to be achieved neither by divine intervention nor utopian revolution but by painstaking negotiation and the careful use of political organization.

In 1938 another royal commission was appointed, under the chairmanship of Lord Bledisloe, in response to continued European pressure for amalgamation (and independence), particularly from Godfrey Huggins, the prime minister of Southern Rhodesia. Almost all commentators have agreed that the commission's report was scholarly and informative but that its recommendations did not follow from the basic analysis and empirical evidence. It suggested that Northern Rhodesia and Nyasaland should come under a single government and that amalgamation with Southern Rhodesia was sound "in principle" although it could not be carried out immediately because of the differences in native policies in the territories. Nonetheless, it recommended that interterritorial cooperation should be increased and formalized and that an advisory council, to be

known as the Central African Council, be established and seek
to coordinate policies on a number of vital matters.

The commissioners did recognize, quite unequivocally, that
the Nyasaland Africans, and to a large extent those of Northern Rhodesia, were overwhelmingly opposed to closer association with Southern Rhodesia, and they believed that it would
be mistaken to ignore their views.[10] Many Europeans "on the
spot" had a natural enough tendency to discount evidence
that didn't suit their purpose, and quite a few of them said
that the Africans who gave evidence were atypical, that Africans did not, and perhaps could not, understand the issues
and that there was no reason why their views should be given
serious consideration. Mackenzie-Kennedy, the governor of
Nyasaland, thought that Africans were not yet competent to
make a sound judgment on so complex a matter and that
their opposition should not deter the British government
from taking advice that would lead to a much more satisfactory level of economic development.[11] At least one of the commissioners, however, took a markedly different view: "The
average native . . . possesses a knowledge and shrewdness in
matters affecting his welfare, with which he is not always cre-
dited. It would I consider be unwise to assume that his opposition is based, to a very large extent, on ignorance or prejudice, or an instinctive dread of change."[12]

In spite of the cautious view taken by the commissioners and
the clear evidence of African opposition to amalgamation—
which might have been expected to carry more weight in Brit-

10. Griff Jones quotes the Commission Report as saying that while Africans
had an imperfect appreciation of the issues involved, there was "striking unanimity, in the Northern territories, of the native opposition to amalgamation
and their fear of change which would lessen the protection they received from
the British government" (pp. 147–148). Rotberg quotes Governor Maybin of
Northern Rhodesia, writing in 1939 that "a very large number of the natives of
this territory have worked in Southern Rhodesia and have an intimate
knowledge of conditions there . . . and they were unanimously opposed to
amalgamation with Southern Rhodesia" (pp. 111–112).

11. Rotberg, pp. 113–114.

12. Guy Clutton-Brock, *Dawn in Nyasaland* (Netherlands: Hodder and
Staughton, 1945), p. 45, quoting a note by Mr. Fitzgerald at the conclusion of
the Bledisloe Commission Report.

ain, with its role of trustee, than it did with the Europeans in Central Africa—the effect of the Report was to contribute to the cumulative pressure on the relatively disinterested British government to abandon its responsibilities in Central Africa. "It was a major stage," wrote Leys, "in a gradually quickening process whereby the real objections to closer union were finally lost to view in a fog of weak and woolly phrases."[13]

War broke out before anything had been decided. Discussion about the long-run development of Central Africa and about the most appropriate relationship between the races gave way to concentration on the survival of the British Empire, and for the next few years the overriding priority for the administration in the three territories was how best to assist the war effort.

The governors were already sympathetic to moves toward closer association, and the exigencies of war would in any event have justified a close working relationship. Moves were made for the coordination and sharing of costs among the territories with respect to aspects of transport and communications, agricultural research, the prospective development of sources of power, and other matters.

Arrangements of this sort, once begun, often have an internal momentum that does little to reflect any reservations that their creators may have felt. Common services are conveniently maintained although the original need for them has passed, and political institutions may be adapted for quite different ends; whatever the costs involved in establishing them, there is often a cost in dissolving them, and perhaps most important, officials and administrators, to say nothing of politicians, rarely welcome the reduction of influence and power that follows any diminution of responsibility.

The Central African Council proposed by the Bledisloe Commission was established in 1943. Roy Welensky, by this time the leader of the unofficials in the Northern Rhodesia Legislative Council and a powerful force in favor of amalgamation, was at first reluctant to endorse the council and serve on it because he thought it a much feebler instrument than was

13. Colin Leys and C. Pratt, *A New Deal in Central Africa* (London: Heinemann, 1960), p. 10.

needed, but he was persuaded to do so by Godfrey Huggins, the prime minister of Southern Rhodesia and, at that time, the dominant figure among European political leaders in Central Africa. They realized that they must at least appear to give the council a fair chance, or else their later assertions that it was inadequate would not be taken seriously.[14]

The movement toward amalgamation and independence was temporarily slowed down after the war, in part because of the influence of the new colonial secretary, Arthur Creech Jones. He was an unusual figure in the House of Commons as a man of left-wing sympathies, with a good deal of political acumen and political weight, who had a detailed knowledge of colonial affairs, and he had the respect of many of his political opponents among the European leaders in Central Africa.[15]

Pressure was continuously applied upon leading parliamentarians in Britain by the Europeans of South and North Rhodesia (and, though to a lesser extent, by the small European minority in Nyasaland), and during the next few years political opinion in Britain was powerfully influenced by considerations that led it during the early 1950s to discount the opinion of Nyasaland Africans.

British political motives during this period may seem at first sight to be little more than indirectly connected with the central themes of Malawian history, but there are several important reasons why one should attempt to analyze these motives with some care. Three of the most critical events in modern Malawian history—entry into the Central African Federation, withdrawal from federation, and the achievement of independence—owed at least as much to the political calculations (or miscalculations) of British parliamentarians as they owed to what took place in Nyasaland, and one cannot understand what happened in Nyasaland without some understanding of the way in which British politicans thought that events in Nyasaland affected domestic British political strategy. Moreover, the

14. Sir Roy Welensky, *4000 Days* (London: Collins, 1964), p. 25.
15. Welensky wrote of him: "Let me say here and now that I always found Mr. Creech-Jones very frank in his dealings. Many Rhodesians, I know, will be surprised, but I rate him as one of the few men I have met in public life whose word is his bond" (p. 22). Jones refers to the "suspicious and experienced Mr. Creech-Jones" (p. 135).

manner in which the British behaved during these years and the motives that inspired them were closely observed by Dr. Banda, Malawi's future president, and had no small effect on his evaluation of the effective choices before Malawi, at least with respect to foreign policy, during his tenure of office. Whether or not one shares his interpretation of the underlying realities of British political life or of its implications for the terms on which African leaders might expect support in Europe, this period is of considerable importance in understanding Malawian politics in the decade after independence.

In 1948, when Roy Welensky was in London with Godfrey Huggins, he visited both Creech Jones and Oliver Stanley, the Conservative "shadow" on Colonial Affairs. Creech Jones told him that "no Government [in Britain], irrespective of its political hue," would be prepared to endorse amalgamation, but he suggested that some form of federal system might be acceptable, presumably having in mind a constitution which, while making provision for certain forms of economic cooperation, would reserve substantial rights to the individual states. In general terms, Oliver Stanley agreed with him, and Welensky and Huggins felt that some form of federal scheme should be put to their constituents.

Whatever merit Creech Jones might have seen in a federal scheme, Welensky and Huggins were confident that it would mean no more than a temporary set-back to their plans. As Huggins was later to explain to his Rhodesian constituents, it made no significant difference to their long-run strategy: "Once the Imperial Government have granted this Constitution they have lost all control—don't forget that."[16]

A conference took place at Victoria Falls in January 1949, with a view both to renewing pressure on the British government in favor of some form of closer association and to putting the case for federation rather than amalgamation to Europeans in the Rhodesias. Later in that year the Southern Rhodesian government informed the British government that it was withdrawing from the Central African Council, which it regarded as inadequate on several counts, and that formal steps toward closer association were urgently required.

16. Leys and Pratt, p. 28.

Meanwhile, resistance to federation was being organized in London by several people, among whom Dr. Hastings Kamuzu Banda was one of the most articulate and perceptive. He had left Nyasaland as a boy, or a very young man, with a standard-three primary education and had worked for several years in Rhodesia and South Africa as a hospital orderly, mine-worker, and clerk. He attended night school, completing his primary education, and with assistance from the church of which he was a member was able to go to the United States to further his education, raising the money for his passage there himself. He attended Wilberforce College in Ohio, at that time a secondary school, and went from there to the University of Chicago, graduating in politics and history; from Chicago he went to the Meharry School of Medicine in Tennessee and in 1938, having obtained American medical qualifications, he left the United States for Britain, where he obtained medical qualifications at Glasgow and Edinburgh and became an elder of the Church of Scotland. He practiced medicine for some time in the north of England before moving, in 1945, to London. By this time he was a successful and prosperous professional man.

It was a remarkable achievement. Starting his education in what he himself described as a bush school, only a few years after the introduction to his country of even the most rudimentary form of modern education, and obliged for years to support himself by hard physical labor, he had gained entry to, and graduated from, a university of great distinction, and he had sought and obtained medical qualifications of international standing; an African from one of the poorest and most backward countries of the continent, a man who would have been treated by Europeans as an inferior in his own land, he had achieved in the colonial metropolis a position of dignity and influence and had become accustomed to the respect of his British patients and neighbors. Whatever else he was to do in his life, he had already accomplished far more than most people aspire to.

He had also taken an active interest in affairs in Malawi and had been a founding member of, and subsequently a generous contributor to, the Nyasaland African Congress, but it was not until much later in his life that his political activities were to provide him with either status or power comparable to that which he had already achieved outside of politics. Far from seeking eminence by entering political life, he first achieved prominence in politics because of the standing he had acquired from professional success. This was something of which he was keenly aware, and it was to profoundly affect his attitude toward both his European opponents and his African colleagues.

He had long been convinced that any extension of the power of Rhodesian white settlers would have disastrous consequences for Africans, and he believed that it was far preferable that direct control be exercised by the British government, whose members he expected to honor at least some part of their responsibilities to their subject people.

His views were presented in considerable detail in a memorandum written in 1951 and co-authored by Harry Nkumbula of Northern Rhodesia, who was then a student at the London School of Economics. Among the points the authors made were two that were absolutely central to an understanding of the Huggins-Welensky strategy: first, that federation was "only a thin edge of the wedge of amalgamation," and second, that federation would enable the European settlers of Southern Rhodesia "to attain the status of a Dominion."[17]

With the benefit of hindsight, these may not appear to be unusually perceptive observations, but few British parliamentarians at the time, if one is to judge from their contributions to *Hansard,* understood as clearly either what the Rhodesians wanted or how difficult it would be to reverse the process once the first steps toward federation had been taken. Those most directly involved—Banda, Nkumbula, Welensky, Huggins—all understood quite well what was at issue, although their estimates of the desirability of various outcomes differed greatly. Neither their fears nor their hopes were to be adequately or even competently reflected in the debates in the House of Commons and the House of Lords, where few speakers were to acknowledge, perhaps because they did not understand, that the fundamental issue in the debate about federation was the tenure and nature of settler domination in Central Africa.

17. Jones, pp. 149–150; Short, *Banda,* pp. 56ff.

Some years later, Sir Harold Macmillan wrote, with characteristic urbanity, that had he "or indeed any of us" realized how strong were the forces of nationalist sentiment in Africa and how effectively they would be organized in the following decade, the imposition of federation against widespread African opposition would never have been considered a viable proposition.[18] If members of Parliament were unaware of the widespread and deeply felt hostility to federation among Nyasaland Africans, it was because they made little effort to examine the evidence that was already available. They were afflicted by a marked lack of perception about what white Rhodesians wanted or were likely to do. Debates in both Commons and Lords were full of tributes to "kith and kin" in Rhodesia, who would be sure to do the right thing by the Africans, but few members of either major party demonstrated any awareness of what was being said (and reported) quite openly by political leaders in Rhodesia.

Had Creech Jones remained at the Colonial Office, the story might have had a different outcome, but in the 1950 election he lost his seat and was replaced at the Colonial Office by James Griffiths, an experienced negotiator, but a man with little experience of colonial affairs. The Labour party, moreover, had a narrow majority and was faced by an aggressive opposition quite openly determined to wear down the government by prolonging debates and forcing votes at every opportunity, obliging government members to remain in the House for hour after hour, day after day, week after week. Under these circumstances a government is not likely to invite confrontation with its opposition on matters that are peripheral to its central purpose.

Almost as soon as he came into office, Griffiths agreed to a suggestion put forward by Huggins that there should be a conference of officials—colonial officials from the territories concerned and senior civil servants from the Colonial Office and the Commonwealth Relations Office—to discuss the form that a federal structure might take. Griffiths apparently thought that such a conference would be "purely exploratory" and would

18. *Pointing the Way* (London: Macmillan, 1972), p. 133.

"in no way commit" Her Majesty's government.[19] This was to prove a very serious miscalculation.

The conference, which took place in January 1951, was under the chairmanship of G. H. Baxter, the assistant under-secretary at the Commonwealth Relations Office, who was a convinced federation man. The officials argued that closer association would not only bring considerable economic benefits but was urgently required to prevent the spread of *apartheid* policies from South Africa. One supposes that this argument was presented in good faith, but no serious effort was made to examine either its assumptions or its implications. The only effective alternative to *apartheid*, short of revolution, would be the gradual abandonment of European minority rule, but the demand for federation came most strongly from the very people who wanted to extend and guarantee minority rule.

The most influential product of the conference was its working paper, *Comparative Survey of Native Policy*, in which the authors declared: "The most striking conclusion which we draw from our examination of the survey is the degree of similarity between the policy and practise of the three Governments, rather than the degree of difference."[20]

They acknowledged that there were differences but said that they "relate largely to methods and timing" and represented no obstacle to closer association. These differences were, however, as Colin Leys and others have pointed out, "the whole issue at stake."[21] Moreover, the assertion that policy and practice were similar did not rest on detailed examination and explanation of policies and practices but on a supposition that the objectives in each case were the same; the conference, far from providing expert opinion on matters of detail, adopted a political position and one that, moreover, assumed away the very points at issue. In the view of Griff Jones, "the officials knew the solution was rubbish," but "it provided an evaluation [of the problem] which enabled the officials to continue working together."[22]

19. Great Britain, *Parliamentary Debates* (Commons), 8 Nov. 1950. See Griff Jones, pp. 135ff.
20. Quoted by Leys and Pratt, p. 20.
21. Leys and Pratt, p. 20.
22. Jones, p. 137.

Welensky was delighted by the report. "This was a big step forward," he later wrote, "and I don't deny that I was jubilant."[23] He had good reason to be. Great play was made, in the parliamentary debates that followed, of the importance of what Lord Altringham called "the solid testimony of impartial civil servants," which he contrasted with "criticism, coming from students, itinerant professors and politicians of all kinds."[24] Oliver Lyttleton, who became colonial secretary when the Conservatives won the election of 1951, spoke gravely of the expert opinion of men "whose impartiality cannot be questioned."[25]

The Labour party leaders, or at least the two men most directly involved—James Griffiths and Patrick Gordon-Walker (the minister for Commonwealth Relations)—had become convinced that there was a great deal of merit to the proposed federation (for reasons that we shall examine presently), but Griffiths was beginning to have doubts about either the wisdom or propriety of forcing it through against the wishes of almost the entire African population of Nyasaland.

He visited Nyasaland to canvass African opinion, and at a meeting of the Central Province African Provincial Council held at Lilongwe in August, he was addressed by Chief Mwase, who spoke to him "on behalf of the chiefs and people" of the country:

This federation is for Europeans, not for Africans at all. For this reason we hate such a federation. We do not want it to press us down. What we want is to have our own self-government in the nearest future. . . . Africans still refuse federation in any form because the experience has shown that federation can only benefit Europeans to have more wealth, more land and more power over Africans, that Africans should remain hewers of wood without any voice in Government. All what is said is only to bluff the Africans, therefore we refuse federation and we shall refuse it even [if] it will mean death.[26]

Nothing immediately came of his visit and in September Griffiths went to Victoria Falls for another conference with representatives from the three territories and from Britain, in-

23. Welensky, p. 39.

24. Great Britain, *Parliamentary Debates* (Lords), 1 Aug. 1951, column 181.

25. Great Britain, *Parliamentary Debates* (Commons), 4 March 1952, columns 241–242.

26. Pachai, *Malawi*, p. 259.

cluding the two ministers most directly concerned. The day after the conference began, it was announced that another election was to take place in Britain and it was clear that few plans could be made at the conference since a great deal would depend on who won the election.

Griffiths appears to have been rather surprised to find that Africans could comport themselves with dignity, and he returned from the conference with growing doubts about the wisdom of disregarding African opinion. "It is," he later told the House of Commons, "essential for all of us to realise that the Africans are growing up."[27] Welensky thought that Griffiths "leaned over backwards trying to placate the African representatives,"[28] and it is possible, as Creighton has suggested, that the Labour party would have had second thoughts about federation if it had won the election.[29]

Although Africans from Nyasaland were present for the first time at this conference, they stressed that their presence did not indicate acquiescence. Clement Kumbikano told the delegates:

I should make it clear that the presence of the three of us at this Conference does not in any way imply that the Nyasaland African population in our country has any other different view on this question that that which they have expressed before the Secretary of State for the Colonies during his tour of the Protectorate. That view is total rejection of the proposals and total rejection of federation with Southern Rhodesia.[30]

The victory of the Conservatives over the Labour party in the British election, however, banished any hope there might have been that such objections would persuade the British government to change its mind. Griffiths may have been on the point of yielding but his conservative counterpart was more receptive to the representations of Roy Welensky and others like him and was prone to suspect that African protest was the work of a handful of violent malcontents. When another con-

27. *Parliamentary Debates* (Commons), 4 March 1952, column 216.
28. Welensky, p. 42.
29. Thomas R. M. Creighton, *The Anatomy of Partnership* (London: Faber & Faber, 1960), pp. 44–45.
30. Pachai, *Malawi*, p. 260.

ference was called in London in April 1952, the African delegates from Nyasaland and Northern Rhodesia who traveled to
London announced that they were prepared to have private
talks with the colonial secretary but were unwilling to attend
the conference since they objected in principle to federation
and not merely to a particular form of it. In May 1953, following an outbreak of civil disorder, a delegation of senior chiefs
from Nyasaland arrived in Britain, financed by thousands of
contributions from Africans in Nyasaland, to present a petition
to the Queen but, on the advice of the minister, their petition
was not granted.

Within Britain the campaign against federation was supported, and to a large extent organized, by the Church of Scotland, drawing upon the great experience in Central Africa of a
number of distinguished missionaries, while Dr. Banda, an elder
of the church, addressed meetings throughout the country.

Despite all this, the Federation (Constitution) Order-in-Com-
mand received the assent of the Queen in August 1953.

Clement Davies, the leader of the Liberal party, had put it to
Parliament on several occasions that whatever the prospective
benefits of federation, no member of the government had explained why the matter was so urgent that there was insufficient time to consider African objections in detail and at least
attempt to persuade them that the arrangements would benefit
everyone.[31] There was no persuasive reply to this line of argument made in Parliament, although Huggins explained quite
frankly in Rhodesia why he thought the matter was urgent:
"Part of the hurry is that the Africans, if nothing is done, with
the propaganda they have got going, will become more and
more averse to it."[32]

There was evidently a strong feeling in Parliament that there
were powerful strategic advantages to be gained from the formation of a federation in Central Africa. British hegemony in
Central Africa was felt to be threatened for the first time for
more than fifty years. Gordon-Walker, who had made a much

31. "Why is it that all along it has been suggested that this matter is extremely
urgent? What is the hurry? Why is it that we cannot wait for this?" *Parliamentary
Debates* (Commons), 24 July 1952, column 810

32. Reported by *Manchester Guardian*, 5 Feb. 1952; quoted in Leys and Pratt,
p. 33.

more favorable impression on Welensky than had Griffiths, argued that this was no mere selfish national interest: "I take the view that the maintenance of British influence in Central Africa is just as much in the interests of the Africans as it is in our own interests."[33]

There were three principal threats to British interests identified in the debates. Many members of Parliament apparently believed that if Southern Rhodesia was unable to gain the measure of economic and political progress that it expected from a merger with Northern Rhodesia, it would turn south and seek some form of association with the Union of South Africa. Gordon-Walker told the House of Commons that Southern Rhodesia was not strong enough to stand alone; it must either have a closer association with the territories to the north or throw in its lot with the Union of South Africa. A great deal of concern was expressed lest the philosophy of *apartheid* be carried north of the Limpopo, without any serious discussion of the effective alternatives and their implications. But a more realistic objective was to ensure the survival of a community sympathetic to British strategic objectives. For this purpose Afrikaner attitudes to race were largely irrelevant, and awareness that many Afrikaner leaders had supported Britain's enemies in World War II was paramount.

There was, nonetheless, some fear that Central Africa would become the scene of a violent conflict between what Lord Altringham called the two nationalisms at work in Africa: black nationalism on the West African model or white nationalism as exemplified by the Afrikaners. As Lord Alport later said, it was hoped that federation "would help to curb the excesses of both black and white nationalism."[34] "Partnership" between whites and blacks was seen as a last chance to avoid a disastrous confrontation, and because the alternatives were so unpleasant, few of its proponents were disposed to look at the case too closely; no one bothered to explain how "partnership" could be imposed by a very small minority on the rest of the population who had clearly rejected it.

Gordon-Walker hoped that a successful experiment with fed-

33. *Parliamentary Debates* (Commons), 24 July 1952, column 775.
34. Cuthbert Alport (Baron of Colchester), *The Sudden Assignment* (London: Hodder and Staughton, 1965), p. 20.

eration and partnership would make a significant contribution to race relations in the Commonwealth, and this, in his view, was the area in which the free world countries had hitherto been most vulnerable to soviet propaganda. The claim of the Soviet Union to have solved the problem of color was, he thought, "more potent" than its claim to have been successful in dealing with economic and social problems. Whatever merit there might have been to this argument, the success of the experiment depended on acceptance of its validity, and neither Gordon-Walker nor anybody else was able to explain how this particular objective could be achieved by forcing federation down African throats.

There was, however, a *Realpolitik* version of the argument which had, at least in the short run, more substance but which would have affronted many British voters in both major parties. Appearance of indecision in Central Africa might have encouraged African nationalists who, until then, were being held in control; if, as a consequence, there was any significant spread of civil disorder, the chaos that would ensue might provide an opportunity for communists or other agitators to gain a foothold in the area. Sir Miles Thomas, the chairman of British Overseas Airways Corporation, who had previously been chairman of the Colonial Development Corporation (and had, while holding that job, chaired the Victoria Falls Conference in February 1949), held an interview in Salisbury. Welensky said that Sir Miles saw federation "as an important factor in the resistance of the infiltration of Communist ideology into Central Africa." Sir Miles went on to say: "Clearly federation is an economic necessity in the co-ordination of the natural resources of Northern Rhodesia, Southern Rhodesia and Nyasaland. Once a broad principle of this sort is recognised, it would be a tragedy if mere political considerations were allowed to become major obstacles."[35]

The "economic necessity" of the move to federation was asserted frequently, but any assertion of necessity was almost invariably accompanied, as Hazlewood has pointed out, by a bland statement that the economic benefits were self-evident—

35. Welensky, p. 46.

it was not necessary to bore the audience by explaining what they were or who would benefit from them.[36]

There had, in general terms, been hope that successful exploitation of the hitherto undeveloped resources of "British Africa" would rescue the ailing British economy. "The whole future of the sterling group and its ability to survive depends," said Sir Stafford Cripps, "on the quick and extensive development of our African resources." Central Africa was, without doubt, an area with more obvious natural resources than most parts of British Africa.[37]

Lord Chandos who, as Oliver Lyttleton, had piloted federation through Parliament insisted that "the economic reasons for federation have not been seriously challenged," and Macmillan continued to believe that the economic advantages were "overwhelming" even after he had decided that the political problems were insuperable.[38] The arguments that were put forward were for the most part, however, arguments in favor of closer cooperation among the British territories in Central Africa rather than a demonstration of the need for political union. A more persuasive economic argument may have been at the back of Macmillan's mind when he said that the decision to include Nyasaland in the federation was "economically correct (since Nyasaland is not viable)."[39] In Creighton's view, Britain, "faced with need of post-war retrenchment, would not be sorry to be rid of the labour and expense of running [Nyasaland]."[40]

Whatever may be thought of the merits of the arguments in favor of federation, they were less important than the constitu-

---

36. A. Hazlewood, "The Economics of Federation and Dissolution in Central Africa," in A. Hazlewood, ed., *African Integration and Disintegration* (Oxford University Press, 1967). He refers to the frequent assertions that great economic advantages were to be derived from the imposition of federation and comments that "there is nowhere to be found an even remotely adequate treatment of the economic issues" (p. 188).

37. Jones, p. 136. Welensky had pointed out that if Britain wanted access on favorable terms to the mineral wealth of Central Africa it would be well advised to support the establishment of a stable and friendly government in the area (Creighton, p. 60).

38. Oliver Lyttleton [Lord Chandos], *The Memoirs of Lord Chandos* (London: Bodley Head, 1962), p. 385; Sir Harold Macmillan, *Pointing the Way* p. 485.

39. Ibid., p. 135.

40. Creighton, p. 38.

tional arrangements that provided much clearer evidence about what was meant by "partnership" than anything said in the debates before the constitution was made public.

The division of powers between federal and territorial governments was unexceptional, once one accepts the underlying racial bias of the move to federation. The federal government had control over matters of obvious interterritorial concern, such as external affairs, defense, customs, railways and civil aviation, power development and posts and telecommunications, and also matters of particular interest to Europeans, such as primary and secondary education for Europeans. The powers of the federal government had actually been increased since the initial proposals were put forward, in spite of mounting evidence of African opposition. The additional matters within the federal sphere included European agriculture (except in Nyasaland where it was felt to be impracticable to make a clear distinction between matters affecting European and African agriculture, and both remained under the jurisdiction of the territorial government), health, income tax, prisons, roads, and a few other things. Territorial governments were responsible for "matters predominantly or exclusively affecting Africans" within that particular territory, such as provincial and native administration, African agriculture, fisheries, African education, and labor.

The federal government took control of customs revenue and income tax, which had been the major sources of territorial revenue, and the territories were each to receive from the federal government, an agreed share of total receipts from income and profit taxes. Although Nyasaland was to receive a much smaller share than the other territories, it would be a net beneficiary because that small share was larger than Nyasaland's contribution to federal tax revenue, and in addition some federal expenditures in Nyasaland were in effect financed by tax receipts from the two Rhodesias.

The federal government was to be responsible to a federal assembly with a total of thirty-five members. Twenty-seven of these could, ostensibly, be drawn from any race but were to be elected by a predominantly European electorate, and two others (from Southern Rhodesia) were to be Africans but would be elected by an almost exclusively European electorate. There was provision for four African members (two each from Northern Rhodesia and Nyasaland) to be elected by Africans, who could more legitimately be said to represent African opinion and interests, while two Europeans (one from each of the same two territories) were appointed by the territorial government and charged to devote themselves to African interests. This meant that as long as the elected Europeans stuck together on racial issues, as they almost invariably had done in the past, they would have twenty-seven votes out of a possible thirty-five. On the other hand the opposition would have difficulty mustering eight, since only four of them represented an African constituency, two of them were dependent on European votes and two were themselves European.

The original proposals had provided some safeguards against government action that would cause a deterioration in the welfare of Africans. A minister for African Interests, appointed by the governor, would be empowered to intervene to prevent any legislation by the government affecting African interests that the minister felt contravened the spirit of the constitution until the legislation had been referred to the secretary of state in Britain, who would have the power to veto it. The minister was also to have been chairman of an African Affairs Board, which would include representatives of African interests and would review controversial legislation. But under pressure from Europeans in Rhodesia, plans for the Ministry for African Interests were dropped, and the African Affairs Board was set up as a standing committee of the Legislature instead of as an independent body.

Huggins had said that the British government knew that in practice similar "safeguards" in the constitution of Southern Rhodesia were "not worth the paper they are written on." Almost all Africans understood this from the start, but it appears that some apparently sophisticated colonial officers did not and were later deeply shocked by what they felt to be a betrayal of promises made to the Africans.[41]

41. Leys and Pratt, p. 29. Griff Jones, then a colonial officer in Nyasaland, assured his charges that the procedure for safeguarding African interests was quite satisfactory, but "in 1957 Mr. Lennox-Boyd made an agreement with Sir

It was anticipated by the proponents of federation that there would be political opposition to the new federation, but they expected that the government would be able to contain it until the economic benefits became apparent and opposition dwindled away to insignificant proportions. The first few years of federation were years of economic expansion, continuing the trend that had been set in Nyasaland between the end of World War II and the inauguration of federation. In the late 1950s a commission was set up under the chairmanship of D.T. Jack to examine the economic effects of federation on Nyasaland. The authors of the Jack Report wrote that: "[we are] convinced that the country's economic development has been accelerated as a direct consequence of its federal association ... and that the economic benefits which have been enjoyed are substantial ... the evidence is conclusive that the greater rate of development which has occurred since 1953 must be attributed to the constitutional changes which were made in that year."[42]

This was, however, a conclusion that did not follow from the evidence that the commissioners themselves presented. Their evidence, which is broadly consistent with other evidence now available, did indicate that during the first five years of federation there was a considerable increase in economic activity, and in terms of the usual ways of measuring national income— allowing for the fact that the "statistical" resources available to the government were very limited—it is probable that there was a fairly impressive rate of economic growth. There had, however, been a no less significant rate of growth in the five or six years *before* federation. To some extent we are now in a much better position to see this because of published work, such as that of Irvine, that was not available to the commissioners, but there were a few clues that they should have followed up.[43]

Roy Welensky that Federal legislation would not be repealed by the British government. Those who remembered making promises to the village poeple five years before felt a nausea for which the best remedy was cynicism, until the memory faded in longer time" (p. 152).

42. *Report on an Economic Survey of Nyasaland, 1958–1959* (Jack Report), p. 1, par. 4.

43. A. C. Irvine, *The Balance of Payments of Rhodesia and Nyasaland, 1945–1954* (London: Oxford University Press, 1959).

Discussion of the growth rate will, however, be postponed until we have looked at some of the direct economic effects on Nyasaland of the imposition of federation.

A second criticism of the Jack Report is that several of the indices to which it attached great importance were almost exclusively concerned with the economic welfare of the very small (though, in more than one sense, significant) European community. This was a serious error, because the distribution of gain was the central question, with African opposition based on what was expected to happen to Africans: few of them doubted that whites would be better off with federation.

The most direct and obvious advantage that Nyasaland gained from federation was derived from the revenue-sharing arrangements. The sum paid to the Nyasaland government, an agreed proportion (initially 6 per cent) of the total federal revenue from income and profit taxes was substantially more than the amount of tax that was raised in Nyasaland, but unfortunately the amount received by Nyasaland varied in an entirely unpredictable way from year to year, because total federal tax receipts depended a great deal on the federation's principal export, copper, for which world prices were subject to sharp fluctuations. Because of this, the effective value of the subsidy was less than consideration of the aggregate amount that became available over the period might suggest.

Table 4.1. The net benefits to Nyasaland of tax sharing (£million)

	1954	1955	1956	1957	1958	1959	1960	1961	1962	1963
1. Payments to Nyasaland	1.3	2.0	2.2	2.6	2.2	1.9	2.1	2.8	2.9	2.7
2. Revenue from Nyasaland	0.6	1.7	2.5	1.6	1.8	2.3	2.2	2.6	2.7	2.9
3. Net Benefit to Nyasaland	0.7	0.3	0.3	1.0	0.4	0.4	0.1	0.2	0.2	0.2

Source: Derived from table 6, p. 209, of A. Hazlewood's paper in Hazlewood, *African Integration and Disintegration* (London: Oxford University Press, 1967).

Table 4.2. Federal current expenditure in Nyasaland (£million)

1954	1955	1956	1957	1958	1959	1960	1961	1962	1963
1.2	2.2	3.6	3.8	3.3	3.4	4.7	5.3	6.0	5.0

Source: As for Table 4.1.

Since Nyasaland was making no net contribution to federal government revenue, all direct expenditures by the federal government in Nyasaland were an additional net contribution to the resources of the country, and these were quite substantial.

Some costs—especially those for the African population—are not apparent in these calculations but adversely affected the standard of living. When federation was established, Nyasaland became part of a new customs area, and a massive revision of customs charges was designed to encourage trade within the federation. This meant, however, that charges on many imports from other areas, especially cheap textiles from Japan, were greatly increased. Some of the imports on which charges rose sharply had been popular among the Africans in Nyasaland, whereas Africans did not get much benefit from the boost given by the new tariff to manufacturing in Southern Rhodesia. The effect of the revised customs charges on African standards of living was similar to that which would have followed a rise in taxes, but it was not reflected in the figures given in Table 4.1.[44]

The immediate purpose of most federal expenditures was to provide services for predominantly European activities, but benefit did accrue to Africans from some of them. It does, however, seem likely that after making allowance for the fact that Tables 4:1 and 4:2 tend to understate the cost and overstate the benefits to the African population, there was a substantial net economic benefit to Nyasaland as a result of the tax-sharing arrangements, and this has, indeed, been acknowledged by some of the federation's critics. Hazlewood and Henderson, for example, wrote: "That the Nyasaland Government has gained financially from Federation cannot be disputed."[45] The critics have tended, rather, to make the point that though there was some benefit to Nyasaland, it was far less than was needed and was insufficient to bring about any fundamental change in the country's position of poverty and dependence. As Hazlewood later put it: "What is clear is that the

44. On the costs of customs unions, see Arthur Hazlewood and P. D. Henderson, *Nyasaland, The Economics of Federation*, pp. 64ff., and Hazlewood, ed., *African Integration*, pp. 218–219.
45. Hazlewood and Henderson, p. 48.

relative backwardness of Nyasaland could not have been perceptibly affected without a change in the principles on which federal capital expenditure was allocated."[46]

There were at least two other respects in which Nyasaland may have obtained economic benefits from federation. By the late 1950s, Southern Rhodesia, for so long dependent on immigrant labor, was finding that a much larger proportion of its own African population was leaving subsistence agriculture and entering the wage labor force and it appeared that the country might not require immigrant labor. Hazlewood and Henderson believed that the Foreign Migratory Labour Bill, passed in 1958, was intended to give the government of Southern Rhodesia power to enforce severe restrictions on the entry of African workers from other territories and, in their view, it was "fairly certain" that the only reason that restrictions were not applied to workers from Nyasaland was because Nyasaland was part of the federation.[47] There were, however, other views on this matter. Barber, for example, felt that the labor surplus was a temporary phenomenon, a result of recession in Southern Rhodesia, and that the bill was not, in any event, designed to reduce the total flow of migrant labor into Southern Rhodesia but to give the government power to determine which areas and activities were open to migrant workers.[48]

It had been anticipated that as a result of federation both the central and the territorial governments would be able to raise money in the London capital market more readily than had previously been possible, and that there would also be a much larger inflow of private investment. The quantity of money raised in the London capital market during the first years of federation increased, but the extent to which this increase was primarily due to federation has been disputed. The capacity of the Nyasaland government to pay loan charges had been improved by the tax-sharing arrangements, and it is likely that there was an upswing of confidence among potential investors, at least in the early days of federation. The upswing was as-

46. Hazlewood, ed., pp. 216–217.
47. Hazlewood and Henderson, pp. 82–83.
48. W. J. Barber, *The Economy of British Central Africa* (Ibadan, Cape Town, Nairobi: Oxford University Press, 1961), p. 216, n.2.

Table 4.3. Money national income (£ million, current prices)

Year	Money income	Percentage increase
1950	8.8	—
1951	10.2	15.9
1952	12.0	17.6
1953	13.9	15.8
1954	16.0	15.1
1955	17.4	8.8
1956	19.2	10.3
1957	21.6	12.5
1958	23.0	6.5
1959	24.5	6.5
1960	26.8	9.4
1961	27.3	1.5
1962	29.0	6.2
1963	28.5	−1.7

Sources: 1950–1953, *Report of an Economic Survey of Nyasaland, 1958–59* (The Jack Report), Federation of Rhodesia and Nyasaland, C. Fed. 132.; 1953–1963, *Compendium of Statistics for Malawi, 1966* (Zomba: Government of Malawi), table 150, C.S.O figures.

sisted by greater availability of funds in world capital markets which coincided with, but was not caused by, the inception of federation.

There was, as the Jack Report pointed out, a growth in private foreign investment in Nyasaland, but at least part of this would have been expected in the absence of federation. The economy had been booming since the end of World War II, cash incomes were increasing rapidly, a start had at last been made in providing secondary education for Africans in Nyasaland, and there was the much improved railway connection to Beira, completed at so great a cost just before the war; all contributed to making Nyasaland a more inviting prospect for potential investors. In some respects federation made Nyasaland less attractive to businessmen: as part of the federation's customs union, producers operating from Southern Rhodesia would have direct access to the Nyasaland market while at the same time being able to take advantage of the better commercial facilities available in Southern Rhodesia and being able to provide their European senior staff with better social, educational, and health facilities than would be available in Nyasaland.

In seeking to evaluate estimates of economic growth during the federation period, one should bear in mind that estimates of national income are subject to large margins of errors, particularly in countries like Nyasaland, with a large part of its economic activity taking place in the subsistence or semitraditional sectors, with a certain amount of structural change taking place and very few, if any specialists in the collection and collation of national income statistics.

There are, however, some points that come out very clearly from the figures, and it seems unlikely that a distinct pattern could emerge from a random collection of errors. There was evidently a high rate of growth before federation and the healthy economic conditions of the early federation period were following an earlier trend rather than setting a new one.

The value of exports rose sharply from £1,805,000 in 1945 to £7,040,000 in 1953, as a result of both price and quantity increases. The price of both tobacco and tea more than doubled during this period and the price of cotton lint increased three-or fourfold. More significant than the rise in export receipts is the evidence from the pattern of imports that there was the beginning of potentially important structural change. The principal increase in imports came in producer goods and consumer durables, where the increase in value was ninefold and twelvefold respectively, while the value of nondurable consumer goods increased less than fourfold.[49]

After federation many of these trends continued. A substantial expansion of tea production became possible when the limitations imposed by the International Tea Agreement ceased to apply in 1955, and tea became as valuable an export as tobacco. Groundnuts became a major export earner, but the upswing had begun before federation, brought about by government encouragement and the greatly improved marketing arrangements under the control of the Agricultural Production and Marketing Board.

A construction boom in Nyasaland during the early federation period (that is, from 1954 to 1959) and a considerable proportional increase (from a very small base) in manufactur-

49. Irvine, pp. 159ff.

ing may have been caused, in part, by the bringing forward of projects which, had it not been for federation, would have been undertaken later and, to that extent, some decline in the rate of growth would be expected to occur within a few years. There were substantial increases shown by several indicators of economic activity in the modern sector such as savings deposits, railway goods traffic, and electricity consumption, but in most cases the increase in the preceding period had been equally impressive. The evidence, in short, supports one of the conclusions drawn by the Jack Report, namely that "economic development in all sections of the money economy has been rapid and continuous in recent years." This is quite a different thing from the conclusion that the rate of growth had been rapid and continuous as a consequence of federation.[50]

If it is hazardous, in view of the scarcity of information, to pass judgment on what was happening to national income, evaluation of the distributional effects might seem to invite disaster, but some attempt must be made even though the available information is sketchy and subject to wide margins of error.

The recorded number of workers in domestic employment rose substantially up to the late 1950s but did so from a very small base, and the increase in employment opportunities in Nyasaland was insufficient to have any significant effect on the number of Nyasas obliged to resort to temporary migration. The situation deteriorated during the latter part of the federation period, and recorded employment fell heavily, with the 1963 figure being about 20 per cent less than the one for 1959.[51] African wages were low, and virtually all middle and senior positions in industry and the civil service were occupied by Europeans. There was, however, an improvement in both respects during the 1950s and, in addition, the income of

50. Jack Report, p. 27.
51. According to the *Compendium of Statistics for Malawi, 1965* (Zomba: Government Printer), table 8, recorded employment rose from 130,000 to 155,000 between 1954 and 1959 and fell back to 130,000 by 1963. Since the population was increasing by more than 3 per cent a year, wage employment as a proportion of the potential labor force was very much lower in 1963 than it had been in 1954.

smallholders growing tobacco and cotton, although fluctuating a good deal, tended to rise during the period.[52]

There was a very large proportional increase in the provision of educational facilities for secondary and senior primary students, but expansion in the postwar years started from a pathetically small base. There was no secondary school in the country until 1941, and it was not until 1948 that Africans were allowed to enter those teacher-training courses intended to provide teachers for the senior primary standards. The Department of Education felt that this was a major breakthrough and were not inclined to dwell on the marked contrast with several other African colonies, notably in West Africa. In spite of the mission's efforts to bring some form of education to a large number of children, and in spite of the reputation for sound primary education that the country appears to have enjoyed (through the activities of its migrants) in Southern Rhodesia and South Africa, the department was satisfied that "opinion in Nyasaland had previously considered it impossible" for Africans to be capable of teaching adequately in the senior primary classes.[53]

The number of students attending the first year of primary or preprimary education was large compared with most other African countries, but the wastage rate was very high. In 1950, for example, the number of students in the most junior form of approved primary schools was 31,442, but the number in the final year was only 499. Wastage rates were steadily reduced, at least in the assisted schools, but not all the methods adopted to achieve this undoubtedly desirable end would command unqualified approval. Nyasaland must have been one of the very few countries in Africa in which first-year primary enrollment declined between 1956 and 1963, at a time when population was increasing by about 3 per cent per year.[54]

During the same period, government expenditure on health increased more than threefold during the first five years of

52. *Compendium of Statistics for Malawi, 1965* (Zomba: Government Printer), tables 45, 46 and 53.

53. See T. D. Williams, "Educational Development in Malawi: Heritage and Prospect," *Africa Today,* 14, no.2. (1967).

54. First year primary enrollment in 1956 was 113.9 hundred; in 1963 it was 94.1 hundred. Sources: for 1956, *Compendium 1965*, table 21; for 1963, *Compendium 1970*, table 5–1.

federation. But only a small proportion of the benefit went to Africans and Nyasaland, with more than one-third of the population of the federation, attracting only one-sixth of the federal government health expenditure.[55]

In summary, the evidence about the economic impact of federation shows that during the first five years of federation the economy grew and there was a certain amount of structural changes; some economic benefits accrued to Nyasaland, mainly from tax-sharing arrangements and federal government expenditures, but the main causes of economic expansion had little to do with federation; there were probably some benefits gained by Africans as a result of the expansion, but they were of a very limited kind, and in some respects (for example, the increased tariff on cheap imported textiles and bicycles) the standard of living of Africans was adversely affected.

Even if economic growth had been very rapid, had given promise of being sustained, and had produced really substantial spread effects, so that a much larger proportion of the benefits accrued to the African population, it is quite possible that most Africans would have thought it inadequate compensation for the social and political disabilities that they associated with a continuation of federation. Dr. Banda later reported that in the 1963 discussions, which led to the final dissolution of federation, Sir Edgar Whitehead had asked him how he would feed the people of an Independent nation and that his reply had been, "I would rather have my people starve than be fed by you."[56] There is no reason to doubt that he was speaking for the great majority of his countrymen and that the emergence of an effective nationalist movement had the support of all but a handful of them.

55. Hazlewood, ed., p. 215. The figures given by Jones suggest it was even less; at the same time, education expenditure per African child was £6 per annum, while federal expenditure on education of non-African children was £126 per student per year (Jones, pp. 159–160).

56. Some variant of this story was often produced for the instruction of members of the Malawi Parliament. See, for example, *Hansard*, 16 May 1971, p. 1101 and *Hansard*, 23 March 1973, p. 787.

CHAPTER 5

African Resurgence:
The Rise of the Phoenix

African opposition to federation was discounted by many Europeans in Central Africa on the ground that Africans were unable to grasp the real issues and would, providing they were given a firm lead, come to see that the Europeans were right and that great advantages flowed from the new constitutional arrangements. Others argued that the apparent unanimity among Africans was due to the influence of a small but powerful and unscrupulous group of agitators or that the representations were coming entirely from an unrepresentative and muddle-headed collection of pseudointellectuals "receiving . . . directives from an ex-Nyasaland African now in London"— namely Dr. Banda, described by Welensky as "one of the most voluble African critics of federation . . . who has not set foot in Africa for about twenty years."[1]

Only Europeans who were determined to shut their minds to the evidence could doubt the nature or cogency of African opposition to federation. Every channel through which African opinion could be openly expressed was being used repeatedly in an attempt to make clear the unity and depth of African opinion on the subject. The representatives of Nyasaland Africans at the constitutional talks had expressed their unequivocal opposition to federation, had boycotted the official talks in London and had written eloquently to the *The Times* of London. The Nyasaland Council of Chiefs, which had been formed with congress support, demanded an immediate African majority in the Legislative Council and an end to government support for federation. In January 1953 three chiefs and two

1. The Welensky quotation is from Philip Short, *Banda*, pp. 69–70.

senior members of Congress traveled to London at the time of
the final intergovernmental conference on federation and, with
Dr. Banda's help, presented a petition to the colonial secretary.
They then undertook several speaking engagements throughout the country. In February the chiefs asked leave to present a
petition to the Queen, which was denied by the colonial secretary. The following month the Council of Chiefs, after discussing the denial of the petition, cabled the Colonial Office that
"imposition of Federation against Africans' solid rejection will
be opposed at all costs."[2]

In April, Congress and the Council of Chiefs set up a Supreme Council of Action to coordinate a policy of nonviolent
resistance to federation, consisting of strikes, boycotts, nonpayment of taxes and defiance of government regulations together
with appeals to the United Nations and the International Court
of Justice. When the Legislative Council of Nyasaland debated
the motion approving the federal arrangements the two African members walked out in protest.

The Supreme Council sent six senior chiefs to Britain where
they petitioned the speaker of the House of Commons for permission to speak before the bar of the House on behalf of more
than one hundred chiefs. The petition was rejected and their
alternative suggestion that a select committee be established to
examine the state of feeling in Nyasaland was ignored.[3]

In spite of the virtual unanimity of opposition to federation,
Nyasaland Africans disagreed about the tactics that should be
followed. Some members of Congress felt that if representations against federation proved unsuccessful, the movement
should launch a national campaign of nonviolent resistance
against the governmental authorities. This view was not shared
by J. R. N. Chinyama, president of Congress at the time, and
he felt called upon to make public, in January 1953, his disagreement with the proposed strategy of civil disobedience.

In spite of the doubts expressed by Chinyama, an emergency
meeting of Congress in April threatened a nationwide strike,
the nonpayment of taxes, and an appeal to the United Nations.

2. Short, p. 72.
3. Bridglal Pachai, *Malawi*, p. 263; Short, p. 71.

In May the Supreme Council advocated a boycott of all official functions including the celebrations of the Queen's birthday. Shortly afterward, Philip Gomani, Paramount Chief of the Maseko Ngoni, issued instructions that his people were to refuse to pay taxes and were to ignore certain agricultural regulations that, as a result of the sometimes clumsy and insensitive manner in which they were enforced, had caused a good deal of popular resentment and had become a focus for opposition to the government. Gomani was deposed and banished after an attempt to arrest him had brought about a riot in Ncheu.[4] Sixteen chiefs followed Congress advice and declared that they would resign from their positions, but most of them subsequently had second thoughts and withdrew their resignations.

Tempers got worse as African frustration mounted, and in August violence broke out in the Cholo district under circumstances showing that longstanding African resentments over other issues were becoming interlocked with racial attitudes, which had been polarized as a result of federation. The spark in this case was the removal of oranges from a European estate—which touched upon the deeply felt objection to European domination of vast tracts of excellent land in the Shire Highlands—and the mistaken belief that the European planters had killed the Africans who had taken the oranges. Although the immediate cause had no direct connection with federation, the mood of distrust of, and hostility to, Europeans engendered by the imposition of federation was a major factor in the escalation of what was initially a minor incident. In the next few weeks disorders occurred in Chiradzulu, Domasi, Mlanje, and Port Herald—all in the Southern Province. As Griff Jones commented, the immediate causes of the Cholo riot were "fuses . . . [which] might cause explosions when the atmosphere was highly charged by agitation about land grievances and federation." The Commission of Enquiry into the Cholo riots expressed the opinion that "recent political discussions on current issues added to the uneasiness of the African

4. According to Jones he was deposed, not because of his opposition to federation, but because he had encouraged people to disobey the laws and regulations that it was an important part of his job to enforce. Griff Jones, *Britain and Nyasaland,* pp. 180–182.

population and increased the instability of the Native Administration. . . . In the middle of 1953 tension increased; people
were refusing to pay beer fees and other license fees and to
attend native courts."[5]

Congress was divided in its attitude to these events and J. R.
N. Chinyama, its president, who had all along been opposed to
a policy of civil disturbance, was summoned by the governor in
August and sharply reminded that his father had been executed many years before because he had the temerity to challenge British authority.[6] The previous month Mckinley Chibambo and two other militants had been charged with sedition,
and it began to look to the leaders as if resistance was both
more dangerous and less effective than they had hoped it
would be at the beginning of the year. Their attempts at persuading the British authorities to change their minds had failed
to evoke any positive response and seemed instead to harden
the government's attitude. The riots so far from being (as many
planters thought) engineered by Congress leaders, appear to
have been largely if not entirely outside their control, and the
realization that a continued strategy of confrontation could un-
leash violence and perhaps throw up new leaders and new
issues alarmed rather than encouraged them.

Before the end of September, Congress and the Council of
Chiefs had discovered the rioters and brought to an end the
policy of noncooperation; a decision endorsed by the annual
conference of Congress in January 1954. The more militant
members of Congress lost the support of the membership and
effective leadership passed to such men as Wellington Manoah
Chirwa and Clement Kumbikano, both of whom argued that
Congress should put up candidates for the federal Parliament
on the understanding that they would make a protest on behalf

    5. Jones, pp. 217–218.
    6. Short says that his father was Filipo Chinyama, who had led the abortive
1915 rising in Ncheu in support of Chilembwe and who was subsequently
executed; he notes that he was told this by Chipembere (p. 77). According to
Pachai, J. R. N.'s father was another man who supported the rising, Nthinda
Chinyama (p. 223). According to Dr. Banda, J. R. N.'s father was Nduna to
Nkosi Gomani I who was shot by the British in 1896 and that Chinyama was
executed because he supported Gomani in defying the British authorities at
that time (*Hansard,* 12 March 1974, p. 261).

of the people of Nyasaland and then resign their seats. Congress accepted this view, and Chirwa and Kumbikano were elected.

Meanwhile, Dr. Banda had left London in August and gone to live in Ghana, where he was to practice medicine for the next four years. He had been greatly distressed by the failure of the British government to honor what he felt were its clear commitments as trustee for the African people of Nyasaland; he was saddened by the collapse of the resistance campaign in Nyasaland and he believed that Chinyama, Manoah Chirwa, and Kumbikano had betrayed Congress. He was later to say that he felt that if the African people of Nyasaland were prepared to accept federation, it would be better to give federation a fair chance and that, by taking himself away from London and indeed Britain, he was doing his best to ensure that no misunderstanding about his activities could be held to blame for any failure of the federation. He insisted that he had been prepared at all times to return to lead "his" people, providing that they themselves had demonstrated their commitment to getting rid of "the stupid federation." For the time being, however, he withdrew from politics and even declined to answer letters from Congress.[7]

The unity of the nationalist movement had been derived largely from common opposition to federation; there was much less common ground about the nature of the political and economic structure that members would wish to see evolve in Nyasaland. With failure to make impact on the matter of federation and the disputes that arose over questions of strategy, the impetus of the movement was dissipated and the looseness of the nationalist coalition soon revealed. Apart from open and some-

7. Short thinks that personal problems in which Dr. Banda was involved at this time—he was accused of adultery with his secretary and they went to Ghana together—played a more important role than political ones in explaining his "sudden departure" (pp. 75–79). Welensky apparently accepted the view that Dr. Banda, though still opposed to federation, was prepared to give it a chance (*4,000 Days*, p. 83). In the postindependence period, Dr. Banda insisted he believed that Nyasaland Africans should make up their minds as to whether they were prepared to fight federation head-on and that if they decided to do so he would go back to lead them, regardless of what it would cost him (see, for example, *Hansard*, 13 March 1973, pp. 369ff.).

times bitter disputes among the leaders, support in the country fell sharply. In 1953 there had been 300 branches; the following year there were fifteen, only one of which was effective. Sangala resumed the presidency, but it seemed that little could be done except holding together the rump of the organization.

Congress leadership had been drawn largely from a small number of "educated" men. Although they were often concerned with the needs and aspirations of their less fortunate countrymen, these men tended to lack either intuitive or ideological sympathy with the poorly educated peasant farmers who accounted for most of the population. Congress itself did not possess great internal cohesion and had been subject to bitter personal and tribal rivalries. Some senior chiefs were closely associated with the Congress leadership either because they were themselves "educated men" who would, even had they not been chiefs, have been natural members of Congress or because the mutual advantage in the coalition of different types of elite was recognized. But there were significant underlying differences between those chiefs whose principal complaint against colonial authority was that it was destroying their ancient prerogatives and those whose principal objection was that it prevented them or their people from obtaining a fair share of the advantages they felt should become available in a more modern society.

In much the same way, the almost universal hatred of the natural resource regulations, which had been intended by the authorities to ensure that farmers would adopt the best methods of cultivation, reflected several distinct, and in some cases contradictory, impulses. Some opponents were traditionalists who disapproved of attempts to change traditional practices; they were not concerned whether or not these practices were still appropriate as a growing population began to exert pressure on land resources; others felt that they were being forced to do things that, whatever well-intentioned but not always well-informed agricultural officers might have thought, were either not feasible or not worth the cost; some did not always disagree with the regulations themselves but objected to the insensitive manner of enforcement. Still others would have been willing to endorse both the methods and the objectives if only they had been carried out by an independent African government or even by one more sympathetic to African interests, but they were not disposed to accept directions from a government that was part of the hated federation.

The nationalist movement was not to remain in disarray for long, and although its reunification was to have the same narrow focus as before, being based on a common antipathy rather than a common vision of long-term interests, it was now to challenge not merely federation but the colonial presence itself. Instead of appealing to the British government to honor its trust and preserve the Africans of Nyasaland from settler rule by maintaining direct control from Britain, the new men of the nationalist movement were to insist in no uncertain terms that the time had come for the Africans of Nyasaland to rule themselves.

Congress had been earlier revived by common awareness of a formidable threat, in the form of federation, and had faltered when it became aware of its inability to deal with this threat. The new revival was a response to new opportunities. In 1955 many changes were made in the constitution that were to have a far more profound effect on the political climate of the country than had been anticipated by the colonial administration, which had introduced the changes in the hope of persuading Africans that there was a place for them in the federal political structure. Africans had first gained representation in the territorial Legislative Council in 1949. Provision was then made for two unofficial African members to be selected by the governor from a panel of five names put forward by the protectorate council. In the same year the Asian community achieved representation by appointment of one member from a panel of three put forward by the local Indian Chamber of Commerce. Under the new constitution which came into effect in 1955, Europeans and Asians were able to elect six members, instead of having them nominated, on the basis of a common role. The terms that determined voting eligibility, however, effectively barred most Asians from the franchise: a European population of 6,730 produced 1,866 votes, and an Asian population of 8,490 produced 338 qualified for the vote; there were to be eleven official members of the Legislative Council (nominated by the governor or *ex officio,* by virtue of their positions in the administration) and eleven unofficial or elected members. Of crucial importance to the nationalist cause, five of the latter were to be Africans, who would be elected, albeit indirectly, by three provincial councils whose membership consisted mainly of chiefs. Two African members of the council would be elected from each of the Southern and Central Provinces and one from the Northern Province.[8]

At the beginning of the year, the strength of Congress had been considerably increased when its forces were joined by a group of young graduates including the twenty-five-year-old Henry Masauko Chipembere and the twenty-six-year-old Kanyama Chiume. Chipembere, a Yao, was the son of an Anglican archdeacon from the Fort Johnston district and had been educated at Fort Hare in South Africa, where he had obtained an Arts Degree; Chiume, a Togan, came from the Nkhata Bay District and had been to Makerere, where he had gained a Diploma in Education.

In the elections that took place under the new constitution, four of the candidates returned by the provincial councils were members of Congress and the fifth was known to be a sympathizer. The largest majorities obtained by any of the candidates were those of Chipembere and Chiume, both of whom had been recommended by Sangala and Manoah Chirwa.[9] Belonging to the first generation of their people who had gone straight from school to university, neither of them was old enough or experienced enough to win the undisputed allegiance of the elders, despite their election by a body consisting principally of chiefs. Chipembere was, in spite of recurrent illness, an effective and popular orator who combined tactical adroitness with profound concern for the welfare of the people of Nyasaland. He soon became the idol of the younger, better-educated and more radical Africans, but he was keenly aware at this time that he was not yet ready for the role of national leader. Chiume was never to be a popular figure; he did not convey the same sense of moral integrity as did Chipembere,

8. Pachai, *Malawi,* pp. 239–240.
9. Short, p. 80.

but he was a man of great energy, ambition, subtlety, and ruthlessness. The Devlin Report, which was not notably sympathetic to the views of the militant wing of the nationalist movement, recognized both of them as able men.[10] They brought to the nationalist movement a youthful dynamism combined with formidable organizing capacity; within two years they had laid the framework for an adequately financed and well-disciplined mass party.

Congress had been distinctly unhappy about both the number of representatives and the nature of the franchise granted to Africans under the 1955 constitution because both fell far short of its own demand for an African majority in the Legislative Council elected by universal suffrage. Few people, either in Congress or outside of it, could have had any idea of the dramatic change that was about to take place not merely in the detail of the council's deliberations but in the fundamental terms on which debate took place. It was not simply a radical change; it was a transformation. Hitherto, the African representatives, able and honorable men, had conducted themselves as worthy but junior members of a powerful assembly; it had been their practice to pay respect to "Your Excellency" (the governor, or his duly appointed deputy presiding over the council) and, in the most moderate terms, to address themselves to specific matters affecting the interests of Africans in Nyasaland, without touching upon the validity of federation or colonial rule. They accepted the rules of the game laid down by the colonial authorities and, although they played with skill and ingenuity according to the rules, they were unable to express the concern of Nyasaland Africans about the fundamental injustice of the situation into which they had been driven. They were responsible men doing the best they could under difficult circumstances.

The African members elected under the new constitution had a completely different idea of the purpose to be served by African representatives in the council, and they had the confidence, aggression, and ready wit to match their conception of

---

10. *Report of the Nyasaland Commission of Enquiry*, Her Majesty's Stationery Office, Command 814, July 1959 (Devlin Report), par. 24.

what they were there to do. From the moment they set foot in the council chambers, they behaved as men who, far from needing to learn something about the conventions and procedures of an august body, had come to tell the members of council, whether or not they wanted to listen, what had to be done; if the other council members were not prepared to listen, so much the worse for them. Chipembere and his colleagues would speak over their heads to the ultimate power—the scarcely awakened but smouldering and vibrant power of the Africans of Nyasaland. They spoke as men convinced personally that the Congress argument was not only right but was self-evidently right and could not be disputed by reasonable men.

The first day of the new Legislative Council opened with a formidable barrage of hostile questions from Chipembere and Chiume. The administration had little time to recover from that tactic, which was entirely novel in Nyasaland, before N. D. Kwenje, another of the new members, put forward a motion that all land on private estates on which there were African homes should be declared trust land. Chipembere supported the motion and declared that the certificates of claim—upon which the legal right of a great deal of European landholding in the Shire Highlands rested—were invalid. Council members were reminded of John Chilembwe, not as an illustration of African failure but as an example of the consequences of frustration; the clear implication of Chipembere's remarks was that, if there was to be another such occasion, Africans would be better prepared to face the consequences of revolt. Council rejected Kwenje's motion, and Kwenje immediately attacked again, calling for a complete ban on recruiting licenses which enabled Nyasaland Africans to work in Southern Rhodesia or South Africa.

Kwenje used this motion to launch a comprehensive attack on the colonial and federal administrations, and although he was called to order on several occasions (on the grounds that he was not confining himself to the motion) he was able to get in some cogent points on the much broader issue with which he and his colleagues wanted to deal. That motion was no sooner beaten than Kwenje moved that Nyasaland "be extricated from the Federation of Central Africa" on the grounds that "the protected people of Nyasaland did not sanction it." The Speaker of the council had difficulty in confining the scope of discussion on this motion, and Chiume insisted that debate meant "that one must give reasons why Africans oppose federation." Chipembere protested at being "muzzled" and said he had come prepared to speak for "three hours" on the subject. The European members, both unofficial and official, were unaccustomed to this sort of onslaught and unequipped to deal with it but could scarcely have doubted that Chipembere, given half a chance, would have been as good as his word. When he was speaking, however, he gave the definitive answer to those who had hoped that Africans would easily be seduced by the prospect of economic advantage: "Even if Federation were so economically advantageous, as to turn every African in the country into a millionaire, we would not accept it, we would still oppose it if it meant walking naked in the streets of Blantyre or Zomba."[11]

Chiume then reverted to the question of who had a right to land and persisted with his argument in spite of being frequently called to order. Again and again the African members attacked; they were not ignorant of procedural niceties, they chose to ignore them, and they demonstrated conclusively that, far from being overawed by the unfamiliarity of their surroundings and the trappings of imperial power and prestige, they were remarkably articulate and confident men who could think very fast on their feet.

It was a dramatic beginning, and they kept it up, day in, day out, whenever the council met; a small minority, they dominated the proceedings. Some two years later, Chipembere, in frontal assault on the federation position, faced virtually no interjections save of support from his African colleagues, and the question had become not whether Nyasaland Africans would accept federation but whether federation could survive.

CHIPEMBERE: It is clear now, Mr. Speaker, that the child called Federation has come to a stage where it is struggling for its existence. It

11. *Proceedings of the Nyasaland Legislative Council*, 5 Feb. 1956. The last quotation is from p. 61.

has become necessary now for Honourable Members opposite to bring in Motions to try and defend the Federation because the attack on it is coming from every quarter. In other words, the Federation is now fighting a defensive war and. . . . "

KWENJE: A desperate one.

CHIPEMBERE: I would ask Honourable African Members to take note of that. Federation, Honourable Gentlemen, is at bay. It is fighting for its existence.[12]

The consistently aggressive debating style adopted by Chipembere and his colleagues in the council was given a much larger, and very enthusiastic, audience when the government decided to begin publication of verbatim accounts of council proceedings. The *Legislative Council Debates* were soon as widely read in the country as a popular newspaper. Chipembere became a hero to African youths as thousands of them saw with growing pride and self-confidence that their own men were standing on equal terms, and indeed getting distinctly the better of the argument, with the rulers of the country. The success of the young militants did more, however, than arouse the enthusiasm of the public; it profoundly changed the balance of power within Congress, providing the young radicals with enough personal following to mount a challenge to the very men whose support they had needed the previous year.

The argument that Manoah Chirwa had put forward as a reason for participation by members of Congress in the federal Parliament was that it provided an opportunity for elected Africans to put before a wide audience the case against federation. Since this was now being done, and done effectively, by the elected members of the Nyasaland Legislative Council, the presence of Congress members in Salisbury was no longer justifiable. Chipembere and Chiume called for the immediate resignation of Manoah Chirwa and Kumbikano from the federal Parliament and wrote to Dr. Banda asking him to support the campaign to bring about the resignation of the two members. Banda did not ignore this letter, as he had ignored many communications from Congress since he had left London for Kumasi, but he recommended the more cautious approach that Chirwa and Kumbikano be allowed to serve out their terms.

12. *Legislative Council Debates,* 17 March 1958, p. 21.

Chipembere did not accept Banda's advice on this point, and at the meeting of Congress held in December 1956, he and Chiume put forward a motion demanding the immediate resignation of the two members. After a long debate, the motion was heavily defeated.[13]

Chipembere was confident that he knew what Congress should be doing and that he and his young colleagues had the organizing ability and energy to make Congress the first mass party in Nyasaland's history, but he was acutely aware that he was too young to win the allegiance of senior members of Congress or to be accepted as national leader by the more conservative rural elders. It was in these circumstances that he decided that Dr. Banda must be persuaded to return to Nyasaland to lead the nationalist movement. Congress had, on the prompting of Chipembere and Chiume, declared at their annual meeting in 1955 that they would campaign for the secession of Nyasaland from federation. The skill and vigor with which the campaign had been conducted both in the council and outside it should have satisfied Dr. Banda that there was now in Nyasaland the sort of commitment to end federation that he had called for in 1953. Chipembere had admired Dr. Banda in the years before 1953 for much the same reason as many young people in Nyasaland now admired Chipembere: he had thought it was "remarkable that an African could be so courageous or bold in attacking . . . the Colonial Office and the Nyasaland Government."[14] On the issue of federation—the only political issue about which Chipembere was well acquainted with Dr. Banda's views—they were both radicals and militants, and Dr. Banda, even if not yet widely known in Nyasaland, had qualities that would appeal to all factions of the nationalist movement. His age, manifest courage, and eminence would appeal most powerfully to rural elders; his education, his profession, and his success would gain the respect of the young educated militants; he would know how to deal with Europeans—not only was he a doctor, he had been on terms of familiarity with leading politicians in Britain and, for the first time,

13. Short, pp. 80–82.
14. Interview with Short, cited p. 81.

colonial officials in Nyasaland would be faced by a man who could go over their heads and deal directly with influential figures in the House of Commons. The very fact that he had been out of the country for forty years could turn to his advantage. While almost all sections of the African population could identify with Dr. Banda to some extent, he was not so closely associated with any particular group as to risk alienating prospective support inside, or even outside, Congress. Personal unfamiliarity with Dr. Banda might also have encouraged the young militants to believe that he would not wish to concern himself too intimately with the details of local party organization and that he would be obliged to rely on those (such as themselves) who were more familiar with these matters. They may have felt, too, that a man of his age and accomplishment would lack the personal ambition of a younger, less fulfilled man and that he would, before long, be content to enter into a well-earned and highly respected retirement, passing on the leadership to the lieutenants who had served the nationalist movement so capably and selflessly.

There were a number of approaches made to Dr. Banda at this time but, in the words of the Devlin Report, "by far the most urgent of these came from Mr. Chipembere who was in close correspondence with him from November 1956 onwards." The Report continued:

We have seen a number of these letters in which Mr. Chipembere made his attitude very clear. He was dissatisfied with the leadership of congress. There was no outstanding personality. Mr. T. D. T. Banda, who was elected President-General in November 1957 had, Mr. Chipembere thought, "great qualities" which he admired but was lacking in intellectual equipment. What was needed was a kind of saviour: although it is wrong to be led by a single man placed in a powerful position, still "human nature is such that it needs a kind of hero to be hero-worshipped if a political struggle is to succeed." Mr. Chiume and he were too young, he thought, to fill the vacuum—what was needed was a man of about fifty or sixty, an intellectual with honesty, self-denial and a spirit of co-operativeness. Mr. Chipembere said quite frankly that Dr. Banda's reputation would have to be built up. He told him that he was known as a name, as an African highly educated doctor in London of Nyasa birth, that educated people might know a bit about his political feelings and ability, but that little was known about him among the masses. He must not be frightened if he was heralded as the political messiah. Publicity of this sort could be used with advantage; it would cause great excitement and should precipitate almost a revolution in political thought.[15]

At first Dr. Banda responded to these approaches with caution, but he was much influenced by the success of Welensky's trip to London in April 1957, when Sir Roy obtained an agreement from the British government that it would never use its power to revoke federal legislation in a way that infringed the rights of Africans. This was a serious step in its own right but, of greater importance, suggested that the British government was moving toward the granting of Dominion status and independence to the federation.

Once again Dr. Banda began to take an active interest in Nyasaland politics; the affairs of the federation and the need to exert a decisive effect on its future became, again, the focus of his interest. He now wrote a memorandum to Congress urging that Manoah Chirwa and Kumbikano be required to resign immediately from the federal Parliament and that a resolution be passed declaring that Congress would henceforth refuse to have anything to do with that body. Chipembere had already converted several senior members of Congress to this point of view, but Dr. Banda's intervention would in any event have carried great weight. The letter was read at the Annual Conference of Congress in August 1957 and met with general approval. The two members refused to resign from the federal Parliament and were expelled from Congress.

The August meeting urged Dr. Banda to return home to help lead "the struggle for liberation," but T. D. T. Banda had not responded favorably to Chipembere's suggestion that Dr. Banda should be made "cabinet minister *in absentia*." Dr. Banda, on the other hand, was prepared to return to Nyasaland only if he were guaranteed the presidency of Congress, the right to hand-pick the executive—he had no intention, he later said, of presiding over "a fools' cabinet"—and extensive powers to run the nationalist movement in whatever way he thought right. After T. D. T. Banda lost his position of leader-

15. *Devlin Report,* par. 26.

ship early in the following year, the caretaker president of Congress, Mathews Phiri, was more disposed to agree with Chipembere that Dr. Banda's terms should be met. In June 1958, Dr. Banda was in London for talks with Lennox Boyd, the colonial secretary, about new constitutional proposals for Nyasaland put forward by Congress. He was joined there by Chipembere and Dunduzu Chisiza, and was reportedly much impressed by them. He promised them that he would return to Nyasaland as soon as he could wind up his domestic and professional affairs.

On 6 July 1958, Dr. Banda arrived at Chileka airport, Blantyre, to a tumultuous welcome. The young militants had done their job well; the nationalist movement had found not merely a leader but a Messiah, and it was soon to become apparent that Dr. Banda, intoxicated by adulation, was delighted to be cast in that role. At the conference of Congress at Nkhata Bay in August 1958, he was accepted as leader of the party on his own terms. The constitution of Congress was amended to give Dr. Banda, who was elected president-general, sole power to appoint officers of Congress and the members of the Executive Council. To the senior posts, he appointed the three most prominent of the young radicals: Chipembere, Chiume, and Dunduzu Chisiza, and as organizer of the Women's League, he appointed Rose Chibambo. "His choice," said the Devlin Report, "represented a victory for the left wing which had been responsible for securing his return." Dr. Banda "was the undisputed leader of Congress." The Report went on:

Naturally he was looked up to as the greatest of Nyasaland's sons and as one whose gifts made him the equal of the European. But over and above that there had already been created for him a mystique which raised him far above the level of the ordinary African leader . . . he found himself with an unexpected gift of mob oratory; he obviously enjoyed the sensation of power over a crowd. In addition to inspiration he gave the Congress after a period of squabbling a united leadership. He brought with him some new ideas.

In some respects, however, the Devlin Report was to prove a poor guide to the situation in Nyasaland even though the view expressed was probably shared by many young leaders of Congress. "He never concerned himself with detailed administration and as time went on he gave less and less time to the party. He had chosen as his lieutenants young vigorous men, whom he considered to be capable administrators, and he gave them a free hand."[16]

Dr. Banda toured the country, addressing wildly enthusiastic meetings. The Devlin Commission later commented that his "reception in Nyasaland and the reverence and adulation with which he was treated everywhere he went was enough to turn the head of even the most modest man, and Dr. Banda is not that; it would not have crossed his mind that even his unexpressed wish was not law."[17]

The first response of Europeans in Nyasaland to Dr. Banda's return had been quite favorable because they hoped he would be a much more moderate figure than were Chipembere, Chiume, and the other young radicals, but it soon became clear that he was a formidable leader who was not prepared to compromise on the issues of federation and constitutional reform in Nyasaland.

The governor was in a most difficult position. Dr. Banda had massive popular support and the few Africans who had doubts about him faced ostracism or much worse if their views were made public; Congress was demanding an African majority in the Legislative Council, and there was no doubt that such a majority, if granted, would refuse assent to every bill proposed by the governor unless he were to take Nyasaland out of federation and this he was not, of course, empowered to do even had he thought it appropriate. The British public expected the governor to maintain order with the consent of the majority, but the British Parliament had insisted on a policy that was detested by the majority. In mid-August the governor said there was to be no immediate announcement about the government's reaction to Congress's constitutional proposals. In the next three months, wrote Welensky, "the security situation deteriorated rapidly."[18] By October there were demands that the police force be federalized and thus no longer be inhibited by London influence and also that a preventive detention act

16. *Ibid.*, par. 50.
17. *Ibid.*, par. 96.
18. Welensky, p. 98.

should be introduced.[19] There were several incidents, of which the most widely reported was a riot near the Blantyre clock-tower, in October. Europeans were beginning to feel that African nationalists were seeking to intimidate them; they were, indeed, so accustomed to extreme deference from Africans that any form of assertiveness appeared shocking. Schools were closed, for example, because pupils were heard to declare that things would be changed "when Chipembere took over the schools."[20]

In December, Dr. Banda attended the All African People's Conference in Accra, where a resolution was passed that the conference "declare its full support of all fighters for freedom in Africa . . . [and] to all those who are compelled to retaliate against violence to attain national independence and freedom for the people."[21] Speaking at the conference, Dr. Banda referred to reports that meetings of Congress would be banned. He went on to say:

I want to make it quite clear to those responsible for these measures, that if I cannot speak to my people freely and openly, I will find my own ways and means of speaking to them. These ways and means might prove far more unpleasant to those concerned than the open public platform meetings and processions.

With the rest of Africa, Nyasaland is on the move. Nothing can stay its course. Like the rest of our fellow Africans on the continent, we are determined to be free; to be independent and to live in dignity. Neither heaven above nor hell below will prevail against us.[22]

When the conference was over, he returned to Nyasaland by way of Salisbury and took the opportunity to address a political meeting of Rhodesian Africans. The occasion was, he claimed, a great success and gave his audience their first opportunity to see the manner in which a real African leader conducted himself. He set Salisbury "rocking, rocking," as he told his audience: "They can send me to prison. They can kill me. I will never give up my fight for freedom. We have to be prepared to

19. Jones, p. 238; Short, pp. 96ff., on violence in the country.
20. *Legislative Council Debates*, 4 Dec. 1958.
21. Welensky, pp. 99–100.
22. Account given by Dr. Banda to the Malawi Parliament, *Hansard*, 23 March 1973, p. 785.

go to prison. We must fill the prisons, millions of us. . . . I will fight Federation from prison. Even from the grave my ghost will return to fight Federation."[23]

When he arrived back at Chileka airport in Blantyre, he told reporters that "in Nyasaland we mean to be masters, and if that is treason make the most of it."

On 20 January he met Governor Sir Robert Armitage, to press the demands of Congress for reform of the territorial constitution. The least that would be acceptable, he told Armitage, was an African majority in the Legislature and parity with government officials in the Executive Council. The same day brought the first reading of the Riot Act since Dr. Banda had returned to Nyasaland six months earlier. Some women had been arrested for taking part in an illegal assembly after noisily applauding Dr. Banda, who was on his way to meet the governor. Later in the day both Banda and Chipembere condemned the arrests, with Chipembere expressing himself, or so most Europeans thought, in a highly intemperate and offensive manner. After the speeches, large crowds gathered outside the police station where the women were detained. The act was read, tear gas was used, and a baton charge made by the police, while the retreating crowd hurled whatever they could lay their hands on at the police.[24]

Lord Perth, minister of state in the Colonial Office, was due to arrive shortly in Nyasaland to discuss constitutional proposals and other matters on behalf of the Cabinet. It was already clear, however, that any serious constitutional reform would inevitably put both the administration in Zomba and the British government to a severe test. If a constitution on the only lines that would be acceptable to Congress was introduced and if Congress were then to win all the African seats—as by now everyone realized that they almost certainly would—their majority in the Legislative Council would demand secession and would refuse to cooperate in the passage of any legislation that implied acceptance of the federal constitution. The governor, who was obliged to follow the policy laid down by the British

23. Short, pp. 104–105.
24. Short, pp. 107–108.

Cabinet, which was in favor of federation, would then be obliged either to suspend the African members or to ignore them, and in either event would almost certainly be soundly abused for his pains in Britain, to say nothing of the furor that would occur in Nyasaland. "The Governor," wrote Griff Jones, "stripped of the veil of the official majority, would be exposed as a naked autocrat."[25]

Congress planned to call a general strike if its constitutional demands were not met, and some of its leading members were losing patience with what they felt was the unresponsiveness of the government. Among them were some who believed it necessary to raise the level of violence and force a direct confrontation with the government. Contingency plans, including widespread and systematic terror, were discussed at an emergency meeting held outside Blantyre on 24 and 25 January 1958, but since great efforts were naturally made to screen the participants and no one was allowed to take notes, it is very difficult to establish precisely what took place. The evidence later produced by the government was drawn from the accounts of paid police informers. There is no doubt that there were many inflammatory speeches, and it is not unlikely that some of the delegates favored a campaign of extreme violence, including murder, but most delegates appear to have returned to their respective congress branches throughout (and outside) the country believing that agreement had been reached on a policy of comprehensive and intensive but non-violent resistance to colonial rule.[26]

Reports reached the government, through its special branch informers, that there was a two-stage plan. The first stage was to be nonviolent, but was nonetheless expected to be so disruptive that it would lead to the arrest of Dr. Banda. The second stage would then be reached. Leadership would be exercised by a council consisting of Chipembere, Chiume, Dunduzu Chisiza, and Rose Chibambo, and they would launch a campaign of open violence, recruiting "hooligans, criminals, and known murderers," who would assist in the comprehensive murder

25. Jones, p. 239.
26. Short, pp. 108ff.

and mutilation of Europeans and uncooperative Africans; there would be mutiny in the army and in the police force, and all means of communication were to be sabotaged.[27] Both the federal government and the Nyasaland administration were disposed to believe these reports, but even had they been more skeptical, they could scarcely have taken the risk of discounting them altogether; if nothing else had been learned from the Chilembwe rising in 1915, the governor and his officials were aware that failure to take seriously the early rumors about Chilembwe's plans had cost lives when the rising occurred.

During February the level of violence increased, and several Congress members and sympathizers were killed in clashes between the police and demonstrators throughout the country. Chipembere, whose speeches were increasingly prone to flamboyant threats of violence, declared that "we mean to die for this country or win liberation."[28] Troops were flown in from Southern Rhodesia, to the fury of Dr. Banda, who accused the government of pandering to federal Prime Minister Welensky.

By this time Governor Armitage had become convinced that decisive action was an immediate necessity and on 25 February, anticipating the steps he was about to take, asked the British government to postpone the visit of Lord Perth. The following day the governor of Southern Rhodesia declared that territory to be in a state of emergency, apparently in response to events in Nyasaland. In Nyasaland itself, a number of Africans were killed in clashes with the security forces and just after midnight on 2 March, Armitage declared a state of emergency. "It has day by day become increasingly apparent," he said, that the leaders of congress were "bent on pursuing a course of violence, intimidation and disregard of lawful authority. This policy constitutes a threat to all law abiding persons and to property throughout the country."[29]

The Nyasaland African Congress, the Youth League, and the Women's League were proscribed; the penalty for continuing to organize any of these bodies was to be fourteen years' impri-

27. Welensky, pp. 118ff.
28. Quoted by Short, p. 115.
29. Welensky, p. 126.

sonment, and the penalty for continuing to be a member or knowingly allowing a meeting to be held was to be seven years.

In some parts of the country, the reaction to "Operation Sunrise," the name given to the rounding up of Congress leaders, was a violent one. This was particularly so, as the Devlin Commission pointed out, in areas such as Nkhata Bay where there had previously been very little violence and where, consequently, the seizure of the leaders and supporters of Congress was both unexpected and seemed grossly unjust. More than forty Africans lost their lives in clashes with the security forces, but order was restored over most of the country within a few days; by the end of a month, during which another half dozen Africans were killed, it appeared that resistance had been overcome even in the most stubborn areas.[30]

Dr. Banda and all known Congress activists were placed in detention. With the proscription of Congress, the only channels for the expression of majority African opinion appeared to be effectively blocked for the time being. But it was soon to become evident, even to those Europeans who had so far managed to persuade themselves that they were dealing with no more than a handful of malcontents, that the nationalist movement had mass support.

The authorities in Nyasaland, reinforced to the fullest extent by federal and Southern Rhodesian forces, might have been able to prevent the situation from degenerating into one of complete anarchy and lawlessness, but they could have done so only by totally abandoning all claim to regard for African opinion. The British Parliament, casual though it might have been in its concern with African opposition to federation, had not bargained for anything as dramatic as this. Events in Kenya had already shaken the British public, the Conservative party was on the defensive about its colonial policy, and after several years in opposition the Labour party had shed its earlier enthusiasm for federation and was not at all hesitant about making Central Africa one of its election issues.

30. Welensky's account says there were six deaths (p. 127); the difference between this figure and the larger ones presented by Jones (p. 241), and Short (p. 116), is that Welensky's figure relates to deaths directly related to arrests; many of the casualties were in the riots in protest against the arrests.

The very remoteness of British parliamentarians from the situation in Nyasaland, which had made it relatively easy for them to discount the profound and widespread concern of Africans about the imposition of federation, now led them to underestimate the difficulties that were faced by the governor and his subordinates, who were obliged to deal with the consequences of Parliament's earlier decision to ignore African opinion. The news of Operation Sunrise and the subsequent killing of more than forty Africans by the security forces was received with profound disquiet in Parliament, where, under considerable pressure, Lennox-Boyd announced that a Commission of Enquiry into the disturbances in Nyasaland was being set up under the chairmanship of Justice (later Lord) Devlin.

The commission began work on 11 April. It spent five weeks in Nyasaland and one in Southern Rhodesia, and published its Report on the 16 July. In view of the nature of its task, the speed with which that task had to be carried out, and the difficulties the commission faced (in the absence, for example, of power to summon witnesses) it is not surprising that the Report was, in Welensky's words, "one of the most publicised and one of the most controversial State Papers of modern times."[31]

The Report was, perhaps, a little unfair, by implication if not directly, to Sir Robert Armitage and his subordinates. They were faced with a very difficult situation not entirely of their own making, because the earlier decision of the British Parliament to impose federation on the Africans of Nyasaland had left its representatives with little choice except between repression and anarchy. In imposing federation, the government had lost its moral authority. If it was going to continue to govern on the same terms, it could scarcely afford the loss of its physical authority as well.

The commissioners acknowledged that "in the situation that existed on 3 March, however it was caused, the government had either to act or to abdicate," but the general impression

---

31. Welensky, p. 130. This was the kindest thing he had to say about the Devlin Report, which, he said, "was moulded by British prejudices, rooted in ignorance or misunderstanding of African thought, feeling and customs." He went on to refer to its "careless glibness" and "incomprehension of African realities."

conveyed by the Report was one which rather understated the difficulties with which the governor was faced, and the commissioners' confidence that there was no basis to the massacre plot was quite remarkable. It was in the nature of the situation that really hard evidence would have been very difficult to obtain. Proof, of the sort that would be acceptable in a British court of law, would not be available unless the situation had got completely out of hand.

The main thrust of the Report was, however, both perceptive and immensely influential. The maintenance of law and order is not an end in itself but a precondition of the more important objectives of justice and freedom. If the administration could maintain order only by massive repression, it was time to think carefully about the policies that had led to that situation. The comment in the Report that "Nyasaland is—no doubt temporarily—a police state, where it is not safe for anyone to express approval of the policies of the Congress party," aroused widespread concern in Britain. Lord Boyle later wrote that "during the whole run-up to the 1959 election, the only area of policy in which Conservatives had found themselves on the defensive was African policy, with particular emphasis being laid on the Opposition on Suez, the Devlin Report and the truly horrible disaster at Hola Camp."[32]

The British government had already decided to establish a Royal Commission to review the experience of federation and to make recommendations about what should next be done, but there was some ambiguity, perhaps intentional, about the precise terms of the commission. There were later to be bitter recriminations from Sir Roy Welensky about what he felt to be a fundamental change in the interpretation of the commission's terms of reference; it was his frequently and forcefully expressed view that the British government had agreed, before setting up the commission, that it would not "associate itself with anything which called into question the continuance of Federation itself."[33] A rather different view was taken by

32. Introduction by Lord Boyle to Nigel Fisher, *Ian Macleod* (London: Andre Deutsch, 1973), p. 20.
33. Welensky's account of the establishment and performance of the new commission begins on page 138; the quotation is from page 150.

Sir Harold Macmillan. It was, he said, intended and hoped that members of the commission, which was to be under the chairmanship of Sir Walter Monckton, would be able to suggest ways in which the intentions of the federal experiment could be fulfilled, but that if they felt that the evidence strongly suggested that federation was no longer a viable proposition, members should use their judgment to make whatever recommendations were appropriate in the circumstances. "It will, of course," he said, "be for the commission to decide what use to make of the material which reaches them." He added, "In these cases I do not think it is ever wise to be specific or rigid in interpretation." The commission, he insisted, was appointed "to try and make federation work in some form or another and find a solution acceptable to all the races in all the territories concerned" but if, in their judgment, the problem was an insoluble one, "I have no doubt that a Commission of this kind will find a way of expressing its opinion."[34]

Welensky's view of the matter, although perhaps reflecting a rather naive appraisal of political realities in Britain, was not an illogical extension of the decisions made by Parliament in 1953. When it had been decided that federation would be forced down the throats of Africans in Nyasaland, both Sir Roy Welensky and Dr. Banda had believed that this decision was, in Dr. Banda's words, "the thin edge of the wedge of amalgamation," and a long step toward the establishment of an independent state in Central Africa dominated by settler interests. That Dr. Banda was deeply distressed, and Sir Roy gratified, by these prospects was due not to any significant difference in their interpretation of what had happened, but to their very different assessment of the desirability of such an outcome. Sir Roy had hoped, and Dr. Banda feared, that the British Parliament knew what it was about, but it is the essence of the particular political genius of the British that formal logic has never counted for very much either in their deliberations or, more important, in their evaluation of policy options. When the plans for Central Africa which had appeared to be so convenient a few years earlier threatened to

34. Quoted in Sir Harold Macmillan, *Pointing the Way, 1959–1961* (London: Macmillan, 1972), p. 141.

become a serious political liability, the government, with neither more nor less regard for logic than it had displayed in 1953, decided to look at the matter again. It had no more compunction about abandoning the commitments apparently implied in the 1953 arrangement than it had when it abandoned earlier and equally binding commitments to Nyasaland Africans in 1953 and insisted upon imposing federation against the manifest opposition of Nyasaland Africans.

Macmillan hoped that it would be possible to include in the commission at least one representative of the many distinguished Asians and West Indians who had the same qualities that were to make Lord Monckton so admirable a choice as chairman. Apart from the intrinsic merits of the selection, it might have gone some way toward providing a sympathetic hearing for the work of the commission in the Commonwealth, and particularly in Africa, but Macmillan felt it was necessary first to have the agreement both of Welensky, the federal prime minister, and of Sir Edgar Whitehead, the prime minister of Southern Rhodesia.

Though neither Welensky nor Whitehead appeared to be aware of it, the response from Whitehead illustrated very clearly the impenetrable racial bias of European leaders in Central Africa. Welensky wrote that his colleague "strongly resented being told that his country's representation had to be chosen for the colour of their skin, and that he would regard the appointment of a Malayan or West Indian . . . as quite intolerable and would refuse to take any part in the Commission's proceedings."[35]

Rhodesian racial attitudes were, however, becoming a political liability in Great Britain and, although Macmillan accepted the veto from Whitehead and Welensky on this point, the government was beginning to lose patience with Welensky. It was agreed that, as an alternative, there should be some African representation on the Commission, but this gave rise to a great deal of dispute as to who should represent Nyasaland. Nearly all the leaders of Congress, the only men who could have most

35. Welensky, p. 149.

accurately reflected African opinion, were in detention, and the European leaders in Central Africa were unwilling to accept anyone likely to have the confidence of Nyasaland Africans. When Orton Chirwa was released from detention, his name was suggested, but Welensky "hit the roof" and the idea was dropped. Later, Manoah Chirwa, who had been expelled from Congress for his refusal to resign his seat in the federal Parliament and who had virtually no support among Nyasaland Africans, was reluctantly accepted by Welensky, "provided it was made clear publicly that Mr. Chirwa had always been a staunch opponent of federation," and that he should consequently be treated as a hostile witness.[36]

While these discussions were going on there had been a very important change in the British Cabinet. It had been known for some months that Lennox-Boyd was going to retire from politics, but the name of his successor was not known until after the election in October 1959. Welensky very quickly realized that "a new and disconcerting opponent" had appeared on the scene and was later to say of the new man that "for good or ill he was probably the most powerful holder of the office since Joseph Chamberlain."

The appointment of Ian Macleod reflected Macmillan's belief that the rapid growth of nationalism in Africa required "a change of timing [that] was so radical that it amounted to a change of policy." Macmillan himself was given fresh evidence of the need to reach an accommodation with the nationalist movement when he revisited Nyasaland in January 1960. "The prevailing impression left upon me was that in Nyasaland the cause of Federation was almost desperate because of the strength of African opinion against it. The only grounds for hope seemed to lie in so rapid an advance to self-government in all matters of territorial interests as to reconcile Dr. Banda and his supporters to continue to work within the Federation framework."[37] He had no doubt that "so long as [Dr. Banda] remained in detention, the Malawi Congress Party, organised

36. Welensky, p. 163.
37. Macmillan, *Pointing the Way*, p. 148.

by Orton Chirwa, as Dr. Banda's lieutenant, was clearly gaining in power and strength every day."

Macleod came to the conclusion that any hope of political stability in Nyasaland would depend on the release of Dr. Banda from Gwelo prison, where he was in detention. "It was," writes Fisher, "very much his own decision, taken against all official advice in the Colonial Office and in Africa. The governor, Sir Robert Armitage, thought it unwise; so did the governor general of the Central African Federation. Sir Roy Welensky and his Cabinet were strongly opposed to it, and it was against the feeling of a number of Macleod's own Cabinet colleagues at home, including the Prime Minister himself."[38]

Macmillan had already gained a firsthand impression of the way things were going in Nyasaland, and although, in his imperturbable manner, he had been less alarmed by the level of violence than many British journalists, he no doubt felt that some move toward accommodation was necessary.[39] He had, however, been persuaded by Welensky that Dr. Banda should not be released until after the Monckton Commission had reported, and Macleod was able to get his way only after he made it clear that he was prepared to resign over the issue. Members of the British government were still hoping that they could convince Africans in Nyasaland that some form of federation was in their interests, but they had at last begun to realize that they were unlikely to be successful, and they were no longer willing to force through a policy in the face of widespread and intransigent African opposition. They decided instead to ignore Sir Malcolm Barrow, a Nyasaland European in the federal Cabinet, who warned that 10,000 Africans would be killed in riots if Banda was released.[40]

There were increasingly acrimonious disputes between Welensky and the British Cabinet as Welensky became more apprehensive of British intentions. He tried hard to limit the

38. Fisher, *Ian MacLeod,* p. 157.
39. The behavior of the crowd at Blantyre during Macmillan's visit had occasioned some colorful writing in sections of the British press. Macmillan's own comment was that "to anyone who had been accustomed to electioneering in the North of England in the twenties it seemed a very tame affair" (p. 149).
40. Fisher, p. 157.

terms of reference of the new commission, insisted that if detainees were allowed to appear before the commission they should do so on their own and not with legal council, and he claimed for the federal government the right to prosecute witnesses appearing before the commission if it believed that the evidence they gave involved sedition, libel, or perjury. "I would not agree," he said, "to providing a public forum for sedition, criminal libel or perjury."[41] On each of these matters he had to give way, although some effort was made to provide a form of words that would give the appearance of agreement between the British and federal governments. As it turned out, however, the Malawi Congress Party (MCP) decided to boycott the commission hearings because the MCP leaders felt that the commission was heavily biased in favor of the profederation view and that the report its members were to write would turn out to be a whitewash of the federal scheme.

Lord Home, the minister for Commonwealth Relations, had already met the federal Cabinet in February 1960 and told them that the Monckton Commission might not be able to confine itself to its terms of reference "in the hypothetical event of an overwhelming volume of evidence being in favour of secession."[42] When members of the federal Cabinet insisted that this was quite contrary to the assurances given them by Lennox-Boyd, they were told that conditions in Nyasaland were now so different that it was necessary to consider them with a fresh mind.

Dr. Banda was released on 1 April and he promptly joined Orton Chirwa in appealing for calm. Almost immediately he left the country for discussions in Britain and the United States, but he was back the following month to begin an intensive political campaign designed to lead Nyasaland out of the federation. The state of emergency was not formally ended until 15 June, but restrictions were much reduced before then. The MCP had been formed while Dr. Banda was in detention, but its first leaders, Orton Chirwa and the young Aleke Banda, made it clear that the party was the successor to the banned

41. Welensky, p. 164.
42. Lord Home to the federal Cabinet, quoted by Welensky, p. 183.

Nyasaland African Congress and that Dr. Banda was to be the
official as well as the de facto leader as soon as he was released
from detention. The government had sanctioned the MCP
either because they hoped it would be a more moderate organization than the proscribed NAC or because they felt that it
was desirable that the overwhelming majority of Nyasaland Africans should have some means of expressing their views without being forced into conflict with the law.

On 5 April, Orton Chirwa handed over the presidency of the
MCP to Dr. Banda, and the following month the party held its
first national conference in Blantyre. Two weeks later Dr.
Banda was granted permission to tour all three of the country's
provinces; in each of them he was greeted by large and very
enthusiastic crowds. The government had not yet released all
of the detainees, however, and Chipembere, the Chisiza
brothers, and about twelve other people were still being held
because the government regarded them as particularly prone
to the incitement of violence.

In July, Dr. Banda left for London to attend the Nyasaland
Constitutional Conference. With him, as fellow delegates, were
Chirwa, Aleke Banda, and Kanyama Chiume, together with
three chiefs, including Willard Gomani, who was about to become paramount chief of the Ncheu Ngoni. Two Asian delegates, Sacranie and Antao, were mandated to support the
MCP. The United Federal Party also had four delegates (including one African) and two chiefs as advisers; the Congress
Liberation Party, a small African group, had a single representative; the Nyasaland government was represented by the governor general and several of his colleagues, and there was a
delegation of chiefs and representatives of the African members of the Legislative Council.

The Congress party proposals dominated the conference.
Dr. Banda was not able to get terms as good as those he had
initially demanded, but as these would have represented total
and immediate victory for the MCP, it is unlikely that he really
expected to get them. What he did obtain was enough to provide virtual certainty of complete success in the near future.
The electorate was to be much larger than ever before, though
still well removed from universal suffrage. There were to be

two electoral rolls, which would be distinguished by educational and income qualifications, but the majority of elected members would be chosen by lower roll. The upper roll, which would be predominantly European, would elect eight members; there would be twenty members of the new Legislative Council elected from the lower roll, and five members would be "officials" who would be there by virtue of their position in the administration.

The minimal qualifications for voting even in the lower roll were substantial and excluded most of the population. It was necessary to belong to certain occupational or related groups (chiefs, headmen, members of native authorities or district councils; master farmers; soldiers or pensioners) or have certain income levels (£120 per year, property valued at £250 or have been on the tax register and paid taxes for the previous ten years) together with certain literacy requirements. The upper roll qualifications were still more demanding, and few people, apart from Europeans, would be able to meet the income requirements.

The Executive Council was to consist of five official members and five elected members of the Legislative Council. Three of the latter were to be drawn from members elected by the lower roll, two elected by the upper roll, and two of the five officials could be replaced at the governor's discretion by elected members. The governor was to have a casting vote if deadlock were reached in the Executive Council.[43]

Dr. Banda had good reason to be satisfied with the results of the conference because they made it virtually inevitable that Congress would have an overwhelming majority in the Legislative Council and that, in turn, would make it extremely difficult for the executive to act in defiance of congress opinion. It was difficult for Dr. Banda to convince all of his followers, even if he were convinced of it himself, that the British government and the administration in Zomba were moving fast enough, and there was bitterness over the failure of the administration to release the "hard-core" detainees, particularly Chipembere and the Chisiza brothers. There were fresh outbreaks of vio-

43. Pachai, *Malawi*, pp. 242–243.

lence, which included assaults on Africans who had reservations about the MCP.

Whether in response to this renewed pressure or because it was what the administration had already decided, the last of the detainees were released at the end of September. Chipembere was immediately appointed treasurer general of the party, Dunduzu Chisiza was appointed secretary general, and Yatuta Chisiza became the administrative secretary. At the same time, it was decided that annual elections for the presidency of the party should cease, at least for as long as Dr. Banda wished to continue as party leader. He was appointed life president, so that even if any opposition to him were to emerge it would not be possible to remove him from the presidency of the party without a fundamental change in the party constitution.

As so often happens, violence was markedly reduced when the principal complaint was met, but it was soon to be stimulated by another grievance. Dr. Banda had been insisting that elections should take place by December 1960, and the administration had been equally insistent that it was not practicable to hold them until sometime later. In these somewhat tense circumstances many people feared that the administration was simply being devious, but Dr. Banda made an urgent appeal for calm. "There is too much at stake," he said. "We must have elections."[44]

The administration felt it necessary to take stern action to control the rising tide of violence. In the short period since his release Chipembere had made a number of flamboyant speeches that, whatever their intention, could certainly be interpreted as incitement to violence, and early in the New Year he was arrested, put on trial, and sentenced to three-year imprisonment on a charge of sedition.

Meanwhile, the Monckton Report had been issued in October 1960. It made a number of recommendations of a fairly specific kind, including some that would enable fairer representation of Africans both in the federal assembly and in the legislature of Northern Rhodesia, but the real impact of the report, which led Welensky to refer to this "terrible piece of

44. Short, *Banda*, p. 142.

high explosive," came from its guarded but nonetheless highly significant speculation about the future.[45] After noting that there was continued, widespread, and very strong opposition to federation among Africans of the northern territories which had reached an "almost pathological" intensity, it suggested that the right of secession should be conceded if any territory was still opposed to federation after an appropriate trial period.

This suggestion was, of course, very much milder than the demands made by Dr. Banda. It should, however, be recalled that largely because of the suspicions harbored by opponents of federation about the function of the commission and their consequent refusal to take part in its deliberations, most of its members were assumed to be very sympathetic toward the idea of a federal state in Central Africa. That men of distinction, experience, and political acumen with a predisposition in favor of federation should have accepted, however cautiously, the main thrust of Dr. Banda's argument, carried far more weight than would have been achieved by the report of a commission that had included open representatives of the federation's critics. Welensky was quite right in his judgment that "its mere publication will make the continuation of federation virtually impossible," but it took time before some of the principal actors, including Welensky, adjusted themselves to the new situation.

Toward the end of November, Dr. Banda went to London, accompanied by Chirwa and Dunduzu Chisiza, to take part in the Federal Review Conference. His position was, as everyone expected, entirely straightforward: "I am here to demand secession and secession now, not in five years."[46] No decision was reached at the conference, but Dr. Banda was quite right when on his return he told a meeting of his supporters at Blantyre that federation was dead and all that remained was for the corpse to be buried.

The MCP began its drive to register voters in the new year. The registration period ended in the middle of March; 107,076 people were registered on the lower roll, and there were 4,401

45. Welensky, p. 270.
46. Short, p. 145.

on the upper roll, of whom 471 were Africans. Dr. Banda himself registered for the lower roll. Toward the end of May, Dr. Banda produced his party's list of candidates. He nominated twenty candidates for the lower roll and two for the upper roll. The last two were standing respectively in the Northern Province and for a constituency that covered a large part of the Central Province outside of Lilongwe, in both areas the influence of the Livingstonia mission being particularly strong. There were also four Europeans standing as independent candidates on the upper roll who were known to be very sympathetic to the MCP and who contested their seats with Dr. Banda's blessing. In five of the lower roll seats no candidate ran against the MCP and for some of them it had proved impossible to find the ten people required to sign the nomination papers of an opposing candidate.

Dr. Banda had already assumed a far more dominant position, in terms of effective rather than nominal power, than he had before the declaration of the emergency. He may have felt that it was necessary for him to assume a tighter control over the party because his lieutenants had not kept him properly informed about what was being done in the days before the emergency. He would, in any case, have been obliged to take on more of the effective duties of leader while some of the most dynamic of his young men were contained in jail after his own release, and he was probably becoming increasingly aware that their efforts to build him up as "the political Messiah" had been successful even beyond their expectations.

The election took place in August. The principal issue was federation. Do you want, asked Dr. Banda, "slavery within federation or freedom and independence outside the federation?" It was also seen as a personal confrontation between the new African champion, upon whose victory almost every man and woman in Nyasaland had backed every penny they had, and, on the other hand, Welensky, the tough and experienced champion of white rule. Dr. Banda had no hesitation in forcing a confrontation on precisely these terms. When Welensky came to Nyasaland on a tour designed to bolster the sagging support for profederation candidates, Dr. Banda took the opportunity to make the election a personal challenge: "I have been fighting a rabble without a General. Now for at least three days, from August 2 to August 5, I will be fighting a rabble with a General. After August 15 I shall be fighting a General in Salisbury without even a rabble in Nyasaland. Then the beauty of it to me is that the General will have shared the ignominious defeat of his rabble."[47]

The manifesto the party presented to the electorate was not devoted entirely to these federal and personal issues. It declared its support for the cause of African liberation movements, for Africanization of government posts, and for a radical program of social welfare. It was designed to produce something for everyone who might be a potential MCP voter—civil servants seeking promotion, cash crop farmers wanting a better deal from marketing boards, parents wanting better educational facilities for their children, people angry about police harrassment—and there was not any serious examination of the priorities that should be observed after independence had been gained.

The elections led to a sweeping victory for the MCP which took all twenty seats on the lower roll and, more surprisingly, took the two seats it contested on the upper roll, while one of its Independent sympathizers also won a seat. More than 95 per cent of those eligible to vote on the lower roll had taken advantage of their opportunity and more than 99 percent of them had voted for the MCP. On the higher roll, the very limited and predominantly European electorate had recorded an 85 per-cent vote, but of those only a little more than half had voted for a profederation candidate.

The nationalist movement had appeared on the verge of destruction in 1954. But federation, which had at one time appeared as the flame that reduced to ashes the nationalist cause, proved instead to be the furnace to temper a far more powerful weapon.

47. Short, pp. 151–152.

CHAPTER 6

From One Party to One Man

He either fears his fate too much,
Or his deserts are small,
That puts it not unto the touch,
To win or lose it all.

James Graham, Marquis of Montrose (1612–1650)

Its massive victory at the polls ensured for the Malawi Congress Party a measure of representation in the Nyasaland Cabinet—that is, in the Executive Council of the Legislative Council. It was not entirely clear what form the representation should take, because the new constitution had simply specified that three members of the Executive Council should be drawn from those members of the Legislative Council elected from the lower rolls and two from members elected on the upper roll, but had not made it clear whether the representatives of the upper roll should be drawn from the party that won an overall majority or from the one that gained a majority on that particular roll (which would have meant that the party favored by Europeans would have been guaranteed two seats on the executive). There would in addition be five "official" members of the Executive Council.

Michael Blackwood, who had been deputy leader of the United Federal Party in Nyasaland, insisted that the two members drawn from the upper roll should be representatives of his party because it had gained the majority of votes cast on that roll, but the governor, Sir Glynn Jones, took the view that in the face of so clear an expression of African opinion this would be both impolitic and inequitable. It was suggested that the MCP and the United Federal Party should each have one representative from the upper roll on the executive, but Blackwood found this suggestion unacceptable and took his party into opposition in the Legislative Council.[1]

1. Philip Short, *Banda*, p. 153.

Dr. Banda and three other members of his party became ministers in the new administration, while Colin Cameron, who had run successfully with MCP blessing as a pro-MCP Independent on the upper roll, also became a minister. Dr. Banda himself took over responsibility for natural resources and local government, Chiume became minister of education, Bwanausi became minister of labour and social services, Mkandawire became minister without portfolio, and Cameron was responsible for works and transport. Chipembere was still in prison, but it was assumed that he would be appointed to the Cabinet when he was released. Two key ministries—justice and finance—continued under the control of the senior expatriate civil servants who were *ex officio* members of the Legislative Council, but their parliamentary secretaries were both prominent members of the MCP. Orton Chirwa became parliamentary secretary to the minister of justice, and Dunduzu Chisiza, generally considered the most powerful intellect among the younger members despite his lack of formal training, was appointed parliamentary secretary to the minister of finance.

Dr. Banda and his party were, in fact, in a much stronger position than the constitutional position alone might have suggested. There were clear signs that the British government intended to grant complete self-government to the country in the near future and that the MCP ministers, though without a majority in the executive, were being prepared for the role they would play when the MCP was formally in control of proceedings. The transitional period was, moreover, made smoother than it might have been because of the close sense of understanding and mutual respect between the governor and Dr. Banda. The sympathy of the governor was clearly demonstrated when he decided, only three months after the MCP had come to power, to use his discretionary powers to replace two of the nominated members of the Executive Council by elected members of the majority party. In March 1962, Msonthi became minister of trade and industry and Chokani took over as minister of labour, while Bwanausi moved to the newly formed Ministry of Foreign Affairs.

In the first session of the new Legislative Council, Dr. Banda introduced a measure designed to bring about substantial reform in local government. Local councils were henceforth to be elected on a single roll, with a universal adult franchise that would, for the first time, give the vote to women. Blackwood suggested that it would be more appropriate to introduce such a change more gradually and stressed the advantage of staggering the election of members, with only a third or some similar fraction of the membership of each council facing the voters in each election. This system would allow, he said, advantage to be taken of the experience of presently serving members, while making it quite possible to change the entire membership within a few years. Whatever the merits of this type of system, however, most of the existing council had been elected by a very narrow and racially biased electorate, and few members had sympathized with the MCP in particular or with African political aspirations in general. Dr. Banda was, not surprisingly, unwilling to waste much time with this proposal: "I must be blunt," he said. "It has never been my style to beat about the bush. We mean to make a clean sweep." He went on to comment, with that rather odd mixture of apparent good humor and underlying menace that was one of his hallmarks, on the great changes that had taken place in the membership of the Legislative Council itself as a result of the recent election, telling Blackwood: "Certain heads are not to be seen and you are lucky to be here."[2]

On the following day he began to set out his plans for encouraging more efficient practices in agriculture. Previous policies had frequently occasioned great distress in the rural areas. In their attempt to improve agricultural practices, preceding administrations had sought to enforce regulations by imposing heavy punishment on those who broke them: farmers who disobeyed (or were simply unaware of) planting rules were subject to having their crops destroyed and to the levying of fines or other penalties. These punitive measures, said Dr. Banda, had proved both harsh and ineffective because it was not possible to "legislate or even punish people into being good farmers"; what was needed was patience and education: "Given a long

2. *Debates of Legislative Council* (Zomba: Government Printer), 28 Nov. 1961, pp. 45–46.

time, education, patience, sympathy and understanding will bring better results than punishment."[3]

He was not prepared, said Dr. Banda, to tolerate a situation in which "his" women were obliged to hide in the bush for fear of the police and to suffer these indignities, moreover, as part of a campaign that had no chance of achieving its objectives. When, in May 1962, the Land Use and Protection Bill was introduced, and included severe penalties for disobedience, the opposition were quick to point out what they felt was a contradiction. Dr. Banda insisted that a distinction could properly be made between manifestly antisocial behavior, such as the diversion of water on which other people rely, for which severe punishment was appropriate, and general agricultural practice, where the emphasis should be on "persuasion not coercion." "You cannot terrorise people into good farmers, you can only embitter them."[4]

It was a businesslike start to the proceedings of the new Legislative Council. Dr. Banda conducted himself like a man who, whatever his formal title, was the effective political leader of the country; he had addressed himself to matters that affected large numbers of the African population and, if his words and actions were notable more for their psychological than their material effect, the psychological bruises he was attempting to heal were both of long standing and of considerable practical importance. Moreover, several new members, with little or no previous experience of similarly formal assemblies, had shown a most commendable and promising ability to adapt themselves to the new environment.

A few incidents, although they may not have attracted much attention at the time, could be seen in the light of later events to foreshadow the crisis about to burst within the MCP. Commenting on the capable performance of the new MCP members of the Legislative Council (whose conduct drew a graceful tribute at the end of the proceedings from the experienced Speaker), Dr. Banda, interrupted by shouts of "hear, hear!" and applause and laughter, went on to say: "Under our cus-

3. *Legislative Council,* 29 Nov. 1961, p. 102.
4. *Legislative Council,* 31 May 1962, p. 247.

tom, Sir, I am the father of all my boys behind me. For every mistake they make I am personally responsible, because when I leave the house I go home, I talk to them like children and they shut up."[5]

It was later to become clear that some of the people to whom he was becoming accustomed to refer to as "his boys" were a good deal less than enthusiastic at being treated with such open contempt. Nor were all of them as callow and inexperienced as Dr. Banda was wont to believe. Chiume and Chipembere had both proved themselves very skillful debaters in the Legislative Council some years before Dr. Banda himself had his first experience of parliamentary debate; they had, together with the Chisiza brothers, inspired and organized the party and had been largely responsible for engineering Dr. Banda's triumphant return to the country.

There were signs, albeit muted, that at least some of the younger men in the party were moved by more radical impulses than those reflected by Dr. Banda himself. The party was becoming increasingly identified with the personality of Dr. Banda, but some spoke with veneration of Chipembere. Dunduzu Chisiza paid a long and warm parliamentary tribute to him while he was still in prison serving the three-year sentence for sedition imposed before the election. Before he was called to order by the Speaker, for suggesting that the courts had been at fault in finding Chipembere guilty, he had spoken of those "valiant sons of Malawi who at this particular moment, instead of being with us on this important occasion are languishing in prison," and had insisted that Chipembere should be immediately released and made a member of the Cabinet.[6]

At the next session of the Legislative Council, Kanyama Chiume introduced a debate on proposed improvements in the educational structure. He presented a well-reasoned argument, which included a tribute to the work done by missionary groups in Malawi, but whenever Chiume spoke there was an indefinable but recognizable suggestion of menace, unrelieved

5. *Legislative Council,* 29 Nov. 1961, p. 101.
6. *Legislative Council,* 29 Nov. 1961, p. 83.

by the humor and tough pragmatism that were very much a part of Dr. Banda's public image at the time. Chiume frequently spoke as though he regarded any opinion that differed from his own as an intolerable personal affront. But if his performance was abrasive in marked contrast to that of most MCP members of the Legislative Council, it was undoubtedly competent, and Dr. Banda expressed his delight at the success of " 'my boy'; the honourable minister of Education to the rest of you but to me he is just my boy Kanyama."[7]

In March 1962, Dr. Banda put forward a bill to set up the Nyasaland Farmers Marketing Board. This would replace, and improve upon, the Agricultural Production and Marketing Board which had earlier been formed by a merger of the Native Tobacco Board, the Maize Control Board, and the Cotton Marketing Board.

There were, said Dr. Banda, three functions that the former board had been intended to serve. It had provided a marketing agency for African farmers, stabilized the prices offered to farmers and supervised the growth of production on African trust land. The board had, said Dr. Banda, performed a "very useful and beneficial role," but the methods used to enforce new agricultural practices had given it a bad name among Africans, and this would make it difficult to elicit their cooperation in the future. Since, moreover, the board had been the sole buyer of several of the most important African agricultural products but had had no effective African representation, African farmers had tended to feel that the price was being rigged against them. Whether or not they were right, farmers felt that they had not always been fairly treated, and their confidence must be restored if there was to be any significant improvement in the vital agricultural sector.

In the future, said Dr. Banda, provision would be made for the direct representation of farmers on the ruling body of the board; the buying of tobacco, cotton, and groundnuts would be undertaken by cooperative societies, acting as agents of the board, which would make every effort to use the services of

7. *Legislative Council,* 6 March 1962, p. 144.

African transporters and carriers rather than the larger expatriate companies which had always been used in the past.[8]

Another object of legislation to which high priority was attached was the reform of local courts. When Orton Chirwa introduced the second reading of the Local Courts Bill in May 1962, he drew attention to declarations in the MCP's election manifesto and in a number of speeches made by Dr. Banda, concerning the importance of establishing and maintaining "an independent and impartial judiciary" in Malawi.[9] In the past, he said, magisterial functions had been exercised by provincial and district commissioners, and Africans sometimes appeared before a magistrate under circumstances in which their opponent was a European who was (at the least) a social acquaintance of the commissioner, while they themselves would have met the commissioner, if at all, under circumstances that stressed their social inferiority. Even more often, the accused would be charged with breaking a law or regulation promulgated or maintained by the administration to which the commissioner belonged and, indeed, not infrequently was alleged to have acted in defiance of a ruling made by the commissioner himself. If there was an appeal, it typically meant that the case would be referred to the commissioner's administrative superior, who was both his social intimate and a member of the same administration. It was, said Chirwa, "like appealing from one man to his own friend." Speaking in support of the bill, Dr. Banda stressed the importance of an independent judiciary and said that native courts had been brought into disrepute during the colonial era because they had been used for political purposes and had been subject to direct political control: "The Chief was simply told what he was to do and he went out of his way to please his master, because he knew he could be deposed at any time."

The bill was intended to increase the independence of the local courts, to enable them to deal efficiently with a considerable volume of business, and to cut down frequent long delays in dealing with appeals. Chirwa made it clear that anyone appearing before the local courts would be allowed legal repre-

8. *Legislative Council,* 7 March 1962, p. 154.
9. *Legislative Council,* 29 May 1962, p. 192.

sentation; the bill reflected "our desire to pursue and respect the internationally accepted principles of the rule of law."

The measures put forward during this transitional period were primarily sensible and moderate attempts to deal with problems that most people were aware existed; Dr. Banda was insistent that he would look after "his people," but repeatedly assured Europeans that, providing they understood that Africans now ruled the country, they would be very welcome to stay. The discipline of the party had been good, and although there had been a few incidents in which party leaders had been ruthless in their treatment of African dissenters, there still appeared to be opportunities for genuine discussion about serious matters.

It was perhaps inevitable after the overwhelming victory in the August elections that, despite protestations to the contrary by the British government at the time, there would be a fairly rapid move toward self-government even though this meant secession from the federation and very probably the collapse of the federal experiment. But had there been any lingering doubts about the capacity of Dr. Banda and the MCP to provide a viable political leadership, the party's performance during this period of apprenticeship must have gone far to dispel them.

A new constitutional conference was held in London during November 1962 to discuss arrangements for granting complete self-government for Nyasaland, which was to take the name of Malawi. At the same time the British government finally made it clear to Welensky beyond any doubt that the British government accepted the principle of the withdrawal of the territory from the federation and informed him they would soon make a public announcement to this effect. There were to be two distinct stages in the constitutional approach to full independence. In the first, the Executive Council would be replaced by a Cabinet chosen by the leader of the majority party in the Legislative Council, which was to be renamed the Legislative Assembly; the leader would become prime minister and would preside over the Cabinet, which was to assume full responsibility for all matters except public safety and order, and related issues; there were to be ten Cabinet members, at least seven of whom should be members of the Legislative Assembly, and the Assembly was to have the power of rejecting as well as discussing proposals of the Cabinet.

The second stage was to include a reform of the legislature, with the number of members being increased and all being elected on a common roll save for a small number of seats assigned to the representatives of minority groups (that is, Europeans). After the second stage, responsibility for public safety would pass out of the hands of the governor and into those of the Cabinet.

The first stage came into effect in February 1963. At the request of Dr. Banda, a senior expatriate civil servant, Henry Phillips, the financial secretary, was retained in the Cabinet as minister of finance. But with one exception all the other members of the Cabinet were Malawians and members of the MCP. The exception was Colin Cameron, a Scotsman, who had run for election in 1961 on the upper roll as an Independent, but who had been very sympathetic to the MCP and had run with Dr. Banda's blessing. Chirwa became minister of justice, while Chipembere, recently released from prison and elected for a seat that had been held in his absence by his father, was made minister of local government.[10]

Further talks were held in London in September 1963, attended by both the governor, Sir Glynn Jones, and Dr. Banda. It was agreed that there would be fifty members elected by an electorate no longer divided into separate rolls, universal adult suffrage, and another five members elected to represent special minority interests (though this was later reduced to three). A general election would be held in April 1964, and on 6 July of that year Nyasaland would become the independent sovereign state of Malawi.

In the meanwhile the domestic power of the MCP was acquiring increasingly effective constitutional sanction, and within the party the personal power of Dr. Banda was becom-

10. Chipembere had been feted by party members on his release but, writes Short, "Banda was at heart far from happy at Chipembere's release. He had made no attempt to cut short his sentence, as he easily could have done, and although he kept his promise to have Chipembere freed before he completed his term, it was only by ten days" (p. 168).

ing steadily more comprehensive. Whatever might have been the original intentions or expectations of the young Turks of the party, Dr. Banda had no doubt that this power was meant to be used. "There is no dispute in our Party. We don't say: 'What do you want, what is it?' It is what Kamuzu says that goes over there."[11]

Dr. Banda continued to believe, or at least to behave as though he believed, that his ministers were entirely content to be referred to as "my boys" and to be treated accordingly. "Fortunately for me they do not object—they enjoy it—for by so doing I impart to them some of the things that I know and they do not know. Therefore, I am very, very happy, very very happy indeed."[12]

His powers as life president of the party, always substantial, were significantly increased following the report of a subcommittee of the central executive, chaired by Orton Chirwa, set up in July 1962 to provide a more effective way of dealing with dissidents in the party. One of the proposed rules stated: "Any member of the Party guilty of disloyalty, rumour-mongering, deliberate manufacture of destructive stories, invidious whisper campaigns, loose talk and character assassination against any member of the Party or the Party itself shall be dealt with in such manner as the President in his absolute discretion may think fit."[13]

Among the rules adopted in February 1963 was one which forbade ministers to make statements about party policy without first obtaining the approval of Dr. Banda: In effect, no minister was permitted to touch on any subject, even if not a matter of direct governmental concern, in any way that suggested any measure of disagreement with Dr. Banda; no minister could, without resigning his office, take any part in debates on party policy unless he fully agreed with Dr. Banda.

Few, if any, members of the Assembly appeared to question the extent to which the party president could, and did, control the terms on which political discussion might take place. In May 1964, less than four months before he was driven out of

11. *Legislative Council,* 1 June 1962, p. 266.
12. *Legislative Assembly,* 26 Feb. 1964, p. 1272.
13. Quoted by Short, pp. 169–170.

the party, Kanyama Chiume told the Assembly that "there is nothing wrong with dictatorship" and said that he was keenly looking forward to the day when the party would "remove even traces of opposition."[14]

Very occasionally, something would be said that reflected, albeit indirectly, some underlying tensions, perhaps all the more significant for the fact that they could not be expressed openly. Something of this sort occurred shortly after the death of Dunduzu Chisiza in a car crash in 1962. Chisiza's brother Yatuta (who had earlier distinguished himself as the first African to become the head of the police force in Tanganyika and who had been Dr. Banda's personal bodyguard during the campaign for independence and was later to lead an abortive raid into Malawi for the purpose of killing Dr. Banda) referred in the Council (as it then was) to "statements . . . in the Press, on the radio, in private and public which imply . . . or, in my view, are calculated to imply that he was not loyal to his leader, Ngwazi Kamuzu Banda."[15] He vigorously denied that these rumors had any substance, but the fact that he felt it necessary to refer to them at all suggests that there were already some misgivings about the relations between the leader of the party and his principal lieutenants.

The death of Dunduzu Chisiza was a severe loss to the country and the party in general, but in particular to those younger members of the party who had taken the social-democratic trappings of the party manifesto with some seriousness. Dunduzu Chisiza was probably the most consistent and thoughtful protagonist of this element in the party's program, and he had acquired a substantial international reputation among liberal and moderate left intellectuals as a result of several perceptive papers he had written about the political and economic problems facing African countries on the threshold of independence.

He had devoted a good deal of thought to theoretical as well as practical problems concerning the role of the party and the leader in the postindependence era. He had, more particularly, addressed the question of whether glorification of the leader

14. *Legislative Assembly,* 29 May 1964, pp. 124–125.
15. *Legislative Council,* 16 Oct. 1962, p. 90.

for the purposes of the anticolonial struggle, and his consequent domination of the party apparatus, would later enable him to ignore genuine popular aspirations in the newly independent state.

Dunduza Chisiza's reputation among intellectuals abroad had been a considerable asset to him and, though his domestic political following may have been less potent than that of some of the other MCP leaders, his international prestige enabled him to stimulate some public dialogue about policies in Malawi. Colleagues of his shared at least some of his views, but they were more narrowly political in their orientation and, although they may have had a stronger following within Malawi or at the OAU, they lacked the standing that Dunduzu Chisiza had with people in Britain and the United States whose support was valuable to Dr. Banda.

Only someone who had support outside the country, from people whose support was also important to Dr. Banda, would be in a position to raise questions Dr. Banda would rather not have discussed. Dunduzu Chisiza had been the one man in the party whose open alienation would have caused serious doubts among the liberal intellectuals in Britain and the United States, for he had been among the most articulate supporters of Dr. Banda at a time when he still needed all the outside support he could muster.

It has been one of Dr. Banda's greatest assets as a serious political leader that, though he may be disposed to behave with bluster and arrogance and to be contemptuous, abrasive, or intimidating with people whom he controls or regards as inconsequential, he has usually had a clear grasp of the realities of power. When it has been to his advantage to do so, he has been able to display formidable resources of intelligence, coolness, and charm.

Relations between Dr. Banda and Dunduzu Chisiza were not entirely cordial, but the two men were a long way from any open break. It would have been very much in Dr. Banda's interests—at least until independence was achieved—to have maintained the appearance, if not necessarily the substance, of harmony. Chisiza was the one man in the party whose public goodwill was a major asset to Dr. Banda. Had Chisiza lived,

Banda might have had some hesitancy about pursuing policies to which he would have been deeply antipathetic.

The effective restrictions on serious debate before the death of Chisiza and its almost complete absence after his death made it virtually impossible to resolve the tensions within the party. For a long time the disparate and sometimes contradictory ambitions of different sections of the party were concealed by the very real unity of desire to get out of the federation and win freedom from colonial control, but as the country moved closer to independence, that unifying force lost its potency. The party had to think seriously about the policies it would seek to carry out after independence was achieved, and the conflict of sectional interests became both more acute and more apparent. Bringing the conflict into the open might not, of course, have resolved it, and the party might have been torn apart as each faction sought to impose its will on the others, but suppression of the issues and the failure to work out an acceptable order of priorities was to mean that the party, and the nation, lived continuously on the threshold of turmoil when any issue, however remote to the central problems of the nation it might seem to an outsider, might spark off a bitter struggle for political power. In the absence of public debate, many people might feel that the only effective way to influence policy was to seize control of the government itself. These persistent underlying sectional conflicts were intermingled with differences of a more philosophical nature, differences of ideology and of instinct. Added to all these were the conflicts that arose from personal ambition, vanity, greed, and lust for power. In the period before independence, however, there were persuasive arguments for maintaining the facade of unity, and in the negotiations over independence Dr. Banda held a dominating position of advantage over all other members of his party. He was regarded by the British as a comparatively moderate and reasonable man of ability and experience; he may not have outshone Chipembere or Chiume in the Assembly, even though he patronized them, and he did not create as great a stir in the OAU but when it came to negotiating with senior British civil servants and cabinet ministers, no other member of the Malawi Congress Party could match his experience and authority.

The logic of the situation encouraged the continued dominance of Dr. Banda in the party organization, at least until independence had been achieved, and he was not the man to have any doubt that this was the way things ought to be. He did not take lightly to argument from his subordinates. As Chipembere was later to explain with some poignancy, "We all admit, Ngwazi can be frightening and it is not easy to approach him."[16]

Together with the party regulations, which had given such sweeping personal powers to Dr. Banda, these conditions precluded serious discussion within the party, even when the point at issue was the further extension of Dr. Banda's own authority, unless Dr. Banda himself was prepared to sanction it. Discussion of the most trivial point could be interpreted as a deliberate challenge to the party constitution and could be punished by expulsion from the party; the fomenting of "disunity" or the formation of cliques—in short, any behavior that aroused Dr. Banda's disapproval—could be similarly punished. A man such as Chipembere had only two options if he wished to stay in politics. Either he did and said just what Dr. Banda wanted, or he could challenge the party constitution and mobilize his support in the country. The second option, if he chose it, might have brought the country to the verge of civil war and would have endangered negotiations over independence. The reform of the constitution which had enlarged the assembly and provided for universal suffrage based on a common roll came into effect in the early part of 1964 when there were elections for the new assembly. Under the party constitution Dr. Banda had the power, which he did not hesitate to exercise, to decide who should be the MCP candidate in each constituency, and he was able on this occasion to bring in a number of men who, unlike those elected in 1961, were without an independent base of power. No other party was able to put up candidates in any constituency, and all fifty MCP candidates were elected unopposed. The members who were returned to the assembly in April 1964 contained a disproportionately large number of men and women who were very much indebted to Dr. Banda personally for their political advancement.

16. *Legislative Assembly,* 9 Sept. 1964.

In the early years after his return, Dr. Banda had been constrained to some extent, despite the great formal powers given
him under the party's constitution, by the fact that the party
organization had been largely built up by the young men who
were now his Cabinet ministers. Since 1961, however, he had
set about building up a personal organization and had made
less use of the channels in which his Cabinet ministers still
exercised some influence; he took a much greater interest than
anyone appears to have anticipated in internal party organization, and he began to advance men who not only owed him
loyalty for their promotion but who depended on his support
for their political survival.

By the latter part of 1963 it was becoming evident that some
of Dr. Banda's policies were at considerable variance with the
program on which the party had contested the 1961 election,
and the divergence became steadily more marked thereafter.
Some ministers were particularly unhappy about Dr. Banda's
increasingly close association with the Portuguese and with the
slow rate of Africanization. Rumors abounded, but nothing
came into the open before independence was declared.

Lord Alport, who had represented the British government in
Rhodesia during the Federation period, attended the independence celebrations and reported: "I had a long talk with him
that evening and noted the increasing degree to which he was
holding himself apart from the other members of the Malawi
Hierarchy."[17]

Tensions within the party and particularly between Dr.
Banda and the more senior of the young men were, moreover,
building up at a time when the economic situation in Nyasaland
was worse than it had been for years. In 1964 the economy was
in the trough of the only depression that had seriously affected
the country since the end of World War II. A downturn in
economic activity had in fact begun in the late 1950s, well before Dr. Banda had taken power. To some extent this may
have reflected an almost inevitable reaction among Europeans
to the unduly optimistic expectations prevalent earlier in the
decade, when many of them had believed that the imposition

17. *The Sudden Assignment.*

of federation would bring about a transformation of the economy, and as a consequence of which there had been an artificially high rate of investment in some sectors (for example, construction) which was unlikely to be sustained for very long. The slight fall off in economic activity that was to be expected, even in favorable circumstances, was exacerbated by the uncertain political climate, which not only discouraged some potential investors but induced some Europeans to move themselves or their financial capital out of the country. Moreover, the success of Congress's agitation over natural resource regulations during the 1950s had caused serious disruption of economic life in the rural areas, while throughout the country the most dynamic people were devoting a substantial part of their energy and time to political agitation. This last factor became much less significant after the MCP had joined the government in 1961, but Europeans became more apprehensive, and the relatively modern sectors of the economy suffered badly between 1961 and 1964.

Estimates of money national income show that there was an absolute decline in the total figure during both 1963 and 1964, and since there was, at the same time, a high rate of population increase, the fall in average money income during these two years was probably about 10 per cent. Subsistence income may have risen a little between 1961 and 1964, and although aggregate national income did not rise fast enough to keep pace with the increase in population, the people who lived in the least developed areas—those who were most conservative in both an economic and a political sense—were doing relatively well at this time. This may not have been without significance when Dr. Banda was seeking to mobilize political support against his opponents in the party. Manufacturing and construction, on the other hand, were particularly badly hit, and both output and employment fell sharply. Information about the number of Africans earning wages in Nyasaland at the time is far from precise, but the figures provided by the government statistical office at the time indicate that wage employment fell by more than 20 per cent between 1960 and 1964. At the same time the value of remittances from migrant workers in Rhodesia and South Africa was substantially lower in both 1963 and 1964 than the usual annual amount.[18]

All major cash crops suffered during this period. Tea production, which had made a dramatic rise from 17.5 million pounds in 1955 to 31.5 million in 1961, had fallen back to 27.3 million in both 1963 and 1964; tobacco production, which had reached 43.5 million pounds in 1959, was down to 33.1 million in 1964, one of the lowest outputs recorded since 1953; the output of shelled groundnuts, which had accounted for a substantial part of the increasing export earnings during the 1950s, did rather better since it continued to rise until 1962, but it plunged downward in 1963.[19]

The characteristics of depression were reflected in the reduced provision for education and health. Between 1963 and 1964, a time when enrollment in schools was increasing very rapidly in most countries of Africa, the number of students in Nyasaland schools went down, and entrants to the first year of primary school fell by more than 10 per cent. Annual expenditure on health also fell by more than 10 per cent during the year.[20]

Tension among leading members of the Cabinet built up to crisis proportions with the achievement of independence on 6 July 1964, because this removed one of the principal restraints on Chipembere and his colleagues; opposition to at least some of Dr. Banda's policies or practices could now be expressed without risking the odium that would be visited upon anyone who delayed independence. The slightest dissent could be made public only by men and women willing to challenge Dr. Banda's control over the party and the state, and Chipembere and his colleagues were aware that, after being the principal organizers of the mass party in the late 1950s, they were rapidly being displaced from key positions in the party; even worse

18. *Compendium of Statistics for Malawi, 1970,* table 7.9.

19. *Compendium of Statistics for Malawi, 1965,* tea production, table 56; tobacco production, table 40; groundnuts, table 57.

20. Recorded first-year school enrollment fell from 99.1 hundred in 1963 to 89.2 hundred in 1964; in 1956, it had been 113.9 hundred. Sources: for 1956, *Compendium, 1965,* table 21; 1963 and 1964, *Compendium, 1970,* table 5-1. Recorded expenditure on health is given in *Compendium, 1966,* table 150.

from their point of view was the fact that Dr. Banda had built up a personal network of support and control that was independent of the party organization; his vast powers as head of state and leader of the party were being supplemented by the development of a private, informal structure of control with channels of information and command outside the formal party hierarchy. The Cabinet ministers had never greatly appreciated the prime minister's patronizing references to them, but by the middle of 1964 they had sharper and more profound reasons for dissatisfactions. To be patronized was one thing; to be emasculated something else again. The young radicals had been prepared to see a much older man become president of the party for a few years, but now they had reason to fear that the secondary leadership of the party organization was passing out of their hands. When they first heard the public references to themselves as boys they may have been able to persuade themselves that there was an affectionate, if condescending, intimacy between the grand old man and the much younger and less experienced men whom he saw as his natural successors, but by July 1964 it was becoming apparent that this interpretation was not the one Dr. Banda had in mind. The ministers might have felt when they first took office that, whatever their capabilities, they were indeed short of experience and needed a period of apprenticeship, but by July 1964 several of them had spent three years as senior members of the Executive Council, and had carried out their parliamentary duties with considerable credit, only to find that their period of tutelage was to be of an apparently indefinite duration. Dr. Banda had become more rather than less insistent that he alone would make all decisions and made it clear in the most humiliating terms that he was not under any obligation to consider the views of his subordinates.

So what does a Leader do? When I was negotiating a constitution, before my men knew what I was doing I had finished everything. I said: "well, boys, I've done this, that and that, finished." Even when they were with me in London—Chirwa, Kanyama, Aleke and Chokani—they didn't know what I was doing. I had finished everything before they knew anything about it! Last October they didn't come with me to London. I didn't even take Chirwa, Kanyama and Chipembere—what's the use? I left them back home—I do the work myself. A waste of time, why take them? . . . This kind of thing where a Leader says this, but somebody else says that; now who is the Leader? That is not the Malawi system. The Malawi system, the Malawi style is that Kamuzu says it is just *that,* and then it is finished. Whether anyone likes it or not, that is how it is going to be here. No nonsense, no nonsense. You can't have everybody deciding what to do.[21]

Some of the ministers were, however, well aware that Dr. Banda did not have the authority or prestige at the OAU that he commanded in Malawi, whereas they themselves, kept very much in their place at home, were treated with respect at the OAU, where they felt in tune with, and appreciated by, some of the most articulate and well-known spokesmen among radical pan-Africanists.

At the OAU meeting in Cairo, immediately after independence, Dr. Banda was greatly displeased by what he felt to be the liberties taken by, in particular, Kanyama Chiume, his foreign minister. Determined that there must be no further attempts to upstage him, Banda administered a sharp public rebuke immediately after he returned to Malawi.

You, the common people, are the real Malawi Congress Party. Watch everybody! Even Ministers—and I tell you when they are present, right here. Watch them, everybody! If they do what you do not think is good for the Malawi Congress Party, whether they are Ministers or not, come and tell me. It is your job to see that nothing injures or destroys the Party. Ministers are human beings, you know. . . . I am saying this because I know we have strange funny people here very soon, Ambassadors for this country, Ambassadors for that country, and they will be trying to corrupt people in the Party, and they will be starting with Ministers and Members of the National Assembly.

So I want you to be vigilant. One Party, one Leader, one Government, and no nonsense about it.[22]

The ministers to whom he was alluding were not named, but everyone knew which ones he had in mind. It was a humiliation that must have dispelled any doubts the ministers had about the need to confront Dr. Banda before their power had completely melted away.

21. Short, pp. 202–203.
22. Short, pp. 203–204.

Whether or not Dr. Banda was aware of the full extent of dissatisfaction among his Cabinet ministers, he was not disposed to take unnecessary risks, and he issued instructions for the drafting of preventive detention legislation. These powers had, of course, been available to, and used by, the colonial authorities, but in Malawi the ruling party had the support of all but a handful of the population, so that powers of this sort must have been intended for use against members—presumably prominent ones—of the ruling party itself. There appears to be some doubt as to whether the Cabinet ministers fully understood the urgency of the situation, but its implications were not lost on Colin Cameron, who resigned in protest against the decision to introduce preventive detention in these circumstances.

Differences of opinion over foreign policy were becoming more acute as the government moved much closer to a policy of cooperation with Portugal, but the full extent of Dr. Banda's overtures appear not to have been understood by the ministers at the time. Negotiations had begun on the details of a trade agreement between Malawi and Portugal, and a prominent Portuguese resident in Mozambique, Jorges Jartim, was appointed honorary consul for Malawi in Beira.

Dr. Banda insisted that he would "do a deal with the devil" if it would help the people of Malawi, but he proved unresponsive to a substantial offer of aid made by the People's Republic of China at this time. It was never to become entirely clear why this was so. He later insisted that he had turned the loan down because too many strings were attached to it and because he believed that once the Chinese were able to get a foothold in Malawi it would be very difficult to dislodge them. This outcome, however, was implausible: the Chinese had no base from which to exercise continuing pressure on Malawi, in marked contrast to Portugal and the Republic of South Africa, with whom Dr. Banda was quite willing to enter into agreements. In any event, he appears to have made no serious attempt to find out what conditions were attached to the loan or to engage in any bargaining about its prospective terms. He may have felt that to accept aid from mainland China at that time would have jeopardized his chances of getting assistance from the Western powers on favorable terms, but he has never explained his decision in these terms, and he is not a man who has failed to make a point on other occasions, especially after the event, on the grounds that it would embarrass someone else. The most plausible explanation of his refusal to explore the offer is that Kanyama Chiume had been instrumental in bringing about the preliminary discussions about the prospective arrangement and if negotiations proved successful, people in Nyasaland might have been less disposed to believe that Dr. Banda was the only man in the country able to deal successfully with major foreign powers.

Faced by Dr. Banda's head-on attack, the ministers realized at last that there was little time left for them to prevent the total disintegration of their own power base, but they appear to have been unaware that the threat was not of demotion but of disaster. In mid-August, despite Chipembere's absence in Canada, where he was attending an educational conference, the others confronted Dr. Banda at a Cabinet meeting. The agenda was concerned with the establishment of a university in Malawi, and this might in any event have raised some controversial issues. There was a very real difference of opinion about the rate at which Africanization of the civil service should proceed, because of great disparities within the country in the level and range of educational development: the Chewa of the Central Region, kinsmen of Dr. Banda and one of the strongest bases of popular support for his leadership, had—for a variety of reasons—produced very few secondary-school graduates and had reason to fear that immediate comprehensive Africanization would establish their rivals in senior places in the civil service; similar fears were prevalent in many of the more conservative rural areas from which Dr. Banda drew his support. The Northern Region and the Blantyre and Zomba districts of the Southern Region and perhaps one or two other areas would have benefited from immediate moves to Africanization, because they had a relatively high proportion of secondary-school students and graduates; educated young men and women throughout the country and the majority of African members of the civil service were much in favor of Africanization, but these were the very groups that were, in any event, most keenly attracted to Chipembere, Chiume, and Dunduzu

Chisiza. These issues do not appear to have been raised directly in the Cabinet meeting, but the fact that the participants were almost certainly aware of them may have contributed to the hostile atmosphere.

The ministers expressed dissatisfaction with several aspects of Dr. Banda's policy. At first he gave the impression that he was willing to discuss these matters, but two days later the ministers, perhaps surprised at the extent to which their complaints had apparently been accepted as a basis for discussion, moved on to a more fundamental attack on the way he conducted business and accused him of running the government as his "personal estate."

While he was considering the latter and much more serious set of complaints, Dr. Banda recalled John Msonthi to the Cabinet and announced the postponement of the opening of Parliament, due in early September, until the beginning of October. He had decided to buy time while he mobilized support for a decisive battle. He understood quite well that the ministers, had they but the resolution to match their ambition, were still in a position, collectively, to command the loyalty of more men than he could muster; but he knew, also, that they were divided by petty mutual jealousies and that the one man who had the intellectual and personal force to weld them together—Chipembere—was absent. The ministers thought that they had won a great victory and were completely taken by surprise when Dr. Banda, his own troops now at the ready, recalled Parliament for an emergency sitting to begin on Tuesday, 8 September.[23] The day before it was to meet, he dismissed from the Cabinet four of its members: Bwanausi, Chirwa, Chiume, and Rose Chibambo. A few hours later Yatuta Chisiza and Chokani resigned as a token of support for their colleagues,

23. Short believes that "Banda felt compelled to act or face nationwide unrest" as both the ministers and Dr. Banda's supporters sought to mobilize their strength in the party (pp. 209–210). One cannot be sure exactly when Dr. Banda decided on his course of action but if the timing was accidental rather than, as suggested in this chapter, part of a shrewd and very tough-minded battle plan, then Dr. Banda had remarkable luck. It is not simply that his tactics won the day; it is difficult, even with the benefit of hindsight, to imagine how they could have been improved.

but by then their resignation looked more like an act of despair than an affirmation of solidarity. On the day Chiume was sacked, he sent a telegram to Chipembere in Ottawa and then, with the terms of battle already decisively in Dr. Banda's favor, Chipembere returned—the one man among the ministers who could, perhaps, have won the fight if he had directed its tactics and one who was too honorable a man to abandon his friends when their folly had put the issue beyond recall.

The friends he elected to join had seriously misjudged the nature of the enterprise upon which they were embarked; they behaved, for the most part, like men in pursuit of petty advantage who, when called to account, proved desperately anxious to make it clear that their challenge to authority was merely about trivial matters which could easily be resolved; as a consequence, they were quite unable to present an effective argument in the Legislative Assembly or anywhere else. If the burden of their complaint had been justified, Dr. Banda stood convicted of betraying the spirit and aspirations of the nationalist movement; to insist that they were still loyal to him could only mean that they were concerned not about the issues (on which there was, it would appear, fundamental disagreement) but about the way in which he treated them as individuals. Dr. Banda on the other hand, whether because he had a profound contempt for the personal qualities of his opponents or because he was, by instinct, a man for whom the only alternatives were triumph or disaster, had prepared for a confrontation of a much more fundamental kind. In circumstances which, he must have realized, were not entirely propitious, he elected a savage and uncompromising attack upon his opponents. He adopted a strategy which precluded any chance of compromise; the outcome would be either total victory or total defeat, and in first postponing and then bringing forward the meeting of the Assembly, so that his forces were prepared for battle while his opponents were still not sure whether or not a battle was to be fought at all, he had secured a major tactical advantage.

The two-day debate on 8 and 9 September, was to be the only occasion after independence when there was any suggestion that some Malawian members of Parliament might conceivably take a different view of the national interest from that taken by Dr. Banda. It was the only occasion on which the results of the debate were not entirely predictable, although the prime minister had done everything he could to make sure that the odds were heavily stacked against the dissident ministers. Dr. Banda had prepared his speech with great care. He began in a somber mood:

Mr. Speaker, Sir, it is in deep sorrow and grief that I arise this morning. I arise to speak in sorrow and grief because the four cornerstones on which the Malawi Congress Party, the Government yes, even more—our state, the state of Malawi itself was built, has broken down.

I would rather see those benches empty and myself in the bush, dead, than see the four cornerstones destroyed by anyone. Once there is no unity, no loyalty, no discipline, no obedience we are finished. Just as the Congo. It is finished.[24]

He then provided an account of the meetings which had immediately preceded the recall of Parliament. This version of events made no reference to the astute maneuvering in which he had engaged, but left no doubt about the thoroughly autocratic style of leadership which he believed to be appropriate.

It was that draft Bill to create the University of Malawi that sparked off the smouldering embers of disunity, disloyalty, indiscipline, disobedience which I have noticed on my return from Cairo. As soon as I began talking of that paper my Ministers began to attack me. They all attacked me. I was shocked. I was shocked, Mr. Speaker, because there I was, the Prime Minister, isolated, deserted by everyone of my Ministers. No one tried to support me. Not one of them tried to defend me. They all attacked viciously, violently—and most disrespectfully. I could not believe it was my Ministers speaking to Kamuzu. I just couldn't believe it, Mr. Speaker.

He was attacked on several aspects of government policy, all

24. The two-day debate that was both opened and closed by Dr. Banda took place in the Legislative Assembly on the 8 and 9 September 1964. In previous footnotes and in those subsequent to the account of the debate, the reader may be helped by reference to specific pages of the Proceedings, but in this case the reader intending to pursue or question points made in the text will probably read, if not the entire debate, then at least the speeches of the principal protagonists. In these circumstances, a series of footnotes would be both tedious and irrelevant.

of which, according to Dr. Banda, had been previously agreed upon in the Cabinet: the slow rate of Africanization, the imposition of the "tickey" (three-pence) charge for hospital outpatients, relations with Portugal, and the rejection of the Chinese loan.

Two days later, said Dr. Banda, the ministers broadened the range of their attack and accused him of "running the Government as if it were my personal estate. They accused me of nepotism, favoritism, and they demanded equal and even distribution of Ministries. I must confess I was staggered. I, Kamuzu, practising nepotism, favouritism."

Having presented his account of the events of the past few weeks, he launched into a savage personal assault upon the qualities and credentials of the dissident ministers. Several of them were, he insisted, held in such low regard by the people that the only way in which they had been able to find their way into Parliament was because he, Dr. Banda, had "forced them" on the people. That he should have felt that this was a point in his favor (whether or not it was true) tells us more about his attitude toward the practice of government than anything that the ministers were able to say in reply during the first day of the debate. He dismissed the arguments put forward by the ministers, insisting that they had never voiced any doubts when the policies were being formulated and had shown no objection to accepting the hospitality of the Portuguese. The arguments were, he said, merely a cover for more sinister motives.

"Why all this fuss . . . ambition? Yes. Avarice? Yes. But there is something much deeper." Chiume knew he was unpopular in Malawi so he sought to win friends in other African states by denigrating the prime minister of Malawi; the ministers, he said, thought that Peking China would line their pockets: "I am here to tell you that their smouldering embers of ambition have been fanned to inflame them. . . . It was after they came back from [Dar-es-Salaam] that they demanded immediate recognition of China, now, now, now! But they went further than that. They went further than that. They said the Chinese Ambassador had promised them that if we recognised Peking China now, Peking China would give us 18 million Pounds." Insistence that the ministers were greedy, incompetent, and disrespectful would, no doubt, have been sufficient to justify their dismissal, but would scarcely have satisfied the dramatic requirements of the occasion.

Well, Mr. Speaker, that is the story but I have left out something deliberately—I have told you that I have offered to resign and that they refused to accept my resignation. Why did they refuse? . . . The Ministers wanted to get rid of me. That is a fact. That is the story and if they could have murdered me and got away with it and the people accepted them as leaders, they would have murdered me in cold blood without flinching, and if they knew that they could force me to resign and get away with it by people accepting them they would have done it. But they know very well that they could not get rid of me and get away with it; that they could not murder me and get away with it; they could not force me to resign and get away with it, because the people want me in this country.

The prime minister's speech was, of its type, a masterly performance. It was weak in logic and short on facts but, beginning with an account of muted dissent from his assumption that he was the sole repository of the wisdom of the nation and the only architect of its well-being, he built a tale of perverted ambition and irresponsible avarice, finally presenting the hapless ministers as men who were deterred from murder only because their cowardice was more potent than their lust.

His supporters in the Assembly had come well prepared for the confrontation. They vied with each other in shouting threats and insults at the ministers, vowing their loyalty to the *Ngwazi* (Dr. Banda) and declaring, as though ignorance were the epitome of virtue, that they had never so much as heard of some of the most important matters in dispute.

Chipembere was not able to get back to the country until the evening of the first day's debate and had not been publicly committed in the dispute. In his absence the other ministers had to do as best they could on their own, and they appear to have been completely shattered by Dr. Banda's onslaught. Chisiza protested that it was the duty of members of the Cabinet to explain to the prime minister the feeling of the country as they understood it and that they had done this but had never sought to challenge the personal or constitutional authority of Dr. Banda. Within its limited terms it was an honorable speech and a good deal better than most of the ministers were able to produce but, like the others, Chisiza made no sustained attempt to argue the case for policies different from those the government had been following, far less to suggest that there might be any constraints imposed on Dr. Banda's authority. Perhaps the ministers felt that, having been so comprehensively outmaneuverd, the only sensible tactic was to play for time; to avoid, if they could, any more direct a confrontation than had already been forced on them, to mobilize their own support in the constituencies, and to come back to fight another day. The impression they gave, however, was one of irresolution and confusion.

As soon as Chipembere arrived back at Zomba he received a message from Dr. Banda urging him to remain a member of the Cabinet but, although the relationship between the two men was closer to one of mutual respect than that between the prime minister and any of the other members of his cabinet, Chipembere took the view that he was already committed to his colleagues. He did, however, attempt to arrange a meeting between Dr. Banda and the dissident ministers only to be rebuffed by Dr. Banda, who said that it was too late for such a compromise.[25]

When, on the following morning, Chipembere rose to speak from the back benches where he had joined the other former ministers, he began by telling members of the Assembly that he had hoped that a reconciliation could have been arranged before irreparable damage was done. He deplored the breakdown of discipline as much as Dr. Banda did but he put it into a different perspective.

It gives me a heavy heart that Malawi, which was so proud of its unity, so famous for its stability; that Malawi, which people were regarding as a paragon of political organisation and discipline and understanding, has now broken down. Broken down to the extent of the members of one party, the mighty Malawi Congress Party, attacking one another in public here, in the presence of . . . our former enemies, calling one another traitors. Wherever Welensky is today, he must be rejoicing. He must be celebrating. There must be a cocktail party

25. Short, p. 213.

somewhere in Salisbury as a result of what is taking place here. We are in utter disgrace.

Chipembere wanted no one to doubt that he had done what he could to heal the rift in the party. "Let it be recorded in history, for all posterity, that I did make an effort to have this thrashed out before public denunciation." When this effort failed, he had no honorable alternative but to stand with the former ministers:

I would like nobody to believe that I am an outsider in this matter. I was a member of a group of Ministers that approached the Prime Minister to begin with. Although certain things have taken place in my absence, on fundamental matters of principle I was present; everything began when I was here. So nobody should regard me as a man who is not involved. I am together with my friends. I was a participant in the delegation that went for the first time to see the Prime Minister, to approach him asking him to consider the possibility of making certain changes in the system of running of this country.

He reviewed the careers of those who had been savagely attacked in the Assembly; they had all, he said, rendered great service to their people and to the party, but this had been forgotten and they were now being described as traitors. He appealed to members to see beyond the passions of the moment; history, he said, would be their judge.

He went on to say he believed that the approach made by the dissident ministers to Dr. Banda was that of sincere men who had done what they believed to be in the interest of the country and, indeed, of Dr. Banda himself. They were genuinely concerned about matters of policy and about aspects of the way in which Dr. Banda was running the government and the party.

The former ministers feared, he said, that the policy of accommodation with Portugal was being carried further than was necessary for the protection of Malawi's essential economic interests. Chipembere acknowledged that he and his colleagues had attended some parties given for the Portuguese, but only because they did not wish to let their leader down; they had always felt in their hearts that it was wrong to fraternize with the Portuguese. What would Malawians have thought if, in 1959, Nyerere had given a cocktail party for Welensky; the

Malawians had themselves "boycotted a delegation from Nigeria because it fraternized with the Federal Government."

Chipembere said that it was most unfortunate that Dr. Banda should give as much credence as he did to the "reports" of informers about men and women who had served their country and their party well. One of the requests made by the ministers had been, he said, that Dr. Banda should not "listen to every allegation that one man in the Malawi Congress Party makes against another . . . [and] of late . . . a number of people, innocent people, have been attacked or denounced [by Dr. Banda] in public, Anonymous letters should not form the basis of policy." At the very least, a man or woman against whom accusations had been made should have the right to confront his or her accusers.

When the former ministers had been on their way to the Assembly for the debate now taking place they had been cheered by the Zomba crowds, and Chipembere referred to "the crowd which is cheering outside" as evidence that "there is a strong feeling in favour of the point of view of the Ministers." He said, "The clapping [proves] what we say, the complaint we have submitted to the Ngwazi, comes from the people."

There was no dispute about the fact that people in Zomba had aligned themselves behind the former ministers. Dr. Banda himself referred in his closing speech to "all the shouts outside this House and clapping of hands outside there when the ex-Ministers walked out of here," and said that while it would gladden the hearts of Welensky and his followers as well as those foreign journalists who had been writing that Chipembere and Chiume were the real rulers of the country, it would not frighten him.

Chipembere's speech was, without question, the outstanding performance of the second day. Cool and coherent, Chipembere was neither afraid nor spoiling for a fight. The speech did not, however, seek to provide a distinct alternative to the policies pursued by the prime minister; there were differences in points of emphasis rather than about fundamentals, and the speech dealt more with what Chipembere feared might happen in the future than with what he was prepared to claim had actually been done by Dr. Banda. As it turned out, Chipembere had more cause for concern about the direction of foreign policy than he appreciated at the time. Dr. Banda was later to say that "near our Independence, 1963, high Portuguese officials and businessmen began to come and see me secretly. I can reveal this now. Yes! Secretly." On another occasion he was to boast that the former ministers "rebelled against me because I was getting friendly with South Africa, Rhodesia, Mozambique."[26] In 1964, Dr. Banda was more discreet, and Chipembere had little hard evidence to support his argument that accommodation with Portugal had gone too far. In any case, Chipembere seemed unable or unwilling to follow his argument to its logical conclusion, so perhaps it would not have made a great deal of difference if more evidence had been available.

Whether it was due to Chipembere's moderate tone or to the considerably more strident tone of the Zomba crowd, the violence of Assembly speeches directed against the former ministers abated on the second day and, indeed, when Dr. Banda wound up the debate he did so with the appearance of moderation and forgiveness—the headmaster obliged, against his wishes, to chastise some errant pupils. Forgotten, it seemed, were the charges that the ministers would have murdered him if only they had been bold enough, and a number of foreign observers believed that Dr. Banda had decided on a policy of reconciliation, although that view was not widely shared in Malawi.

The ministers immediately went to their constituencies and did what they could, rather late in the day, to muster support. Dr. Banda appointed five new Cabinet ministers and replaced Chirwa as attorney general with a European, Bryan Roberts, who had been a government servant. Several posts, including the one formerly held by Chipembere, were left vacant. As both sides appealed for support in the country, the lines hardened still further. Chipembere was reported as saying that Banda's government was worse than that of Welensky, and Banda described the former ministers as "hyenas in the night." On 15 September, six of the former ministers and Rose Chi-

26. The first point was made in the Assembly on 23 April 1969, p. 376; the second on 20 Nov. 1969, p. 220.

bambo were suspended from the party; charges and counter-
charges were made in an atmosphere of mounting hysteria,
and the faint hope of a reconciliatory gesture which had been
possible while Chipembere's post remained unfilled was stifled
when John Msonthi was moved to that position.

Dr. Banda left Zomba to tour the Central and Northern Regions toward the end of September but banned all public meetings and processions in the Southern Region unless the organizers had obtained police permission; the ban meant, of
course, that Dr. Banda's opponents would not be allowed to
hold meetings. Despite this, there was violence in Blantyre,
Zomba, and Fort Johnston, with the former ministers receiving
a good deal of popular support. Troops had to be brought in
to maintain control and restriction orders were issued against a
number of people, Chipembere among them.

Dr. Banda had the considerable advantage of controlling the
party organization (especially the Young Pioneers and League
of Youth, who were used as storm troops during this period)
and the even greater one that, as head of government, he could
call upon the white-officered army and police forces. He also
had some important sources of support among the general
populace. The Chewa, his own tribal group, were numerous
and, for the most part, poorly educated. They were not in favor
of rapid Africanization because that would have led to the dominance of other tribal groups, especially Northerners, among
whom the advantages of modern education had been more widespread: they feared that the Northerners might have proved far
more difficult to displace than Europeans, who accepted the
temporary nature of their positions in the government.

The very success of Chipembere and his colleagues in appealing to the young, educated, mobile men and women with a
"modern" orientation made them suspect to the more traditional social groups which would, in any event, have favored
Dr. Banda on grounds of seniority. Dr. Banda could also expect support from an important group among the educated
young men: those who were anxious to make a political career
for themselves doubtless found the prospect of a return to
power by the former ministers a forbidding one, because every
position of importance was held by men only a few years older

than they themselves, and, saving acts of God or political turmoil, they could be expected to stay in power for thirty years or more.

The former ministers, particularly Chipembere, had considerable support in the country but they were unable to overcome the advantages in Dr. Banda's favor. Some of the ministers left the country, and one made an abortive attempt to achieve a reconciliation with Dr. Banda, appealing for "mercy and forgiveness"[27] before fleeing, but Chipembere remained in his stronghold in the Fort Johnston area, where government forces were unable or unwilling to track him down.

The party was subjected to a drastic purge. Three out of five MCP district councils in the Northern Region were dissolved, in the Southern Region six out of ten were dissolved, and in both regions several chiefs were deposed or disciplined.

Young Pioneers were able to embark upon a reign of terror which, since Dr. Banda was the head of government, went completely unchecked by army and police; unless the police had first received personal permission from the president, they were, indeed, forbidden from taking action against Young Pioneers for any offense. The police were, of course, likely to be called in if any prospective victims of the Young Pioneers were able to fight back successfully.

The Young Pioneers Amendment Bill was introduced to Parliament on 10 November 1965, the same day that Parliament received a bill providing for public executions. Dr. Banda said that there had been, "to put it mildly, a misunderstanding between the police and the Young Pioneers," and the police had released people arrested by the pioneers. Dr. Banda had ordered their rearrest and was determined there should be no further misunderstanding. "The Young Pioneers cannot be arrested by any policeman without my consent. . . . If a Young Pioneer arrests anybody . . . and brings them to the police station, the police officer in charge of that station must not release them . . . if he does release them, he is committing a crime."[28]

In October a special Party Conference endorsed the reintro-

27. Short, p. 223.
28. *Legislative Assembly* (Zomba: Government Printer), 10 Nov. 1965, p. 263.

duction of preventive detention and heard Dr. Banda insist that "every man and woman will have to be taught how to use a gun . . . even a machine gun." "Vigilance" was to be the order of the day, and the most slender suspicion would justify savage treatment by party members or supporters of people believed to be sympathetic to the dissident ministers.

In February of the following year, Chipembere's supporters around Fort Johnston, who had been successfully defying the government for several months, attacked the administrative center at Fort Johnston and then moved down the road to Zomba. They presumably expected to cross the Shire River at Liwonde by ferry boat, but the boat was on the other side of the river when they arrived, and they had neglected to provide other means of crossing. The rebels retreated, providing no answer to the question that Dr. Banda triumphantly asked: if Chipembere was "a determined man, as he pretends to be, why did he not simply change his route?" He could, said Banda, have attempted to "come to Zomba and assassinate me and my ministers by way of Blantyre."[29] Instead, the rebel forces appear to have lost their nerve; within a few days four hundred known or suspected supporters of Chipembere were taken prisoner.

Although there were several other rebel attacks in various parts of the country which led to some loss of life on both sides, there was no significant rebel success. Chipembere remained in the country for several months, having enough support in his home area to prevent information of his whereabouts reaching the security forces. Even Dr. Banda acknowledged that there were "a number . . . that he really trusts, and they will not betray him,"[30] but all except a small band of committed men and women were seeking to make their peace with the government. G. E. Ndema, the member of parliament for Zomba South, clearly conscious of the widespread feeling that the people of Zomba had supported Chipembere, insisted to the Assembly that this feeling was a misunderstanding and that the great majority deeply deplored attempts to "train civil servants

29. *Legislative Assembly,* 6 April 1965, p. 505.
30. *Legislative Assembly,* 6 April 1965, p. 508.

to fight against the government." It was claimed that in Zomba alone, within a matter of two weeks, some £3,000 had been contributed to party funds—far more than had ever been received before the rebellion.

New security regulations were introduced which, among other things, provided for seven years in prison for anyone consorting with, harboring, or giving sustenance to a rebel. In April, following a fight between young pioneers and a band of rebels who had crossed the border from Tanzania, the death penalty was made mandatory for treason, and treason itself became a very loosely defined offense. Talking to Parliament about the penalties for attempts to overthrow the government, Dr. Banda said: If he even just thinks about it and speaks aloud and somebody hears it, that's treason. He doesn't have to march at all; if he thinks about, talks to others about it . . . no-one should be left in doubt now about what treason is."[31]

It is unlikely that anyone in Malawi could have been in doubt as to what Dr. Banda meant, but no one could have failed to understand the next speaker, N. Mwambungu of Karonga North. "A whisper which would lead to the breakdown of the Malawi government will," he said, "be treated as treason."

Members of the Assembly were well aware that there would be no more debates that would offer any opportunity to question the wisdom of Dr. Banda's policies, and they were anxious to leave no doubt that they approved the constraint. As one member of the Assembly put it: "The coming of members to the Parliament to pass laws is just a formality, otherwise *Ngwazi* himself is enough to make laws for us. We happen to be here, Mr. Speaker, just to fulfil the procedure of making laws."[32]

31. *Legislative Assembly,* 12 April 1965, p. 641.
32. G. E. Ndema, the member for Zomba South. Malawi *Hansard,* 12 April 1965, p. 642.

CHAPTER 7

The Machinery of Control: Politics, Economic Opportunity, and the Law

> We are here to govern, at least I am.
>
> Dr. Banda, 2 December 1970

> Strangely, there was no picture of Dr. Osbong in the bar. He was the President of Malawi. It was against the law not to have his picture in a conspicuous place in every building in the country.
>
> Paul Theroux, *The Jungle Lovers*

Malawi became a republic on 6 July 1966, and the Malawi Congress Party was officially recognized as the only political party allowed in the country. Under the terms of the new constitution, which had been presented to the annual conference of the party in October 1965, the first president was to be elected by the Assembly—and Dr. Banda had been duly elected in May 1966. Thereafter there was to be a two-stage process for the election of a president. A national electoral college, with the same membership as the annual party conference, would select a candidate whose name would be presented to the nation by referendum. If a majority of voters supported the party's candidate, that person would be declared elected; if a majority voted to reject the candidate, the electoral college would put forward another nominee, and so on, until a candidate was found who could command a favorable vote. Elections for the presidency were to take place every five years or at such time as the Assembly was dissolved, if sooner.

There was to be no vice-president. If the president were too ill to carry out his duties, he could appoint a committee of three ministers to act in his place; in the event of the president's death, the secretary-general of the party and two ministers would take charge until a new president could be appointed. All parliamentary candidates were required to be members of the MCP; loss of party membership meant immediate loss of membership in the Assembly, and any member who voted against the government on a motion of confidence would immediately forfeit his seat in the Assembly. The Assembly would normally be dissolved every five years, but dissolution would also occur if the government were to be defeated on a motion of no confidence, or if the president twice refused assent to a bill approved by the Assembly.

Dr. Banda already had virtually unlimited discretionary powers with respect to party membership, and the new constitution allowed him to remove immediately any member of Parliament whose loyalty appeared questionable. The exercise of this power might have aroused sympathy for the dismissed member, and even though the sympathy would be unlikely to lead to any effective action on the member's behalf, it might, if circumstances changed, be recalled—in his (or her) favor—that he (she) had found the courage to stand against the president. The government's extensive powers were, accordingly, supplemented by an ingenious ruling. If any member failed "to retain the confidence and support of a majority of the voters in the constituency where he was elected," the voters would have the right to petition the president, asking him to intercede on their behalf; a committee would be sent to investigate the complaint and report to the president, who was, in turn, to report to the Central Executive of the party and, when appropriate, the member could be dismissed from the Assembly.[1] In practice this procedure gave the president complete discretion in the examination and interpretation of evidence and the assessment of its implications. Neither the terms of the complaint nor the names of the complainants (or even their number) were required to be released; there was no specified procedure for investigating the complaint or of finding out how many people were dissatisfied with the member; no criteria were laid down

1. *Legislative Assembly,* 17 May 1966, pp. 550–551.

to indicate, even very roughly, how various sorts of offenses should be weighted and whether the usual response to a given type of offense would be a reprimand, suspension, dismissal, or whatever; there was no procedure that would enable the accused member to examine the case against him or to allow either the member himself or any of his constituents to appeal against any decision that the president might make. This provision, whatever its intention, in effect permitted the president to remove at will any member of Parliament who no longer commanded his confidence, while insisting that he was simply responding to the wishes of his people.[2]

The new constitution enabled the president both to handpick members of Parliament and to remove them at will if they did not come up to expectations. Members themselves were under no illusions about their position and publicly acknowledged their complete dependence on Dr. Banda. It became common practice for members of Parliament making their maiden speeches to offer profuse thanks to the president for the honor he had done them when he appointed them to the Assembly. More than a few of them, determined to make their loyalty evident, launched into ecstatic eulogies on the president's character, capacity, and achievements.

When Gwengwe, the member for Lilongwe East, rose to deliver his maiden speech, he understood what was expected of him, and what he said brought the expected applause: "Mr. Speaker, I desire with all sincerity to thank His Excellency, Ngwazi Dr. Kamuzu Banda, Life President of Malawi Congress Party, Life President of the Republic of Malawi, the great and beloved political Redeemer of Malawi on behalf of Lilongwe

2. Some observers have taken a most charitable view of this measure. Philip Short, for example, says that it was introduced to compensate the people of the country for loss of other political rights and thus it reflected Dr. Banda's awareness "of the dangers of so completely removing the element of choice from the electorate" (*Banda,* p. 265). The new law provided *no* sanction that could be imposed by a majority of constituents against an unsatisfactory representative and that went beyond the very meager power already available to them (and available in even the most authoritarian states). They could, if they dared, assert that they did not hold their representative in high regard; they had no power—even if 90 per cent were agreed—to insist that the representative be changed.

and the country as a whole." He went on, to laughter and more applause:

I thank His Excellency for nominating me as his candidate for Lilongwe East Constituency. Needless to say, Mr. Speaker, I was returned unopposed on the 28 October 1967 . . . and that is why I am here. Mr. Speaker, Sir, to this end, I have nothing materially which I could show to his Excellency as a token of appreciation for what he has done for me and therefore I will try to show it in a very few words by saying—"a hundredfold of thanks to His Excellency the President of the Republic of Malawi." Through you, Mr. Speaker, I am profoundly indebted to the President and grateful for the wonderful honour which I know I don't deserve but will long be remembered by me."[3]

Gwenge's colleague from Lilongwe West also spoke for the first time in that debate and he was no less determined to show that he was fully acquainted with the duties of a parliamentarian:

Mr. Speaker, Sir, I would like to express my true and sincere gratitude to His Excellency the President, Dr. Kamuzu Banda, for making me Member of Parliament for Lilongwe West. I am really very happy now to be under the Ngwazi's sphere of influence. . . . Mr. Speaker, Sir, I am unable to find suitable words to express my happiness to the Ngwazi, the greatest son Africa has ever produced. There are many things that make our Leader great in Malawi here, in Africa as a whole, and of course, in all countries that matter under the Sun. [Applause.] Here, Mr. Speaker, allow me to name only a few of the things that make our Leader, the Lion of Malawi, the greatest man: (1) He is an upright Christian gentleman; (2) He is a most courageous man; (3) He is the greatest humanitarian; (4) He is the greatest scholar and historian; (5) He is the greatest nation builder Malawi has ever had; (6) He is the greatest orator in Malawi if not in the World [Applause]; (7) He is the greatest teacher. If I have to elaborate this, Mr. Speaker, allow me to do so.

Under the terms of the 1964 constitution there was to have been a general election in 1969. When the country became a republic in 1966, it was decided that the parliamentary elections should be postponed so that they would coincide with the

3. *Legislative Assembly*, 30 Jan. 1968, p. 255. The speech which follows in the text is reported on p. 248 of the Assembly proceedings.

election for the presidency in 1971. As things worked out, there was no election for the presidency. Pachai has described the annual convention of the MCP at Mzuzu in September 1970, where the delegates "resolved unanimously that Ngwazi Dr. Kamuzu Banda was the people's choice for the office of President and demanded that the Constitution of the Republic of Malawi be amended to provide for Ngwazi Dr. Kamuzu Banda to be President for his life time."[4] In accordance with this directive, the constitution was amended by Parliament in December 1970.

For several powerful and quite obvious reasons this arrangement appealed to Dr. Banda, but some of his supporters put forward rather more esoteric reasons for approving the resolution. A. S. Chimphanje, the member for Lilongwe North, said that when Dr. Banda had returned to Malawi, defied the colonial and federal governments and led his people to independence, he had won a victory as remarkable as that of David over Goliath. David, he went on, had been given great rewards in recognition of the benefits that his valor and skill had won for his countrymen; the Malawian people believed, he said, that Dr. Banda should be similarly honored for his great services to his country, but to have offered him a sum of money, however large, would not have met the case, because "he is already, Mr. Speaker, Sir, a millionaire."[5]

The formal terms under which the parliamentary elections were to be held reflected the fact that Malawi was a one-party state; in its actual practice the election served as yet another demonstration of the almost unlimited range of Dr. Banda's personal power. The number of constituencies was to be increased (from fifty to sixty), and in addition to the five Europeans already nominated by the president, there were to be ten Africans who would not represent constituencies but would be nominated solely on the president's discretion. With respect to other members, formal provision was made for some expression of popular views, since there was to be a conference in each district, consisting of representatives of the Malawi Con-

4. Quoted by Pachai, *Malawi*, p. 245.
5. *Legislative Assembly*, 20 July 1971, p. 30.

gress Party, the Women's League, the Youth League, the District Councils, Native Authorities, Chiefs and Sub-Chiefs.

These conferences were to bring together representatives from the entire district and were to choose candidates from the district as a whole to represent particular constituencies. The official explanation was that unscrupulous candidates would find it more difficult to buy support in a district than in an individual constituency, with a smaller area and lower population: "A lot of men can buy all these local people—but it is not easy to buy the whole district," said Dr. Banda.[6] The larger grouping also meant that the local support that a member of Parliament from a good constituency might be able to build up, even if he were considered a little unreliable on national matters, would be dissipated in the larger and more diffuse district committees.

Each district conference was to submit the names of three, four, or five candidates for each constituency and Dr. Banda would then make his choice from among them. If any district put forward a candidate of whom the president disapproved, but who had not been sufficiently conspicuous to lose his party membership, the mistake could be rectified promptly, privately, and in circumstances that allowed no possibility of appeal. To guard against the unlikely event that some committees (thinking they could force the president's hand) might nominate only one man, Dr. Banda made it clear that he would be under no obligation in these circumstances to accept the nomination and that he would have the most severe reservations about all those who had forwarded it. "I will be suspicious, and I will hesitate to confirm him. It so happens that I can keep the whole thing indefinitely, I don't have to confirm anybody. I am giving warning now." Members of Parliament interjected: "We are forewarned, Sir," but Dr. Banda asked, "Is that clear?" "Yes, Sir," was the reply.[7]

There was no shortage of advice to prospective candidates from Cabinet ministers anxious to ensure that they, at least, would win the president's approval. Before Parliament broke up, Chibambo, the minister for the Northern Region, told re-

6. Ibid., 16 March 1971, p. 1104.
7. Ibid.

tiring members that if they were not chosen for the new Parliament, it would be "because there is something wrong that you have done, and that is why you have not come back, because Ngwazi would like his men to be with him who have been loyal to him."[8] and Muwalo, the minister of state in the president's office, advised members not to cause trouble if they found that they were not selected as candidates for the next Parliament. They would, he said, find instructions waiting for them when they returned home after the end of this Parliament and they should follow these out loyally.[9]

The constitution was changed in the same year to give the president still greater powers to determine unilaterally the membership of the Assembly. Until 1968 the president had been able to select a maximum of three Cabinet ministers who were not members of the Assembly; the limitation was removed in 1968, and by 1970 more than half of the members of the Cabinet (seven out of thirteen) were nominated from outside the Assembly. In that same year the constitution was amended to enable the president to nominate fifteen nonconstituency members of the Assembly, and in July 1971 another constitutional amendment provided that ministers who had not been elected to the assemblies would become members by virtue of their Cabinet position. This meant that Dr. Banda, besides having control over M.P.s by virtue of his position in the party hierarchy, and besides being able both to appoint and dismiss constituency members of the Assembly, was now able to add some thirty nonconstituency representatives to the Assembly (that is, the fifteen nominated members plus members of the Cabinet).

The right to nominate members, especially in the Cabinet, who had no connection with the constituencies was not without advantage to Dr. Banda. An elected member of the Assembly was not expected to reflect views of his constituents which were critical of the government, but he was expected to spend a good deal of time in his constituency, talking to the people, presenting the government's case in as sympathetic a light as possible, and eliciting as much popular support for Dr. Banda

8. *Legislative Assembly,* 15 March 1971, p. 1039.
9. Ibid., p. 1049.

as was consistent with the government's ruthless suppression of dissent. Some ministers had been so unpopular that the only conceivable benefit to anyone occasioned by their visits to their constituencies was the exercise gained by their constitutents, who (in some cases, quite literally) chased them out again. Dr. Banda had his own, usually very effective, means of dealing with popular disapproval but he did not court unpopularity unnecessarily, and ministers whose presence in the Assembly was valuable but who were known to be detested by their constituents were well accommodated by this new amendment. At least two other objects were served by the amendment. Some of Dr. Banda's ministers would have found it difficult to attend to their constituencies and still find time to do justice to their ministerial duties; others could manage both tasks but for that very reason might have aroused suspicion in the president's mind that they were establishing a stronger personal political base than he was prepared to tolerate.

The powers of the president to control the political life of the nation, both by virtue of his formal constitutional position and by virtue of his almost total power to direct the machinery of the party, were supplemented by comprehensive control over almost all forms of economic activity, with extensive discretionary powers in his own hands.

The president frequently identified the four "fronts" in the "war on economic inviolability." These were agriculture, business, tourism, and labor. Measures put forward, then and subsequently, to prosecute the "war" gave the government extensive powers not merely to regulate the economy and to significantly affect the terms on which economic activity was conducted but to determine unilaterally whether particular individuals might engage in business at all. These powers of government extended to businesses with only four or five employees and, ultimately, to every person who owned or rented land. The government's power in these matters was unconstrained by rights of appeal or by any requirement to give reasons for its decisions. Whatever the intention of the series of bills passed by the Assembly, their principal effect was to permit the government to provide patronage on a huge scale to its supporters and apply swingeing economic sanctions against anyone whose loyalty was suspect.

The development of monopoly control in the domestic market has been greatly facilitated by extensive licensing arrangements which cover even very small enterprises: no one, for example, is allowed to employ five men (or more) producing shoes unless he has first obtained a license from the government, and this license may be withdrawn at any time if, in the opinion of the relevant minister, the license-holder has abused his position. There is no right of appeal against the minister's decision nor is the government required to provide any explanation of its decision.[10]

A joint arrangement between an expatriate company and the government, with the government owning a substantial proportion, though not necessarily more than half, of the share capital, provided one principal instrument of government control; the government's powers as shareholder were most powerfully supplemented by comprehensive discretionary power to decide the terms on which the company could do business or whether, indeed, it could do any business in Malawi at all.

The National Trading Company was set up as a partnership between the private firm of Bookers and the Malawi Development Corporation (MDC) with the ostensible purpose of assisting Malawians to enter business by providing them with relatively easy and simple access to credit. It was subsequently felt that this arrangement had not given sufficient power to the government, and the government-owned State Trading Company was established, which, it was said, would be able to provide more effective assistance to potential and actual African businessmen through its substantial discretionary powers to affect the volume and composition of imports.[11]

10. See, for example, the speech by John Tembo, *Legislative Assembly*, 15 April 1969, p. 281. The absence of provision for appeal is common to virtually all government measures, and other specific examples will be referred to later in the chapter.

11. The establishment of the partnership was discussed at some length by the president in the *Legislative Assembly*, on 19 Dec. 1968, pp. 155ff. On several occasions comments indicated that the partnership was not working out in an entirely satisfactory manner, but it was never explained clearly what went wrong. John Tembo's speech in the *Legislative Assembly*, on 29 July 1970, pp. 521ff., alluded to a number of problems without clarifying the critical issues. The president launched a sharp attack on Bookers in March of the following year: see next footnote.

The ease with which the agreement with Bookers was dissolved provides a clear illustration of the nature of the government's discretionary powers. Dr. Banda told the Assembly that the company had thought that it could use its partnership with the government as a "shield behind which to hide in raising their prices."[12] He warned all companies that had entered into partnership arrangements with the MDC that their position would be continually under review by the government; the government made no attempt to substantiate the charges against Bookers, and no members of the Assembly showed any interest in hearing the evidence. Whether or not Bookers was guilty of the behavior ascribed to it, the incident demonstrated that any company in similar circumstances would be under considerable pressure to do whatever was necessary to maintain the goodwill of the president, and that without it nothing could save the company's position in Malawi.

Several oil companies had been operating retail businesses in Malawi for a number of years when a local company was established, with the MDC holding a substantial interest; the government became a partner in the Malawi enterprises of Carlsberg brewery, Whitehead textiles, and Gilbey and Mathieson, the distillers; the Commercial Bank of Malawi was set up by the MDC in concert with a Portuguese banking firm and later the government entered into partnership with the expatriate banks, Barclays and Standard, to form the National Bank of Malawi.

The National Insurance Company was established in 1970; the government was to hold a majority of the shares, but the hope was expressed that insurance companies already active in Malawi would also contribute some of the share capital. In case the management of the companies involved had failed to understand what was expected of them, they were reminded that no business could operate in Malawi without a license and that the government could unilaterally withdraw a license without explanation.

An amendment to the Insurance Act, passed in December of the same year, provided that the power to refuse or revoke the

12. *Legislative Assembly,* 16 March 1971, p. 1105.

license of insurance companies to operate in Malawi was transferred from the registrar of insurance, a civil servant, to the minister responsible for insurance. All companies then operating in Malawi, several of which had obtained their licenses during the days of federation, were required to reregister. "Each application," said A. K. Banda, moving the amendment, "will be considered on its merits." He also told members that registration might be refused "because of various reasons or on the grounds of the National Interest."[13]

Members of Parliament were told by the minister that they would be under an illusion if they imagined, as some speeches suggested they did, that government control of the insurance business would enable members to obtain insurance at uneconomically low or deferred rates, but the criteria for acceptability of foreign companies were vague. Those that made "substantial contributions to the development of the country obviously are likely to be looked on more favorably than others which do not meet these conditions." When the National Insurance Company had been set up in July 1970, it was said that the law covering the sale of insurance was to be carefully examined to ensure that there would be adequate protection for the public against the activities of "persuasive but disreputable" companies, and that henceforth "all Ministries, Government Departments and Statutory Bodies will have to show cause why they are not insuring, or should not insure whatever they are insuring, with the new Insurance Company." The law was designed, members were told, to provide for the "protection of our people and for the survival and success of the new company."[14]

In debate on the Business Licensing Amendment Bill in December 1970, Michael Blackwood, the leader of the nominated European members, said that he appreciated that the government might wish to give directions about the running of businesses but suggested that if there were some form of appeal to a recognized and impartial body, justice would not only be done, but would be seen to be done. In reply, J. W. Gwengwe, minister for Trade and Industry, assured members that there

13. *Legislative Assembly,* 2 Dec. 1970, p. 782.
14. *Legislative Assembly,* 28 July 1970, p. 497.

was no need for such an appeal procedure, because "I take very very great consideration of each and every point for cancellation of licences."[15]

In July 1971 the government introduced an Automative Trades Registration and Fair Practices Bill, after frequent and vociferous allegations by members of Parliament and others that privately owned garages were providing services of poor quality at high cost. A system for reporting and investigating complaints was set up which, once again, left the matter in the hands of the appropriate minister, who had virtually unlimited discretionary powers, with no obligation to publish the evidence or explain his decision, and against whose decision there was no appeal to an independent body.

Once again, Blackwood was sympathetic about the government's intention but felt that there was a danger that the legislation would damage business confidence. There was already, he said, a formidable range of weapons to use against businessmen guilty of improper practices, and the best garage-owners might be discouraged from undertaking the investment necessary to provide a good service if they feared that their "licence may vanish" at any time. He went on to say that although he had complete confidence in the way these matters would be handled by the government, the fact that there was no provision for appeal might give rise to unwarranted suspicion on the part of people not so familiar with the government's record.

A. K. Banda, replying for the government, professed himself satisfied that honest men had nothing to fear from the government. He went on to say: "The Honourable leader of the Non African members should by now accredit the Government, certainly His Excellency the President and his Ministers, with good sense and fair judgement in most of these cases, if not all of these cases."[16] Members of the Assembly were under no misunderstanding about their position; no one suggested that if the minister's decisions were right, the government should have nothing to fear from an impartial review board.

Under the terms of another government bill, Asian traders

15. *Legislative Assembly,* 2 Dec. 1972, p. 796.
16. *Legislative Assembly,* 22 July 1971. Blackwood's point is reported on p. 164; the quotation from A. K. Banda is given on p. 177.

had been required to leave the rural areas, where trading was to be reserved for Africans, and confine their activities to urban areas and administrative centers. Nevertheless, the government was not satisfied that Asians and certain other traders fully appreciated the extent to which they depended on the good will of the president, and issued a warning that if the relevant minister was convinced that any trader was abusing his position, his license would be withdrawn; Dr. Banda went out of his way to make it clear that there would be "no appeal to anybody."[17]

It was not only in the modern and intermediate sectors of the economy that the government acquired the power to dispossess, without either warning or negotiation, whoever was contravening the president's view of the national interest. The great majority of Malawians work on the land, and since his first assumption of office, Dr. Banda has spoken frequently of the need to improve the quality of agricultural practice. There was very proper concern about the extent to which traditional methods of shifting cultivation and communal ownership may have engendered a casual attitude toward regeneration of the soil; since traditional practices governing land tenure may have encouraged farmers to exhaust the natural qualities of the soil and then move on to fresh land.

The Malawi Land Bill, presented to the Assembly in April 1965, provided the government with extensive powers of control of the use and ownership of much of the land. The president's exposition of the powers in the hands of the minister was not entirely clear, but the main lines of the bill were not at all obscure. There were three classes of land in Malawi: public, private, and customary. With respect to customary land, as the president explained, "the Minister is given power to lease that land, to assign the land, to anyone who applies for private ownership under lease . . . [and] in some cases, under sale. . . . But once that land has been leased to anyone, it becomes private property and no one has any right to interfere with that land at all."[18] However, "no one" did not include the minister:

17. *Legislative Assembly,* 17 March 1970, p. 238.
18. *Legislative Assembly,* 12 April 1965, p. 655.

"Then once the land is assigned, still the minister retains power. He has the power, he can take it back; he can control it."

If land was leased, the minister would have the power to increase the rent at any time, and he would be under no obligation to take into consideration improvements made on land by individual tenants; anyone encroaching or trespassing on occupied land belonging to a private owner or to the government would be committing an offense. The minister would have the power to tell every private owner of land, whether or not it had formerly been customary land, how he would use that land.

The president insisted that the minister's powers were very similar to those that had formerly been exercised by the colonial authorities. It is a little bizarre that the leader of an independent country should seek to justify behavior on the grounds that it resembles that of a former, foreign, government and an alien race, whose power rested starkly on the right of conquest. But under the colonial regime, there was provision for appeal against rulings by the governor-general, and it was possible, if not of widespread practical import, to take the case to higher authorities, over which the governor-general had little influence. In Malawi no minister would act without first consulting Dr. Banda, and there was no appeal of any sort against the president's decision.

Under the terms of a subsequent act, the minister was empowered to declare that any part of the country was a development area, and all land in the area would then come under the direct supervision of the government. Anyone wishing to acquire land in a development area had to make application to the government, and the matter would be considered personally by Dr. Banda.[19]

19. *Legislative Assembly,* 4 April 1967, and 28 March 1968, pp. 383ff. A tangential point relating to the compulsory acquisition of land in other circumstances may be found in, for example, the *Legislative Assembly* discussion of a bill for that purpose. Chidzanja, the minister of agriculture and natural resources, commenting on the government's power to order the demolition of appropriate buildings and its refusal to allow any appeal against its decision, said: "If we let these matters go into the courts, the court people don't know what they are talking about; they are talking on the things they read in the papers [laughter]. The Minister is well informed before he takes action" (pp. 29–30).

Acknowledging the immense powers this gave him, Dr. Banda explained that "because of my experience in [Ghana], I won't let anyone else try to run this country. I have to run it myself. No matter how small a piece of land is, I'm going to sign the paper myself. I'm not lazy, I can sign millions of papers."[20] The powers he had acquired enabled him, in his own words, to "acquire any land, owned by anyone, in towns or in the rural areas, by force."[21]

In 1970 the president decided that it was time to demonstrate that he was prepared to use his powers to bring to heel expatriate as well as domestic landowners if they failed to behave in the way that he thought appropriate.

A great deal of land had been acquired by Europeans, especially in the early days of British settlement in Nyasaland, in circumstances and on terms that conferred little moral authority on the new owners; Dr. Banda insisted that throughout the colonial period land continued to be seized from Africans under dubious pretexts and that he himself had been dispossessed of land while he was out of the country and it had been handed over to a European, one Milward, who was already a large landholder.[22] Some European landowners had, moreover, taken advantage of the Africans who worked on their estates and had not paid them fairly for the value of the work they had done. To make matters worse, many landowners had never put their land to productive use. The excuse advanced by the landowners, said Dr. Banda, was that much uncultivated land was being held for future expansion. "If the estate owners have not done any expansion in nine years, how much time do they need for their expansion. Twenty years, one hundred years?"[23] The land was being held, said the president, because land was a form of wealth with a steadily rising price, and in the meanwhile the nation was suffering because a valuable economic asset was being wasted. It was soon obvious, however, that putting the land to productive use was to provide no secu-

20. *Legislative Assembly*, 26 March 1968, p. 785.
21. *Legislative Assembly*, 17 March 1970, p. 235.
22. Dr. Banda made several references to this in the *Legislative Assembly*. See, for example: 17 March 1970, pp. 236–237, and 16 March 1971, pp. 1109ff.
23. *Legislative Assembly*, 17 March 1970, p. 233.

rity of tenure. In March 1971, Dr. Banda told the Assembly that land would be taken over if it was kept idle or "when we have any other good reason."[24]

Whatever the strength of the case for taking over idle land from greedy or inefficient foreign landlords who had acquired the land under dubious circumstances, the law empowered the president to decide, without reference to anyone else or without right of appeal to any other body, whether or not the public interest would be served by confiscating land. All persons Malawian or foreign, whose political reliability was suspect could have their lands taken over, whether or not they were efficient and humane landlords. On the other hand, people who, in keeping with the alleged spirit of the law, should have had their land confiscated could be saved from this fate if they were able to persuade the president that they had a proper regard for the conventions and practices of the Malawi people.

The president himself described an incident that clearly demonstrated his discretionary powers, although it is not so clear that either he or any of the members of Parliament were entirely aware of the implications of what he said on that occasion. The president had been contemplating, he said, the confiscation of some land owned by a company whose directors lived in London. The directors were summoned to Malawi, where the president explained to them why the government was about to take over a part of their land. The directors listened to the president, returned to their hotel, talked things over among themselves, and then got in touch with the president to tell him, so he explained to members of the Assembly, that they had been so impressed by the force of his argument that they had decided to donate a part of their land to him personally. The president was delighted by this gesture and changed his mind about the company's fitness to hold land in Malawi. His account does not make clear whether the company was obliged to give up some land to the government in addition to the amount that it presented as a personal gift to the president, but the directors' astuteness and boldness in offering a

24. *Legislative Assembly*, 16 March 1971, p. 1111.

personal gift had transformed them from unsympathetic, arro-
gant aliens into the sort of foreigners whom the government
was content to see owning land in Malawi; their apparent humility and generosity had made a powerful impression on the
president, who told an enthusiastic Parliament that there would
always be a place for foreign investors who did not think themselves superior to the government of the country.[25]

During the course of a debate in March 1971, Blackwood had
suggested, as was his wont, that there might be a formal system
of appeal by landowners whose land had been taken over, to a
judge of the High Court. Dr. Banda—always willing to allow the
nominated European members considerable scope for sympa-
thetically critical comment—replied: "He is assuming that the
Judges of the High Court know better than the Minister concerned, that Justices of the High Court know better than the
Government, that the Minister concerned has to have Judges
looking over his shoulder, that the Government has to have
Judges looking over their shoulder."[26] Judges are, he went on,
only human, as are ministers, and "the courts are not responsible for the welfare of the country." Judges knew only their own
speciality, but the government understood the "global picture."
When his own "ancestor's land" had been seized in the 1940s,
the High Court did nothing to protect the rights of his family:
"They simply gave the stamp of legality to the robbing of my
family by the Government and the Provincial Commissioner and
the District Commissioner in collusion with Milward. So, do you
think I can trust the High Court after this experience?"[27]

The president's bitterness, which may be understandable,
provided a convenient rationalization for a policy that gave him
the power to deprive any citizen of the country who offended
him of the capacity to earn his living in the way to which he
had become accustomed and to make it extremely difficult for
him to earn a living in any other way, even though not a single
charge could have been publicly brought against the man.

The web of power was further strengthened by the transfor-

25. *Legislative Assembly,* 24 March 1970, p. 487.
26. *Legislative Assembly,* 16 March 1971, p. 1108.
27. *Legislative Assembly,* 16 March 1971, pp. 1109–1110.

mation of the judicial system under Dr. Banda's administration. This was to provide the government with a most powerful weapon to use against citizens who had, for any reason, seriously offended the president or fallen afoul of party members who had access to the president.

Almost from the beginning he had possessed most considerable power to influence the outcome of the judicial process—a power that was to be strengthened in the following years until it became virtually absolute. The president's power to shield activists of the MCP who had dealt roughly with anyone suspected of disloyalty to the president was described in the last chapter; he was, in addition, able to use the judicial system to punish his enemies or others whom he "knew" to be guilty of some offense with little regard for the views or decisions of the judges with respect to the alleged guilt of the accused. Although the president could, from the outset, order the retrial of anyone found innocent by a court if in his view the person was guilty. Dr. Banda soon found that radical changes were required in the judicial system if he were to be able to intervene as decisively in the judicial process as he wished.

Party activists have been accustomed to demanding that ordinary citizens, in no way infringing the law, must show that they are in possession of fully paid-up party membership cards or find themselves turned off buses, denied access to markets, and in danger of a beating. As the president blandly pointed out from time to time, there was no law that said people must belong to the party, but anyone involved in a dispute with party members was likely to find himself accused of provocation or something worse. At times, the president's supporters went much further than that, and Dr. Banda never tired of asserting in public speeches during periods of crisis that his enemies, whom he described as "wild animals," should take care lest they end up as "food for the crocodiles."[28]

28. One of the "wild animal" comments is quoted in Short, p. 256; the "food for the crocodiles" comment was a recurring theme, coming up again 10 July, 1973, p. 810, when the president referred, to the apparent amusement of members of the Assembly, to those of his former enemies now in the stomach of crocodiles.

On at least four distinct occasions, systematic and sustained violence has been used against members of the sect of Jehovah's Witnesses.[29] In a speech made in April 1967, the president had this to say:

"Jehovah's Witnesses cannot be allowed to go about provoking people. I want to say here and now that the country will not tolerate this kind of thing. I will not accept every case of Jehovah's Witnesses being beaten up by members of the Malawi Congress Party as a geniune or valid case of assault or battery. I have to be given full facts before I can accept any case as genuine. Otherwise I will release or order the release of anyone from imprisonment for beating a Jehovah's Witness. The Government will protect every law abiding citizen from molestation by anyone or everyone . . . including members of the Malawi Congress Party, Youth League or Young Pioneers. But it will not give licence to Jehovah's Witnesses to provoke anyone—including members of the Malawi Congress Party, Youth League and Young Pioneers. It will not give licence to Jehovah's Witnesses to prevent people paying tax or to prevent members of the Malawi Congress Party from renewing their cards.[30]

When the sect was banned, the president denied that it was because they would not buy party cards and said that stories to that effect were part of "a vicious propaganda against me personally, and the Government in particular." However, a number of Cabinet ministers—none of whom would have dared to carry out a policy contrary to the wishes of the president—had made speeches, which were freely reported in the party press, insisting that everyone must buy cards and prove themselves active supporters of the party. Chakwamba, then the minister of education and deputy chairman for the Southern Region of the MCP, told a Fort Johnston audience: "There are still people who have not yet bought Malawi Congress Party cards. It is the duty of party officials, chiefs and village headmen, members of the Youth League and members of the Women's

29. The party's policies on reporting these incidents has varied considerably from time to time. According to Short, news of the attacks by Youth Leaguers and Young Pioneers on Jehovah's Witnesses during the election campaign of 1964 "were carefully suppressed" (p. 171). The troubles in November and December of 1967, on the other hand, were extensively reported, albeit in a highly partisan way, in the party press.

30. Quoted, *The Times* (Blantyre), 24 April 1967.

League to see that everyone buys cards."[31] Following his speech, the women of the local branch of the MCP sang a composition expressing the view that anyone who refused to buy party cards should also refuse to handle money because all currency in Malawi carried the face of *Ngwazi*, the president.

Five years later, in December 1972, the president was describing another outbreak of hostilities between Witnesses and party activists, which had, according to a number of observers, led to the flight of many thousand Witnesses from Malawi. The president dismissed these reports as inaccurate and malicious, adding that Witnesses "deliberately provoke others," and went on to ridicule Witnesses and suggest that they had no right to police protection against people who felt disposed to beat them. When they are attacked, said Dr. Banda, "they go to the Police. But is not the Police Government?" If they do not get satisfaction from the police, they go to the district commissioner: "Is not the District Commissioner Government?" They go to the chief: "Is not the chief Government?"[32]

Nevertheless, there were some opponents of Dr. Banda against whom it was not so easy to arouse mob violence without some risk of retaliation, and to deal with these people, Dr. Banda set about the total reformation of the judicial system. As was so often the case, there were cogent reasons for embarking on reform, but the reforms produced were much less well suited to the ostensible purposes for which they were introduced than to the further extension of Dr. Banda's personal power. Dr. Banda was probably not alone in feeling that the modern or "British-type" courts sometimes impeded rather than assisted the cause of justice; that the formal laws of evidence and the pomp and ceremony of the courts overawed and confused witnesses; that "clever" lawyers could bully or mislead witnesses, and that as a consequence people who were known to be guilty were able to escape punishment. Many other people may have felt that in some respects the traditional courts not only were more effective but reflected a superior moral code, and still others perhaps agreed with the president,

31. Quoted, *The Times* (Blantyre), 30 Nov. 1967.
32. *Legislative Assembly*, 1 Dec. 1972, p. 363.

that it was part of the traditional code and a credit to it, that "no one was allowed to hide anyone, to defend anyone that he knew himself had committed a crime," even when the guilty person was one's own son or nephew.[33]

Many people may have felt that a man or woman could be judged more effectively by those, drawn from the same small communities, who knew them well than by lawyers, however learned, who had no intimate knowledge of the accused. Lawyers and judges in Nyasaland had almost invariably differed markedly on almost every count from the African witnesses and defendants who appeared before them or as their clients. There were differences not only of race but of class, power, wealth, education, tradition, and expectations—and probably many of these differences survived in the courts of the independent Malawi. It may be possible, and most people would agree that it is, to detect equivocation among those one knows very well, but the likelihood of being able to do so when dealing with people so comprehensively alien to one's style and environment is slender.

As Dr. Banda put it: "Those who were dispensing the justice were steeped in a foreign way of justice and not a Malawi way of justice."[34] There were likely to be mistakes by both lawyers and witnesses, and because of these mistakes, often about technical points of little practical relevance, defendants who had (properly) been found guilty were subsequently released.

In cases involving abuse of government funds, it was often, so the argument went, difficult to provide the sort of evidence that would normally be necessary in a British court to convict an accused person of embezzlement or theft, even if it was widely known that he was guilty of the alleged offense. The standard of record keeping was frequently inadequate, so that it was difficult to prove, in terms that would have satisfied a British court, precisely when or where the money or goods had disappeared. It was often difficult for the prosecution to trace

33. *Legislative Assembly,* 20 Nov. 1969, p. 220. Three days earlier Sembereka had insisted that it was no part of the tradition of the Malawi people to make public funds available to criminals so that they might be able to defend themselves against charges brought by the people's representatives.

34. *Legislative Assembly,* 28 July 1970, p. 501.

witnesses, since few people had regular postal addresses or were otherwise clearly identified as residing in a particular place. To these problems were added ones involving all legal investigations in Malawi; the obligation to a kinsman or member of one's tribe was strong, the fear of witchcraft was great, the conventions and even the appearance of a "British" court were strange and alien, the judges could not discern the telltale signs of truth or falsehood, and so on. The difficulties of establishing a precise legal case did not always help the defendant, but they did introduce a substantial element of chance into the proceedings, so that a legal action took on, rather more than is usually the case, the aspect of a lottery. Nonetheless, it was very important to check and, if possible, eradicate the sort of petty corruption that could easily become endemic among government officials and that would seriously affect efficiency and public confidence.

Most proponents of the British judicial system would acknowledge that some of its practices reflect the historical accidents of a particular kind of social system rather than constituting a unique means of securing justice. Even were the ends of justice deemed to be the same in some other society, they might well be better served by different institutions more appropriate to the customs and social conditions of that other people. It is not, however, a simple matter to disentangle the accidental from the necessary aspects of procedure, and once one begins to hack away this or that, one is in danger of so changing the balance of the judicial process that vital safeguards are lost.

In any event, Dr. Banda was soon to demonstrate that he intended to go very much further than was necessary to prune the courts of alien customs irrelevant to the pursuit of justice. He intended to make the judiciary, like the legislature, a subordinate arm of the executive.

At first he sought to influence the outcome of various cases by making his views known to the judiciary in advance of the verdict, often by way of public speeches, and on at least one occasion called for the death penalty for a man whose trial had not begun. In that case the evidence against the accused appears to have been so compelling that any verdict other than one of guilty would have been most unlikely, even had there been no threat of intervention by the president, but if there had been any doubt, the president's intervention would have seriously jeopardized the defendant's chance of a fair trial. The president had the right to review all verdicts, whether the defendant had been found guilty or not guilty. He showed no hesitation in taking advantage of this prerogative, and on several occasions he overturned verdicts of "not guilty," announcing that he knew perfectly well the man was guilty and would make sure he was duly punished.

The existence of such powers and the convention that they could and should be invoked at the president's pleasure gave him a very powerful weapon against political dissidents. The government possessed, independently, unlimited powers to detain malcontents, but there was always some danger that detainees might evoke sympathy and respect; perhaps few would have been eager to emulate them, but many more, given a shift in the balance of power, might have been ready to accord a hero's welcome to men and women who had suffered so honorably for their cause. A man sent to prison for embezzlement or rape is not as likely to arouse the same emotions, unless the people have lost all confidence in the judiciary or have no respect for established laws.

In the early years of Dr. Banda's regime, there were limits to the influence that the president could bring to bear on the judicial system. Defending lawyers who discredited witnesses for the prosecution were likely to be served with a deportation order, but a few were prepared to take the risk; there may have been constraints on the discretion of judges, but the judges did not believe that it was their duty to be instruments of government policy and sometimes returned verdicts against the publicly expressed wish of the president. Increasingly sharp clashes between the president and the judiciary reached a climax over a prosecution for a series of murders allegedly carried out for political reasons.

In 1969, there were several killings and disappearances in and around Chilomoni, a district of Blantyre, and rumors circulated that men were being killed to provide what was quite literally "blood money" to the South African government in return for its assistance to Dr. Banda. This was an updated version of an ancient and terrible fear among the Malawi people,[35] and the fact that the superstition could be so easily revived may have reflected public unease about the government's policy of accommodation with the Republic of South Africa. Another rumor circulated that the government was kidnapping people and selling them to the South Africans as slaves. The government took the rumors seriously, and both Dr. Banda and Mr. Muwalo, the party secretary, spoke at length in Parliament, denying that there was any substance to the rumors; on the contrary, they insisted the murders had been initiated by agents of the former ministers in order to give credence to the rumors that the former ministers had themselves been responsible for starting.[36]

In March 1970 a man was arrested, and during interrogation he allegedly implicated several others (including a senior Cabinet minister). They were brought to trial, but the prosecution failed to establish its case. In Dr. Banda's view, justice had been thwarted by undue and irrelevant concern for trivia; this was, he said, the fifth case "in which judges or magistrates had acquitted alleged murderers on mere technicalities."[37]

He told Parliament that after the second case he had instructed his permanent secretary (who was also the attorney general) to draw up a bill introducing a jury system in the country, because he thought "it would prevent the kind of thing whereby alleged murderers were being acquitted by judges or magistrates on mere technicalities." This most recent case had, however, been dismissed without any submission being made to a jury because of a technical fault in its presentation. "This," he said later, "was not a case for European judges or magistrates (or even African judges and magistrates) who use technicalities which they were taught in the Inns of Court in London, which are not applicable here."[38]

The legal system, he decided, must be subjected to fundamental reform. Traditional courts that previously had limited powers, being confined to cases where the penalty could not

35. See Shepperson and Price, *Independent Africa*, pp. 9–10.
36. *Legislative Assembly*, 20 Nov. 1969.
37. *Legislative Assembly*, 28 July 1970.
38. *Legislative Assembly*, 7 Dec. 1971, p. 224.

exceed twelve months' imprisonment, were to become very
much more important organs of the judicial process. They
were no longer to be limited in their jurisdiction or subordinate
to the "British-type" courts or appeal system.

The traditional court was to consist of traditional rulers,
chairmen of the existing traditional courts, and a few barris-
ters—the idea being to effect a balance between traditional and
imported practices and philosophies, between "those who are
steeped in Malawian law and the Malawi sense of justice and
those who have or have acquired some knowledge at least of
the other kind of law and other kind of justice. . . . When and
where there is a conflict between the two, the Malawian sense
of justice and the other kind of justice, the Malawian sense of
justice will have to prevail."[39]

This reform greatly increased the already substantial power
of the government (or, more precisely, of the president) to
manipulate the legal system as an instrument of political control. Under the new system, the members of traditional courts
were appointed, and subject to dismissal, by the government in
circumstances in which there was no body of precedent to con-
strain the president's pursuit of political and personal objectives. These courts would be able to try cases according to what
the president deemed to be traditional practices (there was, as
we shall see, considerable room for doubt, among those who
might be presumed to be well qualified in the matter, as to
what constituted traditional practice), the defendants would be
denied the right of legal representation, and the members of
the court would be allowed a great deal of discretion in assess-
ing a defendant's veracity. Traditional courts would be able to
impose any punishment, including the death penalty; there
would be no right of appeal outside the traditional system, and
an appeal to the traditional system's own Court of Appeal
would be allowed only if approved by the appropriate government minister (whose own office, it may be recalled, was entirely at the discretion of the president).

The introduction of this new system followed, as we have
seen, the acquittal of the defendants in the Chilomoni murder

39. *Legislative Assembly*, 28 July 1970, p. 501.

case. It was not, however, the only significant effect of that decision. As soon as Dr. Banda had learned, apparently from a broadcast on Malawi Radio, that the defendants had been acquitted, he got hold of the attorney general, who was at that time an expatriate, and told him "to tell the police not to release those people, no matter what the Judges are saying. [I am] in charge here, not the Judges."[40] The defending lawyer had, in Dr. Banda's view, frightened and confused the witnesses for the prosecution, and since the judge had allowed this unfair advantage to the defense, the outcome of the trial had no moral validity. The lawyer in question had, he went on, been notorious for defending foreign women (that is, African women from Southern Rhodesia) of loose morals in previous cases before the court, and it was high time that he should be deported. The chief justice protested vigorously about the manner in which the government dealt with the case, resigned, and left the country, but Dr. Banda was not, he assured an enthusiastic Parliament, prepared to be given directions (or, as he put it, be blackmailed) by people who thought that the office of chief justice entitled them to tell the government how the business of running the country should be carried out.

In November the president told Parliament that Kamisa, the first man to be arrested and the one who had given police officers the information that had implicated several other people, had now changed his story and said that he alone was responsible for the murders. Dr. Banda was not prepared to accept that the withdrawal of charges was valid; some people, he said, might have influenced Kamisa while Kamisa was in custody and persuaded him to lie in an attempt to save other, more influential culprits. Dr. Banda would not release the other men until the newly established traditional court had dealt with the case.

In the following month the government introduced the Penal Code (Amendment) Bill to put into effect a resolution of the annual convention of the MCP that the death penalty should be extended to burglary, housebreaking, and robbery

40. *Legislative Assembly,* 24 March 1970, p. 482.

with violence. There had been, it was said, a wave of violence unknown in Malawi in the past, which was caused by foreign influence upon Malawian migrant workers who had fallen into bad company while they were out of the country, and much more severe punishment for these and similar offenses was necessary. Henceforth, either the death penalty or life imprisonment was to be mandatory for housebreaking, whether carried out during the day or night. There was some question as to whether the government's chief concern was random vandalism or something much more significant from its point of view. During the course of the debate, Semberake, a minister of considerable subtlety, let drop an unguarded phrase: "Be it political or just merely robbing but the punishment should be the same—namely death."[41]

Toward the end of 1971 the murder case was presented to one of the newly constituted traditional courts. It was tried by the Southern Regional Traditional Court, which comprised three chiefs, one lawyer and a traditional court chairman. The presiding judge was Chief Chikumba of Mulanje. It's verdict was not what Dr. Banda had expected. It found that Kamisa, the first man to have been arrested, was guilty of murder, but that the men whom he had at first implicated were not guilty.

When Dr. Banda dealt with the case in a speech to Parliament in December 1972, he said that the verdict had been received with hostility by people attending the court and that there was a deep sense of outrage throughout the country when the case against the other accused had been dismissed. The verdict, he said, was faulty on three counts. First, only the one man had been on trial and therefore nothing properly could be said about the others. Second, under traditional Chewa law, which he had now decided was not understood by Chief Chikumba, both accuser and accused should be brought face to face, and this was necessary both when an accusation was made and also when it was withdrawn. Having established, at least to his own satisfaction, that under Chewa law an accuser could not withdraw an accusation except in the presence of the accused, he went on to argue that since the other accused men

41. *Legislative Assembly,* 2 Dec. 1970, p. 780.

(who included a former Cabinet minister and another former member of Parliament) had not been brought to court—this having been the trial of the first one only, namely Kamisa—the withdrawal of the accusations was not valid, notwithstanding that the only evidence against the other men appeared to be in Kamisa's original charge, apart from some very loose circumstantial evidence about which Dr. Banda affected to attach great importance. Third, the number of murders of which Kamisa had been found guilty was only eight, whereas thirty-one murders had been committed and were believed to be connected with this same plot. It was, said the president, self-evidently absurd to suppose that Kamisa could have been responsible for all thirty-one: "Where," he asked, "did he get the courage?"[42]

Dr. Banda showed that he would not hesitate to overrule decisions of the traditional court just as he had done with the "modern" courts because "in this country, among the Africans, the court is not above the law, is not above public opinion." He went on to say that if Parliament did not approve of the president's action it could launch impeachment proceedings, although everyone knew perfectly well that any members contemplating such action would be dismissed from the party and lose their seats in the Assembly before they had a chance to vote on the issue, to say nothing of the likelihood that they would find themselves in detention.

In the course of that speech the president put forward, in commendably succinct form, one of the axioms of his legal philosophy. "We have to remember," he said, "that lack of evidence is not proof of innocence."

Throughout this period there were substantial effective controls over the press. There were three principal newspapers, of which two were organs of the MCP. The third was an expatriate-owned newspaper, but its expatriate editors could be deported at will (and sometimes were), while its Malawian staff were subject to harassment and detention if they exceeded the limited freedom of comment or reporting accorded to them by the government.

42. *Legislative Assembly*, 7 Dec. 1971, pp. 221ff. The quotation is from page 223, and the quotation two paragraphs further on is from page 225.

Nonetheless, the president was enraged in mid-1973 by reports published in foreign newspapers that there had been fighting between Portuguese and Malawian troops, and he believed that these reports had been inspired by rumors "leaked" by Malawian journalists and newscasters. Expressing pride in the government's ability to trace the sources of these rumors, Dr. Banda said that "in this country, the police is supported by other means, means that I, myself, know and control." He went on to charge that journalists from the privately owned *Times* of Blantyre and the party's *Malawi News* had been involved, together with officials in the Ministry of Information and other "so-called journalists."[43]

In addition to spreading rumors about the fighting, reporters had told foreigners that the people of Malawi were not happy with their government, that all was not well with the economy, and that two Cabinet ministers were plotting against the president. Both ministers who had been named in the rumors were called up to speak and protested their loyalty.

Several expatriate journalists were deported, even more severe controls on reporting were imposed, and reports made by British journalists leaving Malawi indicated that a substantial proportion of the most respected Malawian journalists had been sent to a detention camp. In late September, there were reports that the government had taken over direct control of all press and radio facilities, that the Ministry of Information and Broadcasting had been disbanded, and a law passed providing that journalists could be imprisoned for life for passing "false information" to foreigners, with the president being the final judge of what constituted false information.[44]

It had never been easy to obtain detailed information about events in Malawi except from the statements of the president himself, and although he was a highly biased source, he was often remarkably candid about matters on which many politicians would have avoided comment. Now, as public opinion became ever more constrained, the president—whether from a new-found political caution or because the burden of his years

43. *Legislative Assembly*, 10 July 1973, p. 802.
44. Reported by *The Times* (London), 29 Sept. 1963.

was heavy upon him—devoted an increasingly large part of his public speeches to meandering recollections of his conduct during the struggle for independence, making little more than allusion, and sometimes not even that, to pressing contemporary events.

On a few occasions he still lifted the curtain on events that plainly suggested that though the country might be orderly its mood was far from tranquil. In July 1973, during the same session in which he castigated reporters for misrepresenting conditions on the Mozambique border, he referred to the activities of a rebel band in the Mangoche (formerly Fort Johnston) area. In 1971 they had killed the area chairman of the MCP, and government forces had failed to track them down until Dr. Banda became "fed up" with the police methods inherited from the British and ordered the arrest, removal to a detention area, and interrogation of the entire population of one village; the people then talked and, after their release, took an active part in the pursuit and capture of the rebels, or so ran Dr. Banda's account. During the same speech, he referred to the attempted assassination of two ministers in Mulanje during 1969.[45]

In November he gave more details about the Mangoche episode, throwing perhaps more light than he had intended on the attitudes of people in the district toward the government. They had not rebelled, said Dr. Banda, because they were dissatisfied with his rule but because they were in fear of hard-core terrorists such as Kanada, a pro-Chipembere fanatic. Kanada and about twenty others were, said Dr. Banda, professional killers, who had learned their trade working for white gangsters in Johannesburg and had returned to Malawi in the pay of the former ministers. "They kept on terrorising the people, not only in Mangoche but in Kasupe. The security forces could not catch them although they worked very hard, because the people would not give information."[46] In November 1971 the gang killed the branch chairman, the branch secretary, and five Youth Leaguers. Dr. Banda then told the commissioner of po-

45. *Legislative Assembly*, 13 July 1973, pp. 949–951.
46. *Legislative Assembly*, 15 Nov. 1973, p. 606.

lice and the head of the Special Branch that the methods inherited from the British would not do. All members of Molo
village and some in Taliya village were arrested and sent for
interrogation. "Those people in part of Taliya village who were
left behind now got the courage to talk." Kanada was captured,
"found guilty and of course . . . " Applause interrupted the
speech. The people of Mangoche had now begged Dr. Banda
to visit them and receive their apologies for their earlier failure
to cooperate with the security forces.

By this time the president had established a network of comprehensive and highly personal control that had the full power
of the law and yet was completely arbitrary. He had the power
to determine unilaterally who might or might not be a member
of the party and of Parliament; the power to determine
whether or not people might hold title to land and whether or
not they might engage in business; he could arraign people
before courts of his own choosing in circumstances that gave
them little chance of acquittal and even if, in spite of this, they
were acquitted, he had the power to disregard the verdict and
insist that they either be retried immediately or be held in
custody while awaiting another trial, which would be held at his
convenience and in circumstances he deemed appropriate. To
supplement this vast range of powers, he had a virtual monopoly of the means of communication and the power to inflict
severe penalties on anyone who uttered anything displeasing to
him.

There were no means short of rebellion by which any form
of dissent could be publicly declared, and the only limitation to
the president's power was that imposed by his declining physical vigor.

CHAPTER 8

Economic Strategy and National Politics: Keystone or Facade?

Poverty and isolation were the most persistent and notable characteristics of the Nyasaland economy throughout the greater part of the colonial period. Improvements that took place during the last two decades of colonial rule, though must welcome to the government and affording much needed relief to the meager and tedious standard of living of much of the population, failed to resolve the fundamental problem of economic viability.

The vulnerability of the Nyasaland economy was one of the most powerful bargaining counters in the hands of supporters of the Central African Federation, and during the 1950s few influential politicians in Britain, of any party, doubted that Nyasaland's secession from the federation would produce an impoverished state, dependent for the foreseeable future on foreign assistance. Secession became a realistic option to British politicians only when the alternative to this bleak prospect appeared to be the even worse one of openly maintaining a colonial police state, actively suppressing the aspirations of every African in the country.

When Malawi achieved independence, the country was in the trough of the first serious economic depression since the end of World War II. It was a somber introduction to what had been expected, under even the most favorable circumstances, to be a desperately hard task, but the very harshness of the conditions under which Dr. Banda assumed leadership of the newly independent state was later to be greatly to his advantage. The perilously weak economy could hardly fail to improve on its 1964 performance; characterized by temporary excess capacity, it was capable of a rapid upswing in production as soon as there was a measure of political stability.

Within a few years Dr. Banda demonstrated to many of his former critics that Malawi had achieved a near miracle of economic development. Foreign assistance was still needed, but the recorded growth rate had been very high, the number of people in recorded wage employment was increasing, the level of investment was most respectable, agricultural output was rising rapidly, dependence on grants from the British government was decreasing, and the president (as he had become) was proclaiming, almost daily, that European businessmen were welcome in Malawi as long as they understood that the color of their skin did not allow them to flout the country's traditional codes of behavior.

The generally favorable impression of Malawi's economic performance, which had been formed as early as 1968, was enhanced by the substantial expansion of output during the late sixties and early seventies. Several observers, not all of them sympathetic to Dr. Banda's style of political control, have felt that economic success has provided its own justification for the harsh domestic discipline imposed by Dr. Banda. This apparent success has also encouraged the view that Malawi has gained major economic advantages from its cordial diplomatic relations with the white-ruled states of Southern Africa and that the roots of Dr. Banda's foreign policy are embedded in astute and fruitful preoccupation with his country's economic needs.

The economy recovered quickly from the depression of the early sixties, and even if 1960 is taken as the base year (that is, the year chosen as a starting point is one before the downswing really got under way), the rate of growth during the 1960s and into the mid-seventies has been a respectable one. What is rather more contentious is whether this achievement may properly be ascribed to the policies of Dr. Banda's government or whether it was due to favorable circumstances in the economy which produced continuing stimulus for increased output in key sectors.

One should not expect a conclusive answer to a question of this sort, but some light may be thrown on the issue by comparing the growth rate since 1960 with that before it, since this would provide evidence on the rates of growth achieved by different governments pursuing different policies: if the policies were the crucial factor, the rates of growth should be very different; if favorable economic conditions were the major factor, performance would probably not be very different when the government changed.

Evaluation of Malawi's economic performance since independence raises several other important questions about the long-run development implications of the government's strategy, about the distribution of gains from growth, and about the extent to which the government's commitment to national economic development is subordinated to its search for political advantage.

Because of a large inflow of foreign capital (relative to the value of national income), in the form of foreign assistance and of commercial investment, it may be felt that maintaining a high rate of growth has been relatively easy, over the short run. Few people dispute the desirability of foreign assistance, and some believe that a different government in Malawi might have been able to obtain even more help than Dr. Banda has managed to do, but apart from the possible ill effects in the long run of heavy dependence on foreign capital, it has been suggested that the present government has taken too much credit for an economic boom that owes a great deal to investment generated by foreign governments, foreign companies, and international agencies.

There has also been concern that the government's economic strategy has concentrated too heavily on the relatively easy short-term gains derived from exploiting the bargain sectors of the economy, while postponing the most difficult tasks that will have to be undertaken if the country is to achieve long-term viability.

Some of Dr. Banda's critics have taken the view that there has been serious inequity in the distribution of both the burdens and the benefits of economic change during the past fifteen years, and that despite the remarkable progress in raising aggregate national income since independence, a sizable proportion of the population has benefited very little, if at all, from the nation's prosperity.

These reservations about the country's economic performance do not necessarily call into question the government's commitment to achieving a high level of economic growth, but questions may quite properly be raised about the government's effective priorities when pursuit of political ambition is best served by policies likely to reduce the efficiency of the economy. There is ground for concern that the methods by which the government exercises control over the economy are more readily adapted to the demands of political patronage than to careful consideration of economic options, and that critically scarce resources have been allocated to projects better suited to the president's political strategy than to the development of the economy.

In examining the economic evidence available, one must be cautious in interpreting figures, whether from official or other sources. The precision and the objectivity of any estimate of economic growth are always subject to dispute, but contention about both factual and conceptual matters is particularly acute in an underdeveloped country such as Malawi, which has a large subsistence or semitraditional sector and in which, because of recent structural changes, many important economic activities are more likely now than hitherto to be recorded and therefore "counted" in the National Income aggregates.

Problems inherent in estimating rates of change in the Malawian economy are compounded by the frequent changes in the scope and method of statistical enquiry and evaluation in Malawi during the past twenty years. The government has greater access to resources, and the survey and statistical services of the government have expanded; these changes have widened the scope of coverage and improved the quality of data. Yet frequent changes in coverage, weighting, and definition make it difficult to evaluate long-term trends in real income. An apparently significant difference between the estimate for one year and that for the next might be due to a change in coverage or methodology rather than to any real difference in economic activity.

The general pattern of economic growth both before and after independence has been rather consistent, and it is likely that the general trend portrayed by the official figures is a reasonably good approximation of what has taken place, but virtually all specific figures, whatever their derivation, are subject to a considerable margin of error.

The recorded estimates of national income, expressed in current prices, show a large increase since 1964. Between 1964 and 1970 national income nearly doubled, and in the next three years it increased by another 50 per cent. What is more, the increase in real per capita income—that is, after making allowance for the increase in prices and in population—may have been as high as 20 per cent between 1964 and 1970, and between 1970 and 1973 there was another increase of more than 15 per cent.

There are several different series of figures emanating from different government sources. Even the most conservative of them show a high rate of growth since 1964. Table 8.1, which is taken from the *Economic Report*, indicates a higher rate of growth than the figures in Table 8.2, taken from the publications of the Reserve Bank of Malawi.

The high rate of growth can be attributed in no small measure to the depression of the early 1960s, which interrupted the steady expansion of the economy that had taken place in the fifteen years after World War II. According to some official estimates, gross domestic product fell in 1964, but even if an alternative estimate of a rise of one percent were accepted there would have been a drop in per capita income, because population was increasing at upwards of 3 percent a year.

The depression, which reached its low point in 1964, was caused, at least in part, by uncertainty among investors and expatriates about the political future of the country, and some recovery was virtually inevitable as soon as the political situation stabilized, because there was spare capacity in the economy. Many of the Europeans who remained in, or came to, Malawi after 1964 no doubt preferred Dr. Banda to his rivals (or to what they had heard of his rivals), but any reasonably stable regime, providing it behaved with some discretion, would have been likely to attract some investors and skilled people sympathetic to its own style of political leadership. The economic situation in Malawi during the balance of the 1960s was, in any event, still much influenced by factors similar to those which had stimulated the rate of growth during the late

Table 8.1. Gross domestic product, per capita (constant prices)

	(1964 prices, Kwacha million)	(1964 prices, per capita)
1964	151.4	39.5
1965	175.8	44.8
1966	194.4	48.3
1967	198.0	48.0
1968	191.6	45.3
1969	208.8	48.2
1970	222.7	50.1
1971	255.8	56.2
1975 (est.)	275.5	59.1
1973 (est.)	280.5	58.5

Sources: Figures for 1964–1969: *Economic Report, 1972;* figures for 1970–1972: *Economic Report, 1973; Economic Report, 1974* (Zomba: Government Press), table 3.1.

Table 8.2. Gross domestic product, 1964–1973 (Kwacha million)

	Current prices		Constant (1964) prices	
	(a)	(b)	(a)	(b)
1964	149.5		149.5	
1965	180.9		163.5	
1966	187.3		175.3	
1967	199.0	215.5	184.1	221.7
1968	214.4	225.4	185.0	198.0
1969	235.2	246.4	197.1	218.4
1970	258.4	272.0	204.1	223.3
1971		335.9		264.3
1972		373.6		284.1
1973		428.9		306.6

Sources: (a) Reserve Bank of Malawi, *Economic and Financial Review,* 111, No. 3 (March 1971), table 5.1; (b) Reserve Bank of Malawi, *Financial and Economic Review,* VI, no. 2 (1974), table 5.1.

The figures provided by the Reserve Bank of Malawi show a clear distinction between two series of figures; one begins in 1964 and the other, more comprehensive one, begins in 1967. The figures from *The Economic Report* cited in the text had been retrospectively adjusted to show a common series running from 1964 to 1973: the figures for each of the years following 1964 were raised upward, largely because of higher estimates of subsistence income, but the 1964 figure was, rather surprisingly, scarcely affected.

Table 8.3. Growth of national income, 1950–1964, current prices (£million)

	Money National Income[a]	Percentage increase		GDP at factor cost[b]		Percentage increase
1950	8.8					
1951	10.2		15.9			
1952	12.0		17.6			
1953	13.9		15.8			
1954	16.0		15.1	31.6		
1955	17.4		8.8	33.6		6.0
1956	19.2		10.3	36.5		8.5
1957	21.6		12.5	38.3		5.0
1958	23.0		6.5	40.9		7.3
1959	24.5		6.5	42.9		5.0
1960	26.8		9.4	45.2		5.5
1961	27.3		1.5	47.1		4.0
1962	29.0		6.2	48.9		3.5
1963	28.5	31.0		−1.7	50.9	53.0	2.1
1964	27.5	30.3	34.2	−3.5/−2.3	50.6	53.4	55.2	−0.6/0.8

Sources: a. 1950–1953, Jack Report, p. 51; 1953–1964, first column, *Compendium of Statistics, 1966,* table 150, C.S.O. figures; 1963–1964, second column; ibid., N.S.O. figures; 1964, third column, *Compendium of Statistics, 1970,* table 20.2.

b. First column, *Compendium of Statistics, 1966,* table 151, C.S.O. figures; second column, ibid, N.S.O. figures; third column, *Economic Report 1968,* figure for GDP at market prices less net indirect tax.

The estimate for "Money national income" completely excludes the value of subsistence output; that for GDP (Gross Domestic Product) includes an estimate much lower than the amount subsequently estimated for the overlapping year of 1964.

1940s and 1950s, and further improvement in productive capacity was to be expected.

Expansion of cash crop farming in the postwar period, due in large part to the improved access to world markets provided by the Zambezi bridge that gave direct rail access from Blantyre and the lake shore to Beira, on the Indian Ocean, had not yet been restrained by shortage of either land or labor. Some parts of Malawi may have been suffering from population pressure, but good agricultural land was still available for cash crops, domestic transport facilities were improving, and agricultural extension work was being carried out under favorable circumstances; there were still many farmers whose efficiency could be improved by the introduction of relatively simple and cheap techniques and who were becoming increasingly responsive, as they witnessed the success of their neighbors, to the opportunities to be gained in cash-crop farming.

The manufacturing sector was still small. The proportionally large increase in output during the fifties had encouraged the development of such ancillary services as banking and transportation but had not been sufficient to exhaust such relatively easy production lines as beer and soft drinks, tobacco products, textiles, and shoes, which are almost invariably the soft options for the least developed of the less developed countries. The large numbers of Malawians who had been temporary migrants in the Republic of South Africa and in Rhodesia provided potential employers with a skilled and disciplined labor force, and with the end of federation companies that had previously had assured access to the Malawi market from their branches in Rhodesia were now under pressure to set up branches in Malawi itself.

The small urban population could hardly fail to increase considerably if there was any economic growth at all, with the result that urban construction, another soft option, would be faced with bouyant demand. Several important projects had been discussed during the federation period, particularly the implementation of a hydroelectric scheme on the Shire River, and schemes such as the development of sugar production in the Lower Shire, which had already obtained prospective backing, were likely to come to fruition as soon as Malawi achieved both independence and a reasonable degree of political stability.

There are, in short, plausible reasons for supposing that in the period since independence the economy would be expected to have a high rate of growth. Insofar as the depression was of a temporary and easily reversible character, one would expect a fast rate of recovery and continued growth, which would return the economy to the growth path that would have occurred if the trend rate of the fifties had been uninterrupted by the politically inspired downswing of the early sixties.

Making use of the best data available for the purpose, rough and ready as it is, one may compare indexes of per capita real income for the fifties, sixties, and early seventies with the indexes which would have been realized on the assumption that the rate of growth through the fifties had been maintained, without any downswing, into the early seventies.

The results are shown in Table 8.4. The projected figure for 1974 differs by less than two percentage points from the index based on recorded per capita income in 1973. In view of the range of error in the estimates, no particular significance should be attached to the fact that the final figures in columns 2 and 3 (albeit with a year's difference between them) are so very close; any projection made from 1959 which provided an estimate within 15 per cent of what was actually reported fifteen years later would, for most purposes, be considered a remarkably accurate prediction. In view of the political upheaval in the six years following 1959, the similarity between prediction and achievement offers strong support for the view that the underlying economic forces influential throughout this period were remarkably consistent.

The fact that the economic achievement since independence has been less singular than the president's admirers insist does not mean that it has been negligible. An incompetent and corrupt government, or one altogether uninterested in economic growth, might have failed to take advantage of the opportunities available or might have alienated the various governments, commercial concerns, and individuals whose investment played so crucial a role in the development in the sixties and seventies, without attracting support from other sources. Some governments, faced by the same circumstances, would have led the country to economic disaster. Discussion about Dr. Banda's economic policy has not, however, turned on whether or not it has been a disaster but whether or not it has been sufficiently successful to justify the tight control that the government exerts over the economy.

Few countries are able to achieve a high rate of growth without a high level of investment and either the capacity to produce intermediate and capital goods domestically or possession of sufficient foreign exchange to buy them abroad (together with the consumption goods necessary for incentive purposes). Investment requires the use of resources, which accordingly must be withdrawn from consumption; that is, it requires "savings," which are achieved either by limiting consumption or, in

Table 8.4. Indexes (actual and projected) of real per capita income, 1954–1973 (1954 = 100)

	(a) Recorded income 1954–1964	(b) Recorded income 1954–1964	Income projected on the assumption that growth rate of 1950s continued without interruption
1954	100		100
—			
1956	105		
—			
1958	108		
1959	109		109
1960	109		
1961	112		
1962	109		
1963	104		
1964	97	97	119
—			
1966		119	
—			
1968		113	
1969		118	130
1970		123	
—			
1973		144	
1974			142

Sources: The figures in column 1 for 1954–1963 are based on the *National Accounts and Balance of Payments of Northern Rhodesia, Nyasaland and Southern Rhodesia, 1954–1963* (Salisbury: C. S. O.), cited by W. L. Taylor, in P. Robson and D. A. Lury, eds., *The Economies of Africa* (London: George Allen and Unwin, 1969) p. 388. The figure for 1964 is based on the C.S.O. figure cited in table 3, adjusted to allow for a population increase of 3.3 per cent per year.

The figures in column 2 are based on the figures in Table 8.1, which show a faster rate of growth after 1964 than the sources used in Table 8.2. The (Table 2.4) figures are converted to a 1954 base by taking the 1964 figure as representing an index number of 97 (from column 1) and calculating post-1964 indices accordingly.

Column 3 is a projected estimate based on the trend between 1954 and 1959. There are no comparable figures available for earlier than 1954; 1959 is taken as the terminal year partly because the following years were heavily affected by political turmoil (even though the rate of growth between 1959 and 1961 continued to be high) and partly because a five-year period has the useful property of providing an estimate for 1974.

the short run, by borrowing from abroad (or, better still, receiving subsidized grants or loans).

Failure to overcome the savings and foreign exchange constraints has been one of the principal causes of economic stagnation in the less developed countries. A saving rate much below 10 per cent of national income usually means stagnation or deterioration; upward of about 15 per cent would be consistent with, though no guarantee of, a respectable rate of growth.[1] Consequently, an increase in resources available to the community on the order of 6 or 7 per cent of national income, if put to proper use, could make all the difference between bleak failure and the appearance, if no more, of considerable success. This task is frequently far beyond the capacity of the domestic economy to achieve.

It is, not surprisingly, most difficult to persuade people suffering from a low standard of living that it is sensible for them to reduce still further their meager consumption so that resources can be released for investment and the improvement of future incomes at the expense of present ones. The attempt to achieve forced savings through taxation is a potent source of political instability, as is a sharp reduction in the import of consumer goods in order to save foreign exchange; many governments have fallen while attempting to impose severe restrictions on consumption, whether of domestic products or of "in-

1. These sorts of figures, suggested by convention, are based on the following reasoning: if, as is often supposed, the capital output ratio is of the order of 3:1, an increase of savings, which is translated into investment, equal to 3 per cent of national income will increase output by one per cent; 9 per cent of savings/investment will produce an increase in national income of 3 per cent; if, as is often the case in less developed countries, population is increasing by about 3 per cent, a 3 per cent increase in aggregate income is just enough to maintain per capita income stable. In these circumstances, anything less than 3 per cent increase (requiring 9 per-cent-savings/investment) will lead to a fall in per capita income, while a 4-per-cent increase (requiring 12-per-cent savings/investment) will provide an almost one-per-cent increase in real per capita income . . . and so on. A country able to achieve a substantial increase in productivity would be able to get a larger output from its 9-per-cent savings/investment, and one that chooses its investment inefficiently—or that suffers from bottlenecks in crucial sectors—may not be able to increase output by much even though it raises the level of investment. In general, however, the figures are probably not unreasonable.

essential" imports, and others have abandoned serious attempts to achieve economic growth because of the political risks.

To a considerable extent, the government of Malawi has been able to avoid this dilemma because relatively large capital inflows have provided both the investment resources and the foreign exchange needed for the expansion of the economy. In the years immediately following independence, domestic saving was actually negative; that is, the total domestic consumption of both imported and domestically produced goods exceeded the total value of domestic production, including both investment and consumption goods. Put in another way, it would have been necessary to borrow money from abroad, or obtain grants, simply to maintain the level of consumption even if there had been no investment at all; foreign capital made it possible not only to maintain this level of consumption but also to establish a high rate of investment and to finance an import surplus. The country ran a substantial annual defecit on the balance of trade and for several years the government was heavily dependent on grants-in-aid from the United Kingdom in order to balance its domestic current account budget.

The percentage of investment that is externally financed has dropped quite substantially since 1964, but as late as 1972 domestic sources still accounted for little more than 40 per cent; if it were not for the inflow of foreign capital, Malawi would have found it very difficult to prevent a fall in per capita income and there would have been virtually no chance at all of an impressive increase.

The foreign grant component in the government's domestic financing has decreased sharply and, although there has been a substantial increase in foreign borrowing, the proportional significance of foreign sources of finance has diminished; even so, foreign loans and grants applied to government finance amounted to more than 35 per cent of the sum raised by the government from domestic sources. Put in another way, the government had, by the early seventies, managed to cover its current account expenditure, but the entire program of government capital expenditure was being financed from abroad; in the absence of capital inflow on a relatively massive scale, the government could not possibly have undertaken expenditure that was central to its economic strategy.

Table 8.5. Sources from which investment financed, 1964–1972, current prices (Kwacha million)

	1964	1965	1966	1967	1968	1969	1970	1971	1972
Domestic savings	0.9	3.8	6.2	8.7	5.2	13.7	9.7	27.8	35.3
Net factor payments from abroad	−6.2	−4.3	−5.6	−7.8	−7.0	−5.7	−4.9	−1.2	2.7
National savings*	−5.3	−0.5	0.6	0.9	−1.8	8.0	14.8	26.6	38.0
Net foreign transfers	18.1	27.2	16.9	17.7	16.5	15.6	13.1	10.4	10.1
Capital inflow	7.2	9.9	16.1	14.3	25.3	27.8	48.1	32.8	35.9
Total investment resources	20.0	36.6	33.6	32.9	40.0	51.4	76.0	69.8	84.0
Percentage financial externally	126.5	101.4	98.9	97.3	104.5	84.4	80.5	61.9	54.8

Sources: Compiled by D. Humphrey, from *Economic Report, 1972* and N.S.O. publication *Monthly Statistical Bulletin* and *Balance of Payments.* Humphrey's table appears as table A3 in "Malawi since 1964: Economic Development, Prospects and Problems," Occasional Paper No. 1, Dept. of Economics, University of Malawi.

*Both the capital inflow figures and the savings figures differ substantially from those given in the publication of the Reserve Bank of Malawi. The precise figure for "percentage financed externally" differs according to the source used, but the general pattern in each case is similar.

Table 8.6. Government finance (Kwacha thousand)

	Current account expenditure	Total government expenditure	Revenue plus foreign grants	Foreign borrowing	Foreign borrowing plus grants
1964	27,484	32,854	33,240	−62	17,228
1965	28,254	37,662	39,548	−208	20,902
1966	32,646	45,406	34,170	5,380	16,764
1967	36,944	47,058	37,790	6,096	17,206
1968	38,426	52,386	38,736	7,972	17,216
1969	37,186	51,264	38,168	13,854	19,948
1970	42,130	73,494	47,986	30,930	40,318
1971	44,020	71,535	49,638	14,535	18,260
1972	52,849	83,214	55,435	15,807	18,800

Source: *Financial and Economic Review,* VI, no. 2 (1974), table 3.1.1.

Inflow of foreign capital has enabled the country to import goods and services that could not be paid for either by the country's exports or by its assets abroad. During the first ten years of independence, defecit on the merchandise and services account ran at approximately 20 per cent of the gross domestic product. Capital inflows from foreign investment or loans (even if subsidized) will eventually give rise to claims on Malawi's resources, as loans are repaid and profits (or some part of them) are repatriated, but even if there was no future cost to normal capital inflows, Malawi's dependence on foreign capital would be notable. Any country able to maintain a *deficit* on its merchandise and services account which is greater than the value of its merchandise exports is operating, at least in the short run, in very favorable circumstances. A high rate of growth can be achieved with little effort as long as goods can, in effect, be imported free, and the test of economic strategy does not come until the costs of attracting foreign capital enter the calculations.

The import surplus has been crucial to the development pro-

Table 8.7. Balance of payments on current account (Kwacha million)

	1964	1965	1966	1967	1968	1969	1970	1971	1972	1973 (est.)
Merchandise										
Exports	24.4	28.5	34.6	40.4	40.0	43.2	47.9	58.3	62.6	75.8
Imports	−28.6	−40.8	−54.1	−50.2	−57.0	−61.0	−68.3	−75.3	−89.4	−98.9
Net merchandise(1)	−4.2	−12.3	−19.5	−9.7	−17.0	−17.8	−20.4	−17.0	−26.8	−23.1
Net services(2)	−14.1	−14.4	−17.6	−27.7	−37.5	−38.9	−41.9	−37.2	−48.0	−44.2
Transfers(3)	17.4	27.0	16.8	17.9	16.6	15.7	12.9	10.5	10.8	11.4
Balance on current account (1+2+3)	−0.9	0.3	−20.3	−9.8	−20.9	−23.2	−29.0	−26.7	−37.2	−32.8
Defecit on merchandiseand service account as % of GDP	12	14	20	17	24	23	23	16	20	16

Sources: Data for 1964–1966 from *Economic and Financial Review*, III, no. 3 (March 1971), and for 1967–1973 from *Financial and Economic Review*, VI, no. 2 (1974); table 4.1 in each case. The last line is calculated from the data given in these tables and from the GDP figures for the relevant years in table 5.1 of the two publications.

gram of Malawi, not only because it is of advantage to a nation to have more resources at its disposal than it is able to produce itself but because the imports the country has been able to obtain are, to a very large extent, capital, intermediate, and other goods which Malawi can not presently make for itself. Since the end of World War II there has been a steady fall in the proportion of imports devoted directly to consumer goods. This trend has continued since independence. In 1964 consumer goods accounted for more than one half of total imports, and in 1973 they accounted for less than one third.

Table 8.8. Composition of imports (Kwacha thousand)

	Total Imports	Consumer goods and commodities for consumption	Plant, machinery, equipment and materials for industry	Means of transport
1964	28,640	14,660	8,064	3,658
1965	40,804	21,150	11,666	4,604
1966	54,292	21,456	21,274	7,098
1967	50,852	19,440	19,560	7,222
1968	58,180	19,722	23,734	9,072
1969	61,478	19,070	25,578	9,440
1970	71,367	19,746	34,537	10,626
1971	89,750	27,036	41,456	12,490
1972	102,913	30,638	43,837	16,770
1973	114,651	33,368	53,634	16,358

Source: *Financial and Economic Review,* VI, no. 2 (1974), table 4.6.

Looked at from one point of view, the fact that a large part of Malawi's import surplus is devoted to investment goods is a healthy sign, but it probably means that in the short run the economy is particularly vulnerable to external economic pressures. A substantial reduction in imports, which would be necessary if there was any serious diminution in capital inflow, would not only reduce the general standard of living but would have a sharply deleterious effect on economic activity in the small but important modern sector in manufacturing and on the even more important estate sector in agriculture. These sectors already provide between them a substantial proportion of total income and of wage employment and are the sectors in which the most rapid growth of output is likely to be achieved, but being relatively capital-intensive, they have a high import component in production costs.

Conventional strategies of development are concerned not only, in some cases not even primarily, with immediate rates of growth but with establishing the conditions in which long-term growth may be achieved, and this often demands that a high priority be attached to diversification of the economy and, in particular, to a broadening of the export base. There are three principal reasons why this diversification may be advantageous.

First, if export earnings are heavily dependent on the sale of one or two agricultural products, for which world prices may fluctuate sharply from year to year, foreign exchange earnings, which are an important component of national economic strategy, may be highly unstable, and the amount available in any particular year will be very largely outside the control of the domestic government.[2]

Second, the consumption of most agricultural products does not increase very much as people become wealthier, and as world incomes increase there is a less than proportional increase in expenditure on basic foodstuffs; on the other hand, the demand for manufactured goods is more responsive to increased wealth, so that as the income of less developed countries increases, expenditure on imported manufactured goods increases more than proportionately; with the demand for imports increasing more rapidly than the demand for exports, the balance of payments problem gets steadily worse. To avoid this dilemma, less developed countries seek to produce a larger proportion of manufactured goods themselves or develop an export trade in more exotic foodstuffs, which people are more inclined to buy when their income increases.[3]

2. Earnings may be greater in the long run through concentration on a small number of crops that are in demand on the world market, and a judicious use of reserve funds may provide a large measure of stability, in spite of annual fluctuations, but there is a strong temptation to take immediate advantage of the years when export earnings are high and to hope, in the face of all experience, that prices will not fall.

3. A particular country may be able to increase its exports of traditional primary products by more efficient marketing and increase its own export earnings at the expense of rivals, but this strategy could not be pursued effectively by more than a very small proportion of the less developed countries and is, in any event, subject to widespread retaliation.

The third reason for favoring diversification is that agricultural products tend to have few linkage or spread effects, in contrast to successful industrial ventures, which are much more likely to possess the attributes of a "leading sector"; that is, its own success directly stimulates other industries, through increased demand for their products as inputs to the leading sector or, if the leading sector is itself an input for some other industry, by reducing the costs of production.[4] Other external effects may occur: the labor force trained by the leading sector may subsequently make a valuable contribution to other industries, as may banking and insurance services stimulated by the emerging leading sector. Typically, however, the expansion of agriculture in less developed countries creates little additional demand for inputs and has no more than a modest impact on the cost structure of other industries.[5]

Attempts to examine the changing pattern of industrial composition are bedeviled by frequent changes in sectoral coverage and definition, particularly when comparing pre- and postindependence experience, but the available evidence indicates a substantial fall between 1959 and 1964 in the proportion of national income originating in manufacturing, building, and construction; since 1964 these sectors have grown rapidly and assumed a greater proportional significance in the national economy, but some part of this growth is attributable to recovery from the depression of the early sixties, in which these sectors were particularly badly affected. If a linked index is constructed from available (official) statistics, manufacturing falls from 100 in 1959 to 76 in 1964 and rises to 144 in 1973; construction falls from 100 in 1959 to 66 in 1964 and rises to 132 in 1973. Table 8.9 shows government estimates of the pro-

4. The "leading sector" concept is particularly associated with the work of W. W. Rostow. Awareness of the importance of actual or potential leading sectors does not, however, depend on, or imply, acceptance of the broader Rostovian framework.

5. The government may choose to encourage agriculture as the surest way to achieve a significant short-run increase in aggregate income and subsequently tax it quite heavily (usually through some form of export tax, because this is administratively easier than the alternatives), using part of the proceeds for encouragement of industries that have a good growth potential but that require assistance in the early stages.

portion of income in the monetized economy produced by various sectors in 1959, 1963, and 1964.

The table excludes subsistence income which, if included, would substantially increase the significance of agricultural output and might also give a greater relative weight to construction than found in the monetized economy alone.

Table 8.9. The industrial origin of money GDP at factor cost (percentages)

	(a)		(b)		(c)	
	1959	1963	1963	1964	1964	1973
Agriculture	29	26	27	27	25	22
Building and construction	9	7	6	5	4	8
Manufacturing	10	9	13	11	10	19
Distribution	17	21	20	17	16	18
Transport and communication	9	10	9	8	7	9
Public admin. and defense	8	9	9	14	16	8
Education	3	4	4	4	4	3
Health	3	2	2	2	1	1

Sources: (a) C.S.O. figures, based on *Compendium of Statistics, 1966,* table 150; (b) 1963 based on N.S.O. figures in same table, and 1964 based on *Compendium of Statistics, 1970,* table 20-2; (c) 1964 figure based on *Economic and Financial Review,* III, no. 3 (March 1971), table 5.1, and 1970 and 1973 (provisional) figures based on *Financial and Economic Review,* VI, no. 2, table 5.1.

Several minor items are not included in the table, which in most years account between them for about 10 per cent of money GDP. There have been some changes in classification, so that (for example) the 1973 figure for distribution includes banking and finance figures that had previously been included in a section not shown in this table. Some of the tables on which these figures are based give more detailed breakdowns, for which the disparities among estimates were greater than for the aggregates. For example, the C.S.O. and the N.S.O. figures both yield the same (rounded) percentage estimate for the contribution of agriculture, but according to C.S.O. figures, 48 per cent of the monetized agricultural output came from the estates while the N.S.O. estimate was 36 per cent.

Most of the manufacturing industry that has been established is, in international terms, on a small scale, and total employment in manufacturing during 1973, though higher than ever before, was less than 26,000.[6] Factories were established during the 1960s and early 1970s by several foreign companies, acting in concert with the Malawi Development Corporation, to cater to demands formerly met by imports. Textiles, shoes, tobacco, soft drinks and beer, for example, are the easy first options for a country with a very poorly developed industrial base. Firms producing these goods have a relatively simple, though often capital-intensive, technology; they do not require a sophisticated labor force; demand already exists for their produce, and they can be established in relatively small units. Industries of this type may give the economy a boost by providing some employment and sometimes (but not necessarily) saving foreign exchange,[7] but in most cases they provide little stimulus to other sectors of the domestic economy.

The government of Malawi has decided to shift the emphasis of new investment in manufacturing toward "supply-based" industries: that is, toward the development and exploitation of industries that can be supplied by raw materials produced within Malawi. The development of a pulp-and-paper industry and of a furniture-producing industry (for example), both based on the timber resources of Malawi, particularly on the Vipya plateau, would, if successful, provide the linkage effects that could, in turn, stimulate more fundamental changes in the economy than have yet taken place. It is too early to pass judgment on the success likely to be achieved in these new ventures.

To some extent the new strategy has been forced on the government, since the bargain sector options are soon exhausted once a country begins to develop, but it is a necessary one for long-run development. The strategy has a higher risk factor than the simple "demand-based" strategy; the possibility of failure will no longer be negligible, but the rewards for success will be higher.

6. *Financial and Economic Review,* VI, no. 2 (1974), p. 43. The annual average level of employment in manufacturing was 25.8 thousand, but in the second and third quarter of the year it went higher, falling in the last quarter to 23.8 thousand.

7. "Import substitute" industries sometimes spend more foreign exchange on capital and intermediate goods and the salaries of foreign specialists than would be spent on importing the final products.

Agriculture remains a very important sector of the economy, providing employment or subsistence income for the great majority of the population, accounting for a substantial part of total national income, and being responsible for 90 per cent or more of export earnings. Tea and groundnuts had been responsible for much of the increased value of output during the fifties; production of both these commodities has flourished since independence, but the most striking increase has been in production of tobacco.

Even before his return to Malawi, Dr. Banda had been very conscious of the need to improve the quality of agriculture in Malawi and to encourage Malawians to become master farmers. He had looked forward to the day when Malawians would be running their own estates, and it was his intention that they would be helped by the government to produce the superior grades of tobacco which had formerly been the preserve of Europeans.

The centerpiece of the government's agricultural program has been the development of more sophisticated tobacco farming among Malawians. Before 1961 flue-cured tobacco was a European preserve, with Africans confined to cruder techniques and less delicate plants which fetched a lower price, albeit at lower cost. Dr. Banda was determined that this European monopoly should be concluded, and began taking steps toward that end as early as 1962.[8]

Dr. Banda has also insisted that a great deal of effort and substantial resources should be devoted to agricultural research and extension work, and to providing credit and other facilities to approved farmers. This would enable the farmers to extend

8. Dr. Banda has been insistent that he played the decisive role as early as 1962 in making provision for Africans to acquire the skills required for flue-cured tobacco production. See, for example, *Legislative Assembly*, 29 Oct. 1974, p. 11. An extensive description of the new scheme is provided in *Legislative Assembly*, 19 July 1971, pp. 9ff. There are extensive exhortations to ministers, M.P.s, and party leaders to follow his own example and set up "gardens": In the *Legislative Assembly*, 17 April 1969, he asserted that "every minister must have a garden, an estate if you like" (p. 249); other examples include: *Legislative Assembly*, 13 March 1973, p. 373 and *Legislative Assembly*, 11 March 1975, pp. 616ff.

the range of their operations and to employ more advanced (and, in the short run at least, more expensive) techniques.[9] One of the largest of these government-sponsored projects has been the Kasungu flue-cured tobacco scheme. Malawian growers are trained to produce the high quality leaf and use the expensive and sophisticated curing process which had been a monopoly of European farmers before 1961, and the government has made arrangements to provide the land and credit to enable the growers to settle on holdings of 150 to 200 acres. Approximately 120 Malawians have been selected and will be trained under this scheme, for which the training program lasts six to seven years and for which the expense to the government has been estimated at a little over 1 million kwacha.

There is no likelihood that an objective assessment of the Kasungu scheme, and others of a similar nature, will be carried out and published in the present political climate in Malawi, but it seems that many people who are not otherwise disciples of the president have been favorably impressed by the success of the country's agricultural program.

In at least one respect the very success of tobacco cultivation has increased the potential vulnerability of the country's economy. In 1964 and 1965 tobacco accounted for 37 and 38 per cent, respectively, of the country's export earnings, but by 1972 and 1973 it accounted for 45 and 44 per cent, respectively. The country has indeed been more fortunate than many less developed countries because, although its export earnings have been derived almost entirely from a small number of cash crops, they were not crops for which world demand tended to move in concert. In the past, falling revenue from one product tended to be counterbalanced by high export earnings for others; but by the early 1970s the possibility of effective compensating movements was reduced.

9. *Legislative Assembly,* 17 April 1969, p. 249 and *Legislative Assembly,* 9 March 1971, p. 835. There are frequent exhortations to ministers, M.P.s and party leaders to follow his own example and set up "gardens"; see, for example, *Legislative Assembly,* 13 March 1973, p. 373, and 11 March 1975, pp. 616ff.

Table 8.10. Domestic exports, current prices (Kwacha thousand)

	Total	Tobacco	Tea	Groundnuts	Cotton	All other
1964	23,008	8,436	6,676	2,226	1,934	3,736
1965	27,084	10,260	7,536	3,278	2,158	3,852
1966	27,670	9,042	8,898	2,574	2,168	4,988
1967	33,104	8,452	8,982	6,868	1,384	7,418
1968	33,558	10,570	9,700	4,616	1,274	7,398
1969	36,588	12,646	9,526	5,590	1,730	7,096
1970	40,577	16,592	10,916	4,241	2,777	6,051
1971	49,577	22,062	11,905	5,883	2,547	7,176
1972	55,142	24,968	12,022	7,123	2,567	8,462
1973	68,802	30,259	13,721	5,922	1,951	16,948

Source: *Financial and Economic Review*, VI, no. 2 (1974), table 4.4.

Transport facilities have been improved, most notably by the construction of a railway link to the Mozambique line running to Nacala and by continued work on the lakshore highway, which will provide a more effective, albeit expensive, link between the relatively backward North and the richer Central and Southern Regions. The infrastructure has also been improved in other respects, although starting from a very low base: hydroelectric utilization has increased substantially, for example, and there has been gradual improvement in the supply of manpower with secondary and higher level education, but the local university is rather more like a junior college than a university on the British model, and few students are permitted to study abroad for fear that they become politically contaminated.

It may be unreasonable to expect any dramatic and funda- mental structural change in the space of ten years, and the strategy quite explicitly adopted in Malawi has been one of gradual change, at points where it can most readily be afforded and in ways which allow full advantage to be taken of the economy's traditional export products. The infrastructure is, in some respects at least, a good deal more favorable than it was at the time of independence, and there have been substantial in- creases in cash crop agriculture, but the broad pattern of the economy is otherwise very similar. It remains heavily depen- dent on foreign capital.

The rate of investment is high, and presumably will continue to be so unless there is a significant drop in the level of capital inflow.[10] In the short run the aggregate growth rate will probably be substantial, but it remains to be seen whether growth can be sustained in the long run, particularly once the bargain sector investments have been fully exploited. The economy remains highly vulnerable. If net capital inflow falls significantly, either because foreign investors find the country unattractive or because outflow for interest payments and the repayment of debts rise substantially, the country would not simply be faced with a lower rate of growth but might find it difficult to prevent deterioration in its standard of living.

The president has continually urged members of parliament to take advantage of government loan schemes and set up as modernizing farmers. "Every minister must have an estate," he told members and, commending the overdraft facilities provided by the nation's banks, he explained that "I am right up to my neck in debts, but I will pay the debt one day."[11]

There is no doubt that the president has amassed a fortune; he has extensive business interests, many of them controlled through Press Holdings, Ltd., a company initially set up to run the party newspaper and of which Dr. Banda holds almost all the shares, and his own estate management has been assisted by the acquisition of a number of estates formerly owned by Europeans. He has been thanked in Parliament for personally providing schools, dispensaries, and grocery stores for the benefit of families living on his estates,[12] but the very fact that his benevolence in this connection has been remarked upon is evi-

10. Gross Domestic Captial Formation as a proportion of Gross Domestic Production was 18 per cent in 1966, and in the years up to 1973 the annual percentage estimate was, respectively, 14, 17, 20, 22, 18, 19, and 19 per cent. *Sources:* 1964–1969, *Economic and Financial Review,* IV, 3 (1972), table 5.4; 1970–1973, *Financial and Economic Review,* VI, 2 (1974), table 5.4. The tables do not give the same figures for overlapping years—the 1974 publication gives a lower figure for 1969 and a higher one for 1970 than does the 1972 publication, for example—and other publications will provide other variants, so that any estimates of changes from one year to the next is subject to a large margin of error. The essential point, however, is the generally high level of capital formation, and all official sources are agreed upon this.

11. *Legislative Assembly,* 9 March 1971, p. 835.

12. See, for example, the speech of Chatsunda Banda, *Legislative Assembly,* 12 March 1975, p. 641.

dence of the continuing poverty of the mass of the people, obliged to rely on private charity for education, medical care, and the opportunity to purchase simple commercial goods.

The ease with which prominent party members are able to obtain loans from the government raises doubts about the extent to which schemes for the identification and support of master farmers or master fishermen can be divorced from considerations of patronage, but even if the people chosen for these schemes were selected entirely on merit as prospective farmers and managers, it would still be the case that a small number of people have received great benefits from the state while the great majority, who continue to use traditional methods, have gained very little, if any, direct benefit from these modernization programs.[13]

It had been anticipated that some 120 farmers would be settled under the Kasungu scheme by 1976, that the training period would last from six to seven years, and that total investment in the scheme by the end of the decade would be 1.2 million kwacha.[14] If the training program is successful, the candidates selected for the scheme will probably make much more money than the average farmer, and they will, at least in the early stages, have been heavily subsidized by the general public; in other words, there will have been a very considerable transfer of income from people with modest earnings to people who are relatively prosperous. Possibly, in the long run, the emergence of a well-to-do and efficient managerial and master-farmer class will raise productivity, improve the country's balance of payments, and provide secure and decently paid employment, but it is also possible that a handful of politically influential people with little farming or managerial skill will have done very well for themselves, without giving much in return.

In the ten years following independence there was a considerable increase in recorded wage employment and this may have led some people to feel that Malawi has, for the first time

13. From 1974 to 1975 there was a decrease in total marketed output of smallholders (*Reserve Bank of Malawi,* Annual Report 1975, p. 38).

14. *Legislative Assembly,* 19 July 1971, pp. 9ff., and *Statement of Development Policies 1971–1980,* office of the President and Cabinet Economic Planning Division (Zomba: Government Press, Dec. 1971), par. 2.2.6, p. 40.

Table 8.11. Recorded wage employment (in thousands)

1954	117
1958	146
1960	141
1964	114
1968	134
1970	159
1971	172
1973	215

Sources: The 1954–60 figures are based on those given in table 8 of the *Compendium of Statistics, 1966,* but were adjusted to bring them into line with later estimates by excluding domestic servants and reducing the remainder by 4.5 per cent; the 1964 and 1968 figures are from the *Quarterly Report on Earnings and Employment, March 1969;* the 1970 and 1971 figures are from *Economic and Financial Review,* IV, no. 3, unnumbered table on page 15; and the 1973 figure is from *Financial and Economic Review,* VI, no. 2, table III.9.

in the century, been approaching a situation in which there will be a shortage of labor.

The wage-earning base from which the upswing started was however, very low in relation to the total working population and appears to have been well below the level achieved at the end of the 1950s. The population of Malawi had been increasing by over 3 per cent during the late fifties and early sixties and the potential labor force was probably increasing during the 1960s by about the same rate. In order to have the same proportion of the labor force in wage or salaried employment in 1973 as there had been in 1958 (making the quite modest assumption that the government of the day's estimate of the 1958 figure was approximately right, and that the annual increase in the potential labor force was 3 per cent) it would be necessary to have an employment level of about 230,000 in 1973. Recorded employment in that year was 215,000. In view of the range of error in the estimates, no great significance should be attached to the fact that the recorded figure for 1973 was lower than the projection, but it is interesting that the recorded figure for 1973 is not very much higher than the projected figure.

It has always been quite clearly understood that there was a very large surplus of labor relative to domestic demand in 1958; the government's own figures indicate that the demand for wage labor has risen by approximately the same proportion as the rise in the labor force, and the problem of labor surplus is scarcely different in the mid-seventies from that in the late fifties. The number of self-employed farmers may have increased, but, as we have already seen, the government's agricultural policy has been more likely to increase productivity than participation rates. There may, indeed, be some respects in which the employment situation in Malawi has been worse in recent years than previously because opportunities to obtain work as migrant labor in Rhodesia and the Republic of South Africa have been severely curtailed.

The government's policy has been to hold wage levels as low as possible. This is, of course, very much to the private advantage of the president and those of his colleagues who have followed his advice to set themselves up in business, but respectable, if not uncontroversial, arguments have been presented to demonstrate the prospective benefits of such a policy to the national economy.

The policy, it is urged, will encourage investors, stimulate the growth of employment and, in the long run, provide the basis for a viable economy. The government has insisted that minimum wages in the urban areas should not be allowed to rise much above the general level of income in the rural areas; its spokesmen have claimed that both the intent and the effect of this policy have been to prevent the emergence of the kind of income gap between rural and urban areas which has characterized so many countries in Africa and which has been held responsible for the massive flow of rural dwellers into urban areas, with the consequent high level of urban unemployment. It also reduces pressure to raise wages in the rural areas.

Control of the wage level has not, as we have seen, led to a dramatic increase in the demand for labor, but if wages had been higher, the level of employment might have been lower; it is also possible that in the long run the encouragement presently given to employers will provide good employment prospects. In the short run, however, there have been few gains for the majority of the population either from rising wages or from greater opportunities for employment. During the same period a relatively small number of skilled workers and the few Malawians employed in supervisory and managerial positions have done very well out of the developments of the past fifteen years.

A highly skewed distribution of benefit, at least in the short run, has also been associated with the government's strategy of educational development. During colonial days opportunities for postprimary education were meager, but the country and particularly its Northern Region offered introductory primary classes to a much larger proportion of its young people than was being provided in many otherwise more developed countries in Africa, and migrant workers from Malawi, or Nyasaland as it was then called, acquired a reputation in central and southern Africa for literacy and numeracy. Since independence, a small and rather fragile university has been established (whose students and staff, in spite of a docility that would be remarkable in most countries of Africa, have frequently aroused the displeasure of Dr. Banda) and the number of relatively senior secondary students has increased substantially, but although wastage rates in the primary schools have been reduced, the numbers enrolled in the first few standards fell sharply in the first half of the sixties and, in spite of an upswing in the last few years, total enrollment in the primary schools was lower in absolute terms in 1970 than it had been in 1963.[15] The school-age population was increasing rapidly during this period—perhaps by more than 3 per cent a year—so

15. Total reported enrollment in primary schools fell from 367.3 thousand in 1963 to 286.1 thousand in 1966; it then began rising again but did not pass the 1963 figure until 1972, when the reported figure was 430.5 thousand; there was a rapid increase thereafter, with enrollment reaching 611.7 thousand in 1975. Failure to increase total enrollment in the 1960s in spite of greatly reduced wastage rates was due to the sharp fall in entry to the primary schools. Numbers enrolled in the lowest primary standard provide a guide to numbers entering the schools but, in the absence of consistent data on the proportions of students repeating a year, cannot be taken as an exact measure. The numbers enrolled in standard one (the lowest standard) began to fall in the 1950s, when it was decided to exclude new entrants who had already reached an age that made it unlikely, in the view of the authorities, that they would be able to pursue their studies effectively before entering the labor force. Enrollment in standard one was 113.9 thousand in 1956 and then fell steadily to 83.7 thousand in 1965; not until 1972 did first-year enrollment reach the level achieved until 1956. (See *Compendium of Statistics for Malawi, 1965,* table 21; *Malawi Statistical Year Book, 1972,* table 5.1; *Malawi Statistical Year Book, 1975,* table 5.8.) The reported figures make no allowance for "nonintegrated" schools, so it is likely that some part of any reported increase in enrollment is due to the transference of existing schools to the public sector rather than to the creation of completely new educational opportunities.

that the proportion of school-age children actually attending school may well have fallen by nearly 30 per cent during a decade in which access to education was greatly improved in almost every other country on the continent. There has been a big increase in enrollment during the 1970s, but a considerable part of that has simply made up ground lost since independence.

In one respect the government attempted to achieve greater equality of access to education, but this had a distinctly partial political objective. In part because of historical accident, the Northern Region, in many respects the least developed part of the country, accounted for a high proportion of the country's small stock of skilled manpower and throughout the sixties produced far more entrants to the university in relation to its population than any other part of the country did. The northern dominance among the educational elite had long been felt most keenly by Dr. Banda's own kinsmen, the numerically large Chewa, whose own educational achievements, with a few notable exceptions, had been much less impressive.

The government decided that Chichewa should be recognized as the principal language of the country and decreed that a paper in Chichewa be made a compulsory part of the primary-leaving examination. There are few people in the Northern Region for whom Chichewa is the first language, and this requirement should help reduce regional disparities in examination performance; students from the Central Region stand to benefit from the policy, but whether it is good for the country is another matter.

The president speaks eloquently of his enthusiasm for economic progress and may be sincere in doing so, but in his scheme of things, it takes second place to the requirements of political manipulation. The style and method of economic management adopted by the president have placed unchallengeable and, indeed, unexaminable powers of discretion in the hands of ministers, all of whom hold office at the whim of the president, and virtually no economic activity of any sort is safe from arbitrary and sometimes inexplicable intervention by the government.

The system provides almost limitless opportunities for corrupt practice. There is no means of finding out whether members of government take advantage of these opportunities, and never will be unless there is a change of regime, but even if all temptation is firmly resisted, the absence of critical discussion of ministerial intervention means that there is very little general understanding of the economic criteria underlying government decisions. Ministers may act on the basis of inaccurate, biased, or partial information, which the company or individual is unable to correct simply because it (or he/she) does not know what the charge is; companies and individuals are especially prone in these circumstances to opt for low-profit, short-term strategies rather than to seek out and develop long-term growth prospects, which are vulnerable to governmental intervention. Ministers have little opportunity to learn what businessmen and others feel are the problems that need to be tackled, precisely because no forum exists in which matters can be discussed in a reasonably objective manner—the businessman (or civil servants, for that matter) being so much at the mercy of ministerial caprice that the fear of giving offense strongly inhibits plain speaking.

The government has a direct interest in the profitability of one or more concerns in each of the major industrial and commerical groups, and it has the power, of which it unashamedly makes use, to manipulate the domestic market in their favor. It can, and does, insist that all government agencies give their business to these concerns even if normal commercial considerations would suggest some other choice; all private companies and individuals know that they are expected to do business with concerns favored by the government and that imprudent conduct may have grave consequences. The government has unfettered power to grant or revoke the license required for importing goods so that, without exercising any of its powers to put a company out of business by direct action, it can ensure that no company that requires imported goods is able to pose an effective competitive threat against any favored concern.

Whether or not, or to what extent, the government has protected relatively inefficient concerns against potential challenge from more dynamic organizations, is a question that cannot be answered on the basis of information presently available to the public. Indisputably, the government has armed itself with powers that can easily be abused, it has consistently refused to accept any restraint on its own capacity for arbitrary action, and it has never provided any evidence that these powers are needed to further the country's economic interests.

The president has insisted that the country cannot afford, and that he will not tolerate, the diversion of resources toward short-run welfare measures that do improve the productive capacity of the nation. He has not, however, taken so austere a view of all forms of government expenditure. The most expensive project undertaken since independence has been the building of the new capital at Lilongwe, at a cost equal to about one-third of the national income.

For several years, a multitude of apparently reputable economic consultants were invited to visit the country and listen to the arguments in favor of the new capital; they examined the proposed development and, without exception, pronounced it to be an unsound investment. The president then soundly denounced them for their pains, together with the universities or other institutions from which they came, and he sought another opinion—less, perhaps, from any need to have his personal judgment corroborated than from the necessity of convincing potential lenders that the project was worthwhile (a task easier to carry out if some supposedly impartial authority could be cited in support of the argument).

He had appealed in vain to the British government for the financial support needed in order to move his capital from Zomba, where the crowds had cheered Chipembere in 1964, to Lilongwe, where he would be close to his kinsmen and most faithful supporters. He was at last able to find endorsement for the project when there was a visit by consultants from the Republic of South Africa, where the government was anxious to win Dr. Banda's support for its diplomatic offensive in Africa and rightly judged that catering to the president's whims was likely to be more favorably appreciated than serious economic advice. An economic mission from the Republic strongly supported the president's line of reasoning and insisted that building a new capital at Lilongwe would provide a powerful stimulus to economic development in Malawi. Shortly afterward the government of the Republic made it known that it was prepared to advance a substantial loan for the project.

Dr. Banda has vividly described the effect upon him of the refusal by the British government to finance this scheme to which he was so greatly attached: "No one can appreciate to the full the anguish of mind from which I, personally, have suffered since 1964, when our decision to move the capital from Zomba to Lilongwe was painfully frustrated by the refusal to help us by those on whom I had depended most." Of the decision of the South African government to finance the first stage of this plan, he has said: "Nothing proves my point and vindicates me more prominently than the willingness of the Government of the Union of South Africa to respond to our appeal for financial assistance to carry out a decision to move the capital from here to Lilongwe." He went on to refer to "the Government of the Union of South Africa, in every sense of the word, a true friend in need, who is a friend indeed."[16]

When Dr. Banda put forward the project he knew that it "means millions of pounds, and of these millions, Mr. Speaker, Hon. Members, not a pound, not a shilling, not a penny do we have."[17] A loan negotiated on very favorable terms would have entailed repayment commitments running to substantially more than a full year's export earnings, but the president insisted that there was an overwhelming case on economic grounds for the new capital and that so-called experts from Oxford, Cambridge, Harvard, Yale, and several other distinguished institutions who had disputed the point did not know what they were talking about.

Apart from some distinctly esoteric reasons—"it means money to the workers of any country from which we import"—the president's argument in favor of the new capital rested heavily on two points: first, that it would be highly desirable to diversify the location of industry and to stimulate development in parts of the country lagging far behind the high employment areas of Blantyre and Cholo, and that this end could be achieved by siting the capital in the Central Region; and, second, that the stimulus to the construction trade consequent on the building of a new capital—anywhere—would provide a major boost to the level of employment.[18]

16. *Legislative Assembly*, 25 June 1968, pp. 463–466.
17. *Legislative Assembly*, 26 March 1968.
18. The quoted line is from *Legislative Assembly*, 28 March 1968, p. 439. Economic analysis was not one of the president's strong points, and it is difficult to find quotations that express with any cogency the economic rationale of the

In common with much else that the president has set out to do, a good deal can be said in favor of his proclaimed objectives. A greater geographical dispersion of economic activity and more widespread opportunities for employment might have stimulated economic development and would certainly have brought benefits to people who had previously had little share in the gains from economic growth. The ostensible objectives, however (and this was also in common with much else the president did), could have been served much better in other ways. Building a new capital at Lilongwe was not a sensible way of pursuing either objective.

Lilongwe was already one of the most prosperous parts of the country, being one of the principal centers of cash-crop farming, and was already one of the three largest towns in the country. If the objective was to stimulate relatively backward areas, Lilongwe was one of the worst spots in which to locate the capital, and was indeed a poorer choice than the capital at the time, Zomba, which was heavily dependent on its role as the center of government. The extent to which employment would be increased depended largely on the extent to which building the capital would represent net additions to economic activity rather than diversion from other construction projects or a transfer of resources from other economic activities into construction. The problem facing Malawi, however, was not a shortage of actual or potential projects, but the lack of resources to carry them out. Building the new capital was an expensive way of providing employment that could, if the complementary productive factors had been available, have been provided more effectively and more cheaply in a variety of other ways, ways that would also have had a more stimulating effect on the economy as a whole.

Apart from the provision of employment, the building of the capital was not expected to confer significant economic benefits on members of the local community. This fact was acknowledged (though not explicitly) by John Tembo when he told Parliament, on 26 June 1968, that he hoped that foreign businessmen involved in the building of the capital would leave

---

scheme; the argument presented in the second half of this paragraph reflects an attempt to make sense of a series of rambling statements.

the making of bricks to local people because "that is the only way in which they benefit from the construction of the capital, by making bricks."[19]

It has also been argued that Lilongwe was a suitable site—both because of its central geographical location and its generally flat surroundings—for a major international airport, providing a regular stopping point between Nairobi and Johannesburg, and that there would be considerable advantage in having the most important government offices linked by rapid access to an international airport. If the new capital were being offered to Malawi as a gift, benefits of this sort might well be counted to the country's advantage, but for a desperately poor country with a chronic shortage of foreign exchange, there is only a meager economic return to be gained by shifting government offices closer to the country's largest airport. There were rumors that the South African government would be able to use the new airport for military purposes, but these were denied by the government. Any arrangement of this sort would, of necessity, have been an informal one and, with the great change that has subsequently occurred in the politics of southern Africa, we may never have occasion to learn what, if any, arrangements were made for this purpose.

The readiness of the president to devote most substantial quantities of very scarce resources and to incur heavy foreign liabilities that exacerbate the already serious balance-of-payments problem, in order to pursue the political dream of building the national capital among his own Chewa people, cannot easily be reconciled with the view that the economic development of the country was his major priority.

South African investment in the capital nonetheless remains one of the principal economic benefits of the South African connection. Trade with the Republic of South Africa has increased greatly since independence, but although Malawi was importing much more from South Africa in the early seventies than it had in 1964 there was virtually no change in the proportion of Malawi's exports taken by South Africa. Malawi's problem is to increase its export earnings so that it becomes less

19. *Legislative Assembly*, 28 June 1968, p. 541.

Table 8.12. Imports from and exports to South Africa, 1964–1973

	Imports from South Africa as percentage of total imports	Exports to South Africa as percentage of total exports
1964	6	5
1965	5	4
1966	7	3
1967	8	3
1968	11	5
1969	14	3
1970	13	4
1971	11	5
1972	12	6
1973	18	5

Sources: Calculated from *Financial and Economic Review*, VI, no. 2 (1974), table 4.5 (Exports) and table 4.7 (Imports).

dependent on foreign capital to finance an import surplus, while imports, so far as possible, should be discouraged unless they are directly required for productive purposes.

In the early days of friendship with the South African government, the president had made much of the advantages that Malawian migrant workers in South Africa would derive from a more cordial relationship between the two countries. The best estimates indicate that in the early 1970s more Malawians were earning wages outside of Malawi than in it,[20] but it is not easy

20. According to the Malawi Population Census of 1966 there were 266,000 "independent" Malawians outside the country (p. x); the Provisional Census Report had suggested "not less than 225,000" Malawians in employment outside the country, accompanied by "perhaps" 20 per cent of that number of wives and children (p. 3). Table 21 of the census gives a figure of 226,000 Malawians earning wages or salaries within the country, a much higher figure than the estimate of recorded wage employment given in Table 8.11—114,000 in 1964 and 134,000 in 1968. The census figure of 226,000 includes all those who earned some income from employment during the year even though it may have been for parttime or temporary work; the estimate for those in employment outside the country does not distinguish between permanent, fulltime employment and parttime or intentionally temporary activities, but the very nature of the migrant's life—even where no contract is involved—makes it virtually certain that almost all of them are actively engaged in employment or seeking employment. It has always been difficult to interpret the government's annual statistics relating to migrant workers because they refer only to those who have complied with certain government regulations. The *Compendium of*

to tell how many of them were short-term migrants who expected to return home after two years or so and how many
hoped to stay away permanently. The Johannesburg mining area has been particularly attractive to many unskilled migrants because the work, although
hard and sometimes dangerous, is believed to be relatively well
paid. Recruiting for the mines was allowed in Malawi, with
permits being issued to a limited number of workers each year,
on the understanding that they return to Malawi after a two- or
three-year spell in the mines.

An agreement was reached between the governments of Malawi and South Africa that Malawian mine workers receive a
substantial part of their accumulated pay in Malawi instead of
receiving it in South Africa. This might have reduced the risk,
if that is the right word, of the miner's spending money on
frivolous pursuits in Johannesburg but would also have deprived him of the opportunity of buying useful goods there;
the government and the national economy, however, were clear
beneficiaries from the arrangement because the increased remittances provided a valuable source of foreign exchange.

Some people have taken the view that the existence of foreign outlets for migrant labor enabled the authorities in Malawi
to avoid facing up to what should have been their most urgent
task: making productive use of Malawi's one great natural resource, her abundant labor power. There is little doubt, however, that in the short-run restrictions on migrant labor could
have a serious adverse effect on the Malawi economy. The

Statistics for Malawi, 1965 table 13, gives a figure of 62,293 identity certificates
issued in 1965, but no clue is offered about the numbers working outside the
country in that year; of these identity certificates, 39,300 were issued to
workers in or going to South Africa. A later publication, *Malawi Statistical
Yearbook, 1975,* table 7.10, gives a figure of 43,800 Malawian workers under
contract in South Africa during 1965, of whom 41,600 had been "attested" by
the labor office of the Malawi government. The numbers going to South Africa
under contract rose sharply—from 35,600 in 1964 to 123,800 in 1972, with the
numbers attested rising from 34,100 to 76,200. Very large numbers of migrant
workers, with or without contracts, travel without benefit of government attes-
tation. It is not clear either how comprehensive a ban on migration is intended
by the government, or how effective any ban would be in halting migration for
work that could be carried on without the approval of the Malawi government.

reduction in remittances would increase dependence on foreign capital and, because many of the migrants come from the poorer rural areas with few alternative means of obtaining a similar cash income, there would be a fall in income in the poorest districts in the country.

It came as a great surprise to most people when, following an air disaster in which seventy-five Malawians returning from work in the mines lost their lives, Dr. Banda suspended all recruiting for the South African mines in 1974.

During the 1960s, Dr. Banda had used his speeches to Parliament as a means of instructing members on the main lines of argument they were to put to their constituents. By 1974, however, his speeches suggested that he had become obsessed with his recollections of the role he played during the struggle for independence, and matters he would earlier have expounded at length were left unremarked. Although suspension of migration was discussed at the party's annual convention, this discussion was less revealing than the president's parliamentary speeches would have been.

At first it seemed possible that Dr. Banda had decided that a tough line with the mining companies would enable him to negotiate a better deal for the miners, and consequently for Malawi. There would undoubtedly have been considerable risk attached to such a tactic because Malawian workers in the Republic of South Africa were, by 1974, responsible for a large part of the total value of earnings remitted by migrant workers to Malawi, and in that year the total value of remittances was almost one-third the value of Malawi's domestic exports.

Table 8.13. Earnings remitted to Malawi by migrant workers, 1964–1974 (Kw. million)

	1964	1966	1968	1970	1971	1972	1973	1974
Total	3.2	4.3	4.3	9.0	11.5	12.8	21.1	30.9
From S.A.	2.3	3.0	3.5	7.8	10.5	12.0	19.4	29.7

Source: *Malawi Statistical Yearbook 1975,* table 7.11.

There may have been reason to believe that mining companies in the Republic were susceptible to pressure from Dr. Banda because they believed that there were significant risks involved in heavy reliance on alternative sources of supply, such as Mozambique. The length of time which has passed without any resolution of the dispute makes this explanation seem unlikely. It has been suggested by some usually well-informed people that the president set out to reduce the flow of migrant workers so that more workers would be available to take part in Malawi's domestic agricultural development, but this is difficult to reconcile with the evidence about the labor supply in Malawi.

Not long after Dr. Banda took his decision, friction between the new government of Mozambique and the European government of Rhodesia made it very difficult for Malawians to pass through Mozambique in order to find work in Rhodesia. The government's own estimates of the numbers of people in employment suggest that the increase since the late 1950s was approximately equal to the increase in population; nothing indicates that domestic demand for labor is enough to absorb a substantial proportion of the migrant labor force, far less to absorb it in its entirety.

The reasons for Dr. Banda's suspension of South African labor recruitment in Malawi may remain a mystery, but whatever they are, the action demonstrates that the economic benefit derived from migrant labor has not been an important factor in determining the President's policy of detente with the Republic.

The rate of growth of real per capita income since independence in 1964 has been substantial. In the three or four years following 1964 the exceptionally high rate of growth was due, in part, to recovery from a politically induced economic depression, which reached its trough in 1964, but if one estimates the trend rate of growth since 1961 (which include three years of falling per capita real income and provides a base year in which there was relatively little excess capacity) the record is a most respectable one.

In judging the significance of this record, one should remember that the rate of growth in the fifteen years before 1961 was also considerable. There does not appear to be any great difference in this respect in the periods before and after 1961.

The data available, particularly for the early years, are often crude and subject to a wide margin of error, but no evidence leads one to believe that the trend estimates (as distinct from sectoral estimates for a given year) should be considered grossly unreliable. In the absence of such evidence, a fair inference from the data is that Malawi has enjoyed favorable economic circumstances more or less continuously since the end of World War II. Greatly improved facilities for foreign trade have affected an economy that was at a low level of development and that, as a consequence, had scarcely begun to tap its potential "bargain sectors" (simple manufacturing and unsophisticated cash-crop production). In spite of these favorable circumstances, however, steady improvement in national income was not inevitable, and the government and its supporters are entitled to claim that the record reflects some credit on the regime.

Throughout the period there has been a large inflow of foreign capital, whether as some form of assistance or as commercial investment, and this has both provided a large proportion of the country's investment and enabled it to run a large deficit on its balance of payment current account. Without it the country would be in serious economic difficulties and achieving a high rate of growth with the same policies as those that it has pursued would have been impossible.

Two critical questions can be asked about the government's reliance on foreign capital. The first is whether or not the benefits of foreign capital inflow will be sufficient to meet the payments that will eventually have to be made on it; the second is whether or not the pattern of trade and style of life made possible by foreign capital will lead to increasing dependence on the goodwill of wealthier countries even though Malawi itself becomes more prosperous. It is too early to answer either of these questions with confidence, but it is certain that the present strategy does involve costs that tend to be discounted by the president.

In general, economic strategy has been to improve productivity in activities with which Malawi has had long experience rather than to seek rapid structural change. In view of Malawi's lack of raw materials, small market size, and undeveloped economy, the options are not extensive, but there has been a comparatively wide range of choice in the instruments to be used in pursuit of the policy. The government has encouraged the emergence of an indigenous entrepreneurial class in the rural areas to act in concert with, though subordinate to, the state authority, which dominates all sectors of the economy.

This technique provides considerable scope for political manipulation but may also prove to be a relatively effective method of stimulating economic growth in the rural areas. One consequence of this policy, which may or may not have been intentional, is that a small number of farmers have done very well for themselves, whereas the majority of smallholders have not benefited, at least in the short run, to anything like the same extent, and some of them may be worse off as a consequence of the "master-farmer" strategy.

Other evidence suggests that the gains from growth have been unequally distributed and that many Malawians have derived little economic advantage from the efforts of the past decade. The increase in domestic employment has barely kept pace with the rate of population increase despite the government's determination to hold down the minimum wage level and the diminishing opportunities for migrant labor in Rhodesia and South Africa; there has been a great improvement in the standard of life of those Malawians who are now managers or skilled workers, but for the majority of workers, to say nothing of those who are regarded as politically suspect, conditions have not changed much. During the same period there has been a great improvement in the educational facilities available for the small proportion of students who progress beyond primary school, but the proportion of children who never attend any primary school at all is almost as large as it was twenty years ago; indeed, the official figures suggest that the proportion with no access to formal education in the mid 1970s was greater than it had been twenty years ago and included more than 50 per cent of the school-age population.

The attitude of the government (or, more precisely, the attitude of Dr. Banda) has been that economic growth is an important objective, other things being equal, but that some "other things" are much more important. The instruments developed for the ostensible purpose of guiding the economy toward stability and prosperity are better designed to supplement the vast coercive powers that ensure the president's political supremacy. The president may quite genuinely be offended by waste and inefficiency caused by incompetence and carelessness, but the efficient use of resources in pursuit of economic objectives takes a poor second place to the demands of political strategy.

The strictly economic benefits of detente with the Republic of South Africa have been limited, and one needs to look elsewhere to explain that aspect of Malawi's foreign policy.

CHAPTER 9

Foreign Policy: New Initiatives or Variations on an Old Theme?

Dr. Banda's principal concern during the struggle for independence had been, naturally and properly, with domestic issues, and when he had attended the All African People's Conference in Accra during December 1958, he had declined a seat on the steering committee on the grounds that his responsibilities in Nyasaland demanded his undivided attention.[1] During his days as a London doctor, however, he had been closely associated with men who were subsequently to play a dominating role in Pan-African politics, and he appears to have retained his affection and respect for Kwame Nkrumah, perhaps the most "charismatic" of all black African leaders associated with the dream of African unity, long after the two had come into sharp conflict over the conduct of the OAU. There was, indeed, little reason before independence to suppose that Dr. Banda would soon set upon a course of action toward the white-ruled states of southern Africa that would set him apart from almost every other leader in Independent Africa. He had dismissed with manifest contempt the proposition that the Central African Federation might be a viable political entity and he had savagely condemned any Nyasaland African prepared to cooperate with settler rule.

He was at one time interested in a union of Nyasaland, Northern Rhodesia, and several other territories, including what was then Tanganyika, and apparently including areas as

1. Philip Short, *Banda*, p. 102. Sir Roy Welensky's account of the conference says nothing of this but associates Dr. Banda with a conference resolution declaring support for militant nationalists or freedom fighters in all white-ruled states of Africa (*4000 Days*, pp. 99–100).

far away as Uganda. In 1960 Banda and Nyerere agreed to "consider how best our countries in East and Central Africa can forge ahead to greater unity and co-operation." Banda said, in Blantyre, that he looked forward to the time when Dar-es-Salaam would be the capital of the "United States of Central Africa," and he went on to say that he would be prepared to accept a subordinate position in the new state.[2] A few months later he joined Nyerere in calling for a boycott of South African goods.

The election program on which the MCP fought the 1951 elections promised support to African liberation movements, and most of Dr. Banda's principal lieutenants in the campaign were men and women who were committed advocates of the pan-African cause. Dr. Banda was undoubtedly aware that, in the short run, some form of accommodation with Portugal was necessary in order to preserve the rail link to Beira, but his subordinates believed that meant no more than an unfortunate and unavoidable departure from a vigorous policy of support for liberation movements. The party newspaper, the *Malawi News*, was writing as late as January 1962 that "force is the only language the Portuguese know and understand."[3]

By September 1964, however, when the Cabinet crisis reached its climax, Dr. Banda's relations were a good deal more cordial with the Portuguese than with most of his African neighbors. There were several reasons for his shifting alignment, but one can do little more than speculate about their relative importance.

Dr. Banda had discussed with the Cabinet the possibility of a rail link to Dar-es-Salaam; the link would provide a section running from central or southern Malawi to the Tanzania-Zambia railway, which was being built with Chinese help. An American transportation survey team reported to Dr. Banda that the prospect could not be justified on economic grounds. Since he was never a man to be overruled by "so-called experts," this report would not have deterred him unless he already believed that the project did not serve his interests. The

2. Short, pp. 176–177.
3. Short, p. 180.

consequence, whatever the reasons, was continued dependence on outlets to the sea through Mozambique.

There were rumors that he was irked by Nyerere, who did not treat him with the deference he felt was his due, and he was displeased with the favor shown to his subordinates who were treated with more respect in Pan-African circles than they were in his own Cabinet. He was not at ease in the OAU, and he resented the adulation evoked by men who had the facility to arouse enthusiasm at its meetings; these men were, for the most part, ardent protagonists of African unity and the apostles of armed liberation in southern Africa. Dr. Banda's personal dislike of them reinforced his conservative instincts, encouraging his skepticism about millenarian policies of any sort, and induced him to think again about his government's policy toward the white-ruled states of the south.

After the abortive revolt of his Cabinet ministers he found further cause for hostility toward Nyerere and Kaunda, since he feared that both of them, but especially Nyerere, were sustaining his enemies and allowing refugees from his country to establish training bases on their territory. The Portuguese and South Africans, on the other hand, found Dr. Banda much preferable to his domestic rivals and encouraged him to move closer toward some form of alliance between Malawi and Portugal.

In November 1965 the Malawi Parliament was told by John Tembo, one of the most powerful and articulate of the new ministers, that the African nationalist movement in Rhodesia was in complete disarray, divided on tribal grounds as well as by differences of opinion over tactics and increasingly bitter personal animosities. The Rhodesian nationalists would be obliged, said Tempo, to mend their differences and prove that they could operate effectively within Rhodesia itself, rather than in the refugee camps established by Zambia, before they could expect support from the government of Malawi.[4]

Dr. Banda was soon to carry the argument very much further. In January 1966 he expressed doubt as to whether Africans in Rhodesia would welcome the arrival in their homeland of armies from other African states, even if these armies had

4. *Legislative Assembly,* 9 Nov. 1965, p. 213.

been sent there in order to drive out the European rulers of the country;[5] he went on to question the intensity of the Rhodesian Africans' dissatisfaction with the status quo and later suggested that they might be actively opposed to attempts to change the political and social system along the lines envisaged by the guerrillas operating from Zambia. In April 1969 he told Parliament: "We Africans, North of the Zambesi, have no right to speak for all the Africans now under colonial rule. . . . What do we know what the Africans of Mozambique themselves want? What do we know what the Africans of Rhodesia themselves want?"[6] He went on to compare the nationalist guerrilla bands crossing into Rhodesia with supporters of the former ministers who had entered Malawi from bases in Tanzania or Zambia. His own enemies had failed, said the president, because the people of Malawi supported their government and immediately reported to the authorities whenever they heard that rebels were in the vicinity. Similarly, he said, Africans in Rhodesia were reporting the presence of infiltrators to the authorities because they had little sympathy for the strife-torn exiles.

His disenchantment with, or perhaps increasing cynicism about, Rhodesian nationalist leaders did not reflect any great optimism about what was to be expected from Europeans. One of the most persistent themes in his explanation of Malawi's foreign strategy was that European powers simply would not be prepared to send troops to Africa to throw out white rulers and replace them with genuinely independent black ones; the only outsiders who might be prepared to intervene would be those who intended to stake out their own claim to the area. Anyone who imagined that the Russians or Chinese, for example, would endure the risks involved in driving white rulers from Southern Africa and would then simply return to their homes, leaving Africans with genuine freedom to run their own affairs, "needs his head to be examined."[7] Dr. Banda's experience of the world had strengthened his conviction that self-

5. *Legislative Assembly,* 11 Jan. 1966, pp. 284ff.
6. *Legislative Assembly,* 23 April 1969, p. 376.
7. This has been a common theme in Dr. Banda's speeches; this particular formulation is to be found in *Legislative Assembly,* 27 July 1971, p. 208.

interest is rarely less influential than apparently high-minded aspirations about the achievement of a better world and that loyalties to kinsmen, or to members of some other effective community nurtured by tradition and shared experience, are far stronger than attachment to abstract moral principles.

He had long been familiar with the importance of racial and regional bonds in the Western world, and his close involvement in British political life during the struggle over federation had made him acutely aware of the facility with which sophisticated political leaders could stand commitments on their heads when it suited their purpose and of the alacrity with which they stood them up again when the balance of power shifted. He does not appear to have borne any personal grudge against the politicians who paid so little attention to African opinion during that period, perhaps because he had never had any very elevated expectations about the behavior of men whose primary concern was the manipulation of power. His experience had, however, also led him to believe that even the most formidable obstacles could be overcome if only one had sufficient ability, resolution, and patience, and he had no fear that he would be found wanting in any of these qualities.

Both his instinct and his experience led him to a strategic understanding of the situation in central Africa that differed markedly from the views propounded by most African leaders and virtually all of those Europeans who advocated a policy of confrontation with South Africa. He took a more somber view than was fashionable in the mid-sixties of the relative military power of the Republic of South Africa and that of the independent African states, and he was pessimistic about the prospects of finding effective, disinterested support from sources outside the continent.

He insisted that nationalist leaders aspiring to overthrow white rulers in southern Africa should be expected to establish an effective mass-based party within their own country, as had been done in Nyasaland during the 1950s, before earning the support of African leaders in other countries. In arguing his case he did scant justice to the great difficulties faced by nationalist leaders contending with a determined and ruthless settler regime, but he knew from experience that unless Africans could organize themselves effectively, there was little hope that sympathizers abroad would provide anything save good wishes. He believed that the power of racial solidarity was deeply rooted in human nature, and to illustrate the absurdity of the proposition that decisive and disinterested support would be forthcoming from Europe or Asia, he asked members of Malawi's Legislative Assembly to imagine a situation in which the United States was ruled by its Negro minority. Suppose, he said, that the white majority appealed to independent African governments to help them overthrow their black rulers: would African governments, in these circumstances, send troops to overthrow black rulers and put whites in their place? Replying to his own question, he answered, to the evident approval of members of the Assembly, that not only would they not do so, but the proposal would be laughed out of court.[8] Africans, however sympathetic they might be, would not be willing to have their own people killed for a cause that was no more pressing than many others much closer to home. Africans would not behave in that way, and nothing in his experience had led him to suppose that Europeans were any more likely to stifle their own instinctive and inbred racial sympathies. "Would you expect boys from Virginia, Mississippi, Alabama to go to South Africa and shoot other white men in order to put an African in power. . . . Then I lived for nothing in America. . . . Would a boy from Birmingham, Blackpool for that matter, even the East End of London?"[9]

Eastern bloc countries, especially the Chinese, would be only too pleased—in Dr. Banda's view—to involve themselves in African affairs and to stimulate bitter conflict between independent African states and the Europeans of southern Africa. They were aware of great potential strategic and economic benefits to be derived from gaining a foothold on the continent: great mineral wealth to be exploited, bases from which to threaten the trade routes of the Western countries, and, perhaps above all, the possibility of provoking a long and bitter racial war in which, at terrible cost and no benefit to Africans, the power and spirit of

8. *Legislative Assembly,* 9 Nov. 1965, p. 216.
9. *Legislative Assembly,* 16 Dec. 1966, pp. 65–66.

the Western alliance could be dissipated by a slow debilitating struggle. The East Europeans or Chinese would impose their own imperialist control over the area—a control that would prove a good deal worse than the European rule against which Africans in southern Africa were then contending.[10]

Africans, said Dr. Banda, must look to their own resources and they would find little comfort there for a policy of confrontation. An attempt to expel white South Africans would not be like "a game of football"; Europeans in South Africa did not have a "ceremonial army [but] a fighting army, a war machine, the most deadly and most destructive on our continent."[11] Their planes would be able to devastate Blantyre, Lusaka, and Dar-es-Salaam in a few hours of any open conflict, and no country would be permitted to offer sanctuary to guerrilla forces while itself enjoying the benefits of noncombatant status. Any African leader who allowed his territory to be used by forces attacking South Africa would be putting his own people in grave jeopardy. Africans should, he insisted, appreciate that they were dealing with formidable opponents who would behave ruthlessly in defense of their vital interests. Whether or not those interests would commend themselves to a debating society was of little importance; Africans should address themselves to the reality of the situation.

His enthusiasm for the policy of accommodation led him, however, to an endorsement of the Republic's leaders that went far beyond a recognition of the military power at their disposal. In December 1968 he told parliament that he welcomed an increase in the Republic's fighting capacity: "So South Africa is building her own planes, her own submarines, her own everything, even missiles. For myself, Good Luck. I have nothing against her because I know that South Africa threatens no one. Therefore, to me, very, very good luck, even more, more, more."[12]

Whatever the merits of Dr. Banda's views on the conse-

10. Frequent warnings of this sort can be found in Dr. Banda's speeches. See, for example, the reference to "Yellow Imperialism," *Legislative Assembly,* 11 Jan. 1967, p. 284.
11. *Legislative Assembly,* 16 Dec. 1966, p. 66.
12. *Legislative Assembly,* 19 Dec. 1968, p. 163.

quences of a massive racial war in southern Africa, his arguments are largely irrelevant to the policies favored by the more moderate protagonists of confrontation, who advocated sustained pressure in the form of economic and diplomatic boycott with support for liberation movements that would stop short of the level that would provoke military retaliation. Anyone in Malawi who held these views could not have presented them publicly because it was not permitted to question Dr. Banda's intepretation of events, but if Dr. Banda had been obliged to make a reasoned reply to the argument, it would presumably have been that any middle position was impracticable and that the political dynamics of so explosive a situation would have quickly forced a stark choice between accommodation and full-scale confrontation.

There were, in any event, more prosaic reasons influencing Dr. Banda's diplomatic strategy. He was much obligated to South Africa for that country's assistance in removing Malawi's seat of government from Zomba to Lilongwe. The new capital is situated in the heart of the Central Region, which has consistently provided strong political support for Dr. Banda and, until the South African government declared its willingness to provide a substantial loan so that construction work might begin, it had proved impossible to persuade foreign governments or international agencies that the project was economically feasible.

Other considerations may have had a significant bearing on Dr. Banda's assessment of strategic options. The most powerful of his domestic opponents was Henry Masauko Chipembere, a Yao from Fort Johnston. It was in Dr. Banda's interests to remind his people, particularly the Chewa from whom he came and among whom he had his strongest support, that the Yao had, less than a hundred years previously, been the instruments of the "Arab" slave trade, which had ravaged the Chewa and Manganja peoples. The reign of terror that had accompanied their activities had been a brutal reality during the lifetime of his own parents; his sense of antipathy toward its perpetrators may well have been real enough, and the conduct of the "Arabs" was a vivid part of the folk memory of the Malawi people.

In other circumstances the demands of national unity would

have made it more appropriate to emphasize the positive contributions made by the Yao to the development of the new
nation, but this would have dictated circumspection toward the
Arab connection. In his campaign against Chipembere, on the
other hand, it was to Dr. Banda's advantage to exploit, indeed
to inflame, the smoldering embers of resentment. To have
done so by openly castigating the Yao would have presented
too crude a threat to the fabric of national unity and Dr. Banda
found a more subtle strategem: to attack, again and again and
again, the behavior of contemporary Arab nations and to let
the connection with the Yao leader seep slowly into the collec-
tive and unconscious mind, gradually conditioning responses as
though by subliminal message. Dr. Banda had still other reasons for seeking to saddle at least some of the Arabs of North
Africa with the opprobrium of the slave trade. Among the most
prominent Arab leaders in the mid-1960s were the most articulate spokesmen of the policy of confrontation with the European rulers of southern Africa, and men who had been highly
sympathetic to the dissident Cabinet ministers. Their sympathy
reflected, to some extent, a belief that Chipembere and Chiume held views more closely similar to their own than did Dr.
Banda. The Malawi leader brought matters to a head when he
came to believe that some OAU leaders were actively encouraging his opponents within Malawi itself. As bitterness grew,
there were charges that embassy staff members were involved
with seditious or illegal groups inside Malawi and these led to
the breaking of diplomatic relations with both Egypt and
Ghana.

It was perhaps fortuitous that the situational logic of the
domestic power struggle encouraged Dr. Banda to associate the
"Arabs" of the slave trade with his Arab opponents in the OAU
and to identify both groups as the traditional enemies of black
Africans. Ingeniously, he was able to bring together the two
most controversial aspects of his foreign policy: cooperation
rather than confrontation with the European rulers of southern Africa and hostility toward, or at least suspicion of, the
Arab militants and their allies in the OAU.

If there ever had been a group of people, he said, whose past
behavior would appear to rule out any possibility of coopera-

tion with black Africans, it was the Arabs, but (he went on,
rather disingenuously, in view of his attitude toward them) it
had been possible to meet with them and to cooperate with
them at the OAU; if, after the atrocities they had committed in
the not far distant past, they could be treated as fellow Africans, then was it not also possible that in the fullness of time
the whites of southern Africa would come to terms with the
realities of the African situation and that it would then be possible for them to live down *their* past. (This argument might
have a good deal more emotional force in Malawi than in
southern Africa or, indeed, in much of the rest of the world
because experience in Malawi had been that, though European
rule may have been less benevolent and disinterested than its
protagonists claimed, it had been a good deal less brutal and
oppressive than the consequences of the slave trade it had
helped to suppress.) "if my grandfather got out of his grave
today and attended the O.A.U. meeting with me, I don't know
what he would say . . . I don't know what he would say . . . I
don't know what he would say, because, you see, he would find
me, his grandson, me, my grandfather's grandson, embracing
with Arab statesmen as brothers."[13]

Dr. Banda was to return to this theme time and time again.
Two years later he told Parliament: "I, the son and grandson of
Africans in this country who looked upon Arabs in those days
as their greatest enemy and the sons and grandsons of the
Arabs who looked upon my grandfather and father as beings
only fit for enslavement, now we embrace in the O.A.U."[14]

The Arabs *still* looked down upon black Africans, according
to Dr. Banda, and their belief in their own cultural superiority
was as deep rooted as, and in some ways even more unpleasant
and unacceptable than, the attitudes of Europeans in southern
Africa. He made the point on several occasions that Karume,
the late ruler of Zanzibar, was the descendant of a Malawian
family that had been carried away from Malawi as slaves. "The
Arabs" he said "call themselves civilised, they call themselves
superior to us, but they haven't got our code of ethics."[15] In the

13. *Legislative Assembly*, 11 Jan. 1966, pp. 65–66.
14. *Legislative Assembly*, 8 Oct. 1968.
15. *Legislative Assembly*, 30 June 1967, p. 534.

southern Sudan, Africans were being slaughtered during the 1960s because they had the temerity to challenge the supposed legitimacy of Arab rule; his colleagues in the OAU were indulging themselves, he said, in emotional paroxysms about the evils of alien white rule in southern Africa, but they were saying nothing at all about the far more brutal suppression of African aspirations in the Sudan, where, he insisted, tens of thousands of Africans had been slaughtered and no black African ruler apart from himself had made any protest about it.[16]

He was far from consistent in the use that he sought to make of this line of argument. At times the argument apparently served to demonstrate the inadequacy or malfunctioning of the OAU and the failure, through cowardice or hypocrisy, of black African leaders—apart from himself—to stand up to the Arab powers, but often it was used to illustrate his thesis that, in spite of the long and bitter history of racial strife in southern Africa, white South Africans might eventually play a constructive role in the broader African community.

The Arab defeat in the Six-Day War was received with well-orchestrated jubilation in the Malawi Parliament. For Dr. Banda, it served to emphasize the point he had been making for so long about the likely outcome of military conflict in southern Africa: what mattered was not the number of men involved or the volume of sympathetic speeches made at the United Nations but the military efficiency of the respective sides; the South Africans, he had consistently argued, would prove to be as efficient as the Israelis had shown themselves to be.

He was not a man much taken by the virtue of charity and he was not disposed to waste his sympathies regretting the humiliation of his enemies. Members of Parliament, whether because they really shared Dr. Banda's views or because they wished to demonstrate their loyalty to him, vied with each other in pouring scorn and abuse on Arab pretensions. Goliath was just another Arab, shouted one enthusiastic member, encompassing perhaps better than he realized the view that not only were the Arabs, for all their size, ineffective but that they were also on "the wrong side."[17]

16. See, for example, *Legislative Assembly,* 26 June 1968.
17. *Legislative Assembly,* 30 June 1967, p. 511.

The Arab countries were not the only members of the OAU about whose behavior Dr. Banda had severe reservations. Throughout most of the period between 1964 and 1970, relations between Malawi, on the one hand, and Zambia and Tanzania, on the other, were far from cordial. Both governments had allowed dissident Malawian exiles to establish camps in their countries, and it was believed that Malawian exiles either undertook training in these camps or went from them to undertake training in other countries and subsequently returned to them to provide the hard core of infiltrating guerrilla bands.

It was frequently alleged in the Legislative Assembly and in the party press that raiding parties were crossing into Malawi from the sanctuary of these countries, particularly from Tanzania. The most dramatic of these incursions took place in October 1967, when a group of men led by Yatuta Chisiza, who had been Dr. Banda's bodyguard during the struggle for independence, entered Malawi in an attempt to assassinate Dr. Banda. Chisiza was killed in action against Malawian troops because, or so it was widely rumored in Malawi, he had elected to forego escape himself to lead a rear-guard action that would enable at least some of his followers to make good their retreat. Many people who knew him thought the decision typical of the man. Dr. Banda announced that the dead body of Chisiza would be on public display in Blantyre for three days, so that all should know the fate that beckoned those who sought to overthrow him. Before the first day was over, he had reversed his decision, and rumor had it that he had begun to fear that the steady stream of people filing past the dead body were expressing their respect for a brave man rather than derision for a defeated enemy.

Shortly after learning that Chisiza had crossed the border, the president made a nation-wide broadcast expressing his confidence that Chisiza's forces would be destroyed, and his speech left no doubt that, although he anticipated no difficulties in dealing with the present incursion, he would be able to call on allies should he be faced with a more serious threat. "We are not without friends," said Dr. Banda, and these friends either in Europe or in Africa had lost no time in offering their assistance to the government of Malawi.[18] If some people imagined that rebel forces might stand a chance against the Malawian army and security forces, they were reminded that the much more powerful forces commanded by the Europeans of southern Africa were ready to enter the fray. The most formidable army of the continent stood behind Dr. Banda: the policy of accommodation was proving, whatever its other effects, to be a valuable piece of domestic political insurance.

The radicals of the OAU had been attempting to assert their influence in the United Nations and induce that body either to introduce sanctions against South Africa or to order the use of force for the occupation of South West Africa, which was being held in apparent defiance of UN authority; this course of action, said Dr. Banda, had proved ineffective. "The politics and diplomacy of bluff and bluster have failed," he said, and he intended to pursue the only other policy that could avert catastrophe in southern and central Africa; he would show by example that it was possible to "bridge the wall of fear and ignorance" and bring about genuine cooperation among the races living on the continent.[19] The most useful contribution that independent African governments could make to the cause of African advancement in Rhodesia was to demonstrate by example that independent African states could provide stable, efficient, and honest administration.[20]

To support his argument and the extravagant embellishments on it made by his supporters ("What the people in South Africa need today," said John Tembo," is Jesus. . . . Kamuzu, that is the person they need there"),[21] it became necessary to

18. Toward the end of his broadcast to the nation insisting that "Chisiza and his gangsters must not and will not escape," Dr. Banda assured—perhaps "warned" would be a more appropriate term—his listeners: "Already I am receiving messages from some of our friends, asking if I need any help. They are offering us any help, to crush the gangsters. . . . I wanted you my people to know this that, in our fight against the gangsters or terrorists from Tanganyika [sic] or Zambia or anywhere else, we are not without friends" (Nation-wide Broadcast, 9 Oct. 1967; full text produced as Special Supplement to *Malawi News*).

19. *Legislative Assembly*, 29 March 1967.
20. *Legislative Assembly*, 11 Jan. 1967.
21. *Legislative Assembly*, 31 March 1967, p. 349.

insist not merely that things *might* get better in South Africa and Mozambique when the rulers there realized that at least some African leaders, such as Dr. Banda, were capable and moderate men, but that significant improvements were already taking place, thanks to the influence of Dr. Banda.

Aleke Banda, following a visit to South Africa in 1967, made the bizarre claim that many Malawians there were in "top jobs," but he did not explain what he meant, and members of the Assembly knew better than to ask questions.[22] In April 1969, Dr. Banda told Parliament: "The Portuguese in Mozambique have changed their policy towards their own Africans. You do not hear any more harsh treatment of *mbalamototya* and all that, no more of that. Not only that. Even their methods of administration are becoming much more liberal than they used to be. And this is all due to Malawi's policy and Malawi's attitude towards the white man in Mozambique, in South Africa and Rhodesia."[23]

Even so acquiescent a group as the Malawi Parliament must have been a little shaken by this statement. If conditions were improving so rapidly, it was difficult to understand why so few people knew about any improvement, but in July of the following year Dr. Banda supplied at least a part of his answer to the question that was never publicly asked: "Newspapermen are not reporting [the good things that are taking place] because the majority of newspapermen in South Africa are against the government."[24]

In 1971, Dr. Banda was invited by the South African government to pay an official visit to the republic. This invitation was, not surprisingly, presented to the Malawi Parliament as a major triumph both for himself and for his strategy. He had insisted that one of the most pressing reasons whites in southern Africa feared black rule was because they did not understand that black leaders could behave in a civilized and responsible manner. It was, he had said repeatedly, one of the principal tasks of the Malawi government to show them that African rulers could

22. *Legislative Assembly,* 30 March 1967, p. 315.
23. *Legislative Assembly,* 23 April 1969, p. 376.
24. *Legislative Assembly,* 28 July 1970, p. 506.

conduct themselves with dignity, restraint, and intelligence; that, while they were entirely able to bargain hard for their rights, they were fundamentally reasonable men; and that they were formidable enemies but generous friends. How better to demonstrate to the largest possible number of white South Africans these very qualities than by traveling and speaking in South Africa as an official guest of the government?

Of equal importance, Dr. Banda and his entourage not only would be mixing socially with the most prestigious members of the white communities but would be living in hotels and eating in restaurants previously reserved for Europeans; let a single black man in, and let the rule be changed from "no blacks" to (for example) "no blacks unless invited by the government," and the issue would henceforth be changed from one of principle or faith to one of expedience. It would then become a matter about which serious bargaining could take place. Gradually, according to this view, the numbers of exceptions to the rule would increase until the attempt to preserve the distinctions would be abandoned, not on principle, but because their retention was no longer practicable.

Dr. Banda would, moreover, by his presence and his action bring hope and inspiration to the blacks in South Africa; they would see a black leader being treated with all the respect due the head of a sovereign state; he, himself, would be able to speak to them and assure them that, with patience, fortitude, and good sense, their cause would ultimately triumph as had that of the black people in Malawi.

Whether or not these motives weighed as heavily with Dr. Banda as he claimed is not perhaps important, and, even were he moved by more narrow considerations of political self-interest, the course of action he proclaimed may still have been the best option available to the black population of southern Africa. The critical questions about Dr. Banda's visit, to which we are not yet in a position to provide conclusive answers, are whether or not the benefits to black South Africans claimed by Dr. Banda are likely to be achieved and whether or not the visit would diminish whatever bargaining power African leaders in South Africa might otherwise have had. Dr. Banda's supporters frequently claim that he has made a notable contribution to the

cause of the African, and not merely the Malawian, in southern
Africa, whereas many of his detractors insist that he has betrayed the African population of southern Africa and has become a willing instrument of racist domination.
Critics of the visit believed that it endowed the South African
government (and system) with a false sense of respectability, in
the eyes of Western liberal opinion, and that it furnished Western powers with an excuse for continuing inactivity they might
otherwise have found difficult to explain to their own electorate. Most of these governments would have been reluctant, in
any event, to put effective pressure on the South African government because of the strategic and economic interests involved, but liberal opinion might have forced them to take
some action. This possibility was diminished by Dr. Banda's
visit. Many people in Britain and elsewhere who were concerned about both moral and practical aspects of *apartheid,* but
whose interests in the matter were peripheral and whose
knowledge was slight, would be inclined to feel that if the
leader of a sovereign African state, whose interest in and
knowledge of the situation was greater than their own, could be
on such cordial terms with the South African government, then
the question was more complex than they had supposed.
A premise of Dr. Banda's argument is that the majority of
whites in South Africa are fundamentally reasonable men and
women whose concern about the consequences of sharing, even
to a very limited extent, political power with Africans has
rested on a misguided but understandable belief that African
leaders are incapable of intelligent, perceptive, and responsible
behavior. This is not the way in which most African leaders see
the situation; even those who think that a peaceful solution
may be possible in South Africa tend to feel that the principal
requirement for change in the policies of white settlers is a shift
in bargaining power which will make a more reasonable attitude essential for survival. Even if one were to accept as accurate Dr. Banda's assessment of the problem, it would be optimistic to suppose that the misunderstanding could be put to
rights by the example of Dr. Banda and his ministers. South
Africa's own black population has produced leaders whose distinction and moderation appeared clear to the rest of the

world, and it is not easy to discern in what respect Dr. Banda and his colleagues would succeed where Dr. Luthuli and others had failed.

If South Africa's rulers were apparently more receptive to the posture taken by the Malawi ministers, it might have been because they felt that Dr. Banda and his colleagues were primarily concerned with relatively trivial matters of protocol and were not seriously interested in bringing about any significant change in the substance of race relations within the Republic of South Africa. No matter how "responsible," "reasonable," or "civilized" the local African leaders might have been, the majority of the white population were aware that any major change in the pattern of race relations in South Africa would have as its inevitable consequence a substantial loss of economic and social power by the white population. The high standard of living of South African whites is due in no small measure to white control, not only of capital but of land, and to white monopoly in the labor market. Many titles to land and property were obtained as a direct result of the historical pattern of racial domination, and it is unlikely that even the most moderate of African governments would be prepared to tolerate inequities so closely related to the history of white supremacy.

The president received a tumultuous welcome when he visited African townships, and he spoke with characteristic bluntness about the inequities of *apartheid*. He was reported to have addressed whites and blacks alike in a manner that befitted a leader who is as good a man as his hosts and he was everywhere visibly treated with courtesy and respect. He later told the Malawi Parliament "If God chose to take me away tomorrow, I would go perfectly satisfied. . . . [I] had made black and white rub shoulders with each other, push without resentment, without feeling that they were black or white."[25]

If he really did manage what he claimed, it was a formidable achievement, but evidence does not suggest that the experience, if it occurred at all, has had lasting effect on white attitudes. The potential costs of direct confrontation between the

25. *Legislative Assembly,* 7 Dec. 1971, p. 243. The following day Phiri, the nominated member for Nkhata Bay, said of the president's visit: "he was sent there by God" (p. 263).

Republic of South Africa and its neighbors are now much more widely recognized, by virtually all sides, than was the case seven or eight years ago, but although the government of the Republic has shown increasing sensitivity in its dealings with independent African countries, there has been little tangible benefit to the African population of the Republic.

At the very time that the president was consolidating diplomatic links between Malawi and the Republic of South Africa, rumors began to be heard that the relationship with Portugal was subject to increasingly severe strain. A significant change in the balance of power in Mozambique during the early 1970s made unequivocal support of the Portuguese government a less attractive proposition than it had been in the previous decade. During the 1960s two important political considerations had favored a close alliance with the Portuguese and the adoption of a correspondingly cool attitude toward the Frelimo, the militant national movement whose guerrilla forces were operating mainly in the north of Mozambique during the 1960s. These have been discussed in a slightly different context, but it may be useful to recall them briefly in order to bring the shifting balance of advantage in Mozambique into proper perspective.

A real threat to Dr. Banda had been posed by exiled followers of Chipembere who were believed to be undergoing systematic military training; there had been a good deal of sympathy for Chipembere within Malawi, and an invasion or sustained guerrilla campaign might have stretched the military resources of an unsupported Malawian government beyond its capacity to maintain effective control. The rebels were more closely identified with "liberation" movements than was Dr. Banda, even at the beginning of his rule, and he could expect no help from the neighboring African governments. The Portuguese, on the other hand, had a large army on the borders of Malawi and troops could have been put at Dr. Banda's disposal, ready for action, within a few hours notice; many of the troops were, of course, black, and no obvious foreign military presence would have been noticeable to the casual observer (and no other kind of observer would have been tolerated). Apart from this domestic political consideration Dr. Banda was anxious to maintain and develop his rail transport link to the sea at Beira, which was then well removed from the areas of guerrilla activity, and the road link to Rhodesia which ran through the Mozambique province of Tete, which to all appearances was securely held by the Portuguese authorities during the 1960s. Three developments profoundly affected Dr. Banda's strategic assessment of the Portuguese alliance at the beginning of the new decade. Perhaps the most important one was the unintended consequence of a Portuguese initiative designed to strengthen the links between Dr. Banda and the Portuguese administration in Mozambique. A new rail link had been built from Malawi to the more northerly port of Nacala, which provided a quicker and cheaper route to the sea than did the link to Beira, but it ran through an area in which, by the turn of the decade, the Frelimo guerillas were operating much more effectively than they had been able to do along the Beira line. For the first time, the Frelimo High Command were in a position to threaten the flow of Malawian traffic to and from the coast, and Frelimo goodwill began to acquire an economic and strategic significance. At the same time, the construction of the Cabora Bassa dam on the Zambezi River had become the focal point of development plans in Mozambique, and Frelimo had announced their determination to prevent work on the project under Portuguese auspices. The Blantyre-Salisbury road traversed the area around the dam which became one of the principal centers of guerrilla activity. Meanwhile, the threat of effective Malawian opposition to Dr. Banda had been severely diminished, in part because of the ever-increasing powers Dr. Banda had arrogated to himself within the country and partly because the exiled Cabinet ministers and their supporters had lost momentum—they had been unable to exert any effective power in Malawi and had been further weakened by bitter quarrels among themselves.

Early in 1973 the president vigorously denied that any new understanding had been reached with Frelimo, but in May 1973 the Rhodesian broadcasting system reported that fierce fighting was taking place between Malawian and Portuguese forces and that aircraft were being used on both sides. The report indicated that Malawi, which had previously cooperated with the Portuguese by denying sanctuary to Frelimo guerrilla

bands, had allowed guerrillas to seek refuge across the Malawian border and had resisted Portuguese attempts to pursue
them across the border.

In a major parliamentary speech, Dr. Banda referred to
these reports as malicious and inaccurate rumors.[26] As soon as
he had learned of the broadcast, he said, he had called the
commissioner of police. He was told that Jafoo, the secretary to
the president in the Cabinet and the most senior civil servant,
was already at police headquarters, as was Major Matewere, the
commander of the army. These men had met, said Dr. Banda,
as soon as they had heard the news to find out the truth, and
they assured him that the reports were completely without
foundation. (He did not explain why the men who were supposed to be in supreme command of the army and police units
rumored to have been involved in the fighting deemed it nec-
esssary to hold a midnight vigil at police headquarters to assure
themselves that nothing was happening.)

The rumors, he said, had been started by Malawian journalists (or, as Dr. Banda described them, "so-called journalists")
who, although working for the party press, the Ministry of
Information, or the Malawi Broadcasting Corporation, were in
league with enemies of the countries and pandering to sensa-
tion-hungry foreign journalists who had managed to slip into
the country by bribing government officials.

These Malawian journalists, Parliament was told, were also
responsible for other fabrications. They had claimed that the
Malawian people were not happy with the government, that the
economy was not as prosperous as the government claimed,
that members of the National Executive of the party were not
loyal to the president, and, indeed, that two members of the
Cabinet were actively plotting against Dr. Banda.

The president has tended in his later years to digress in his
speeches from the point at issue, but his occasional obscurities
have often turned out to have been astutely judged. On this
occasion, he covered himself carefully when he dealt with the
rumors about the alleged fighting. The borders, he quite
rightly said, are not always clearly demarcated, and one may

26. *Legislative Assembly,* 10 July 1973, pp. 798ff.

easily cross the border unknowingly. It would be surprising if, with the best will on both sides, Portuguese or Malawian troops would not occasionally find themselves on the wrong side of the border. Dr. Banda's statement, though true, begged the question. He did not provide a comprehensive denial that border violations, however inadvertent, had led to serious fighting on any occasion; instead he stressed that there had been no untoward incidents on a specific day: *"On that particular day,* Mr. Speaker, Sir, there was not a single incident of border violation either on our part into Mozambique or on the part of the Portuguese into Malawi"[27] (italics added).

Following this incident, the government tightened the sanctions on foreign journalists, sent a number of Malawians into detention, and introduced legislation that gave the President the power, in law as well as in practice, to impose life imprisonment on anyone passing what the president decreed to be "false information" to foreigners.

The official explanation of this border affair is neither credible nor consistent with the hysteria aroused by those who had publicized it. Whether or not the particular incidents actually occurred, it seems likely that a change in policy was taking place and that the president did not yet want the matter to be public knowledge. He had recognized the shifting realities of power and was seeking accommodation with the Frelimo leadership— at least to the extent of no longer actively opposing all border crossings, and he may have been offering some more positive cooperation—while being careful not to alienate the Portuguese, who were by no means clear losers in Mozambique at the time; the Portuguese for their part might have been willing to accept some modest and discrete arrangement between Dr. Banda and Frelimo as a tactical necessity which did not jeopardize their common interest with the president, but they might well have regarded an open breach, with the inevitable public denunciation, as something less easily forgiven.

The situation was dramatically and irreversibly changed following the coup in Lisbon in April 1974. Ten days after the coup, while the future of the African colonies was provoking a

27. Ibid., p. 805.

considerable amount of dispute in Portugal, Dr. Banda held a press conference at which he "welcomed the change because it could only be for the better."[28] He subsequently claimed that, through his contacts among influential Portuguese officials and businessmen, he was able to bring pressure to bear on the government in Lisbon which made it more disposed to countenance major change in Mozambique. His most influential friend had, he said, once been a reactionary opposed to African independence, but thanks to Dr. Banda's example, he now favored genuine independence. On July 24, Dr. Banda called on the Portuguese to recognize that Mozambique should be an independent state with a government elected by majority rule and that they should immediately begin negotiations with nationalist leaders to arrange the orderly transfer of power.[29]

It is unlikely that Dr. Banda was pleased to find power in Mozambique rapidly transferred to a militant left-wing nationalist regime. He could have no expectations of influential support from the new Mozambique government if his domestic enemies were able to develop effective strength. Frelimo forces no longer wanted bases in his country; he had no resources that could be used as bargaining pawns, and there was no credit to be gained for Frelimo in Africa's corridors of power by maintaining the rule of a cantankerous old man who had gone out of his way to insult most of Africa's presidents. Under the circumstances, Dr. Banda could hope for little more than a policy of benign indifference, and he had done his best to ensure that if, in the event of trouble in Malawi, the government of Mozambique would not intervene on his behalf, it would not intervene on behalf of his enemies.

The unforeseen withdrawal of Portuguese power from both Mozambique and Angola and the consequent emergence of potentially powerful radical regimes in both countries were also to have a profound effect on Dr. Banda's position as the leading protagonist of accommodation in southern Africa. The South African diplomatic strategy had already begun to interest some African heads of state who, if they did not have the

28. *Legislative Assembly*, 29 Oct. 1974, p. 18.
29. Ibid., p. 19.

Malawian president's interest in seeking a South African alliance to buttress their own regimes, were deeply concerned about the wide-ranging consequences of a bitter racial war on the continent and were profoundly skeptical about the good faith of foreign powers that would in these circumstances offer their services to the cause of African nationalism. The opportunities apparently offered by the new regimes for the establishment of effective East European, and possibly Chinese, bridgeheads in southern and central Africa highlighted the critical issues facing both the leaders of the Republic of South Africa and those African leaders, such as President Kaunda of Zambia, who had been much more critical than Dr. Banda of white-settler regimes, but who believed that African interests were best served by some more or less peaceful resolution of the problem.

Far from having established a claim to a leading role in diplomatic negotiations because he had been the forerunner of a strategy of accommodation, Dr. Banda was to find that his cordial diplomatic relations with the Republic were to leave him on the sidelines in the more important discussions of the mid-seventies. If, as he had earlier had every reason to suppose would be the circumstance, the Republic had continued to have a virtual monopoly of military power, and if he had continued to be the only African leader receptive to the Republic's overtures, he would very probably have enjoyed considerable support from the Republic. Political calculation does not, however, depend on services performed in the past but on an estimate of services available in the present or in the future—and few leaders in Africa have understood so clearly the Machiavellian calculus as has Dr. Banda. In the quite different circumstances occasioned by the new power base in Mozambique and Angola, the African leaders whose support, or at least acceptance, was most important to the government of the republic were those who presented—either in their own right or because of those to whom they were allied—a serious threat or those who might be expected to have some influence with hitherto uncommitted African leaders. Dr. Banda was beaten on both counts: Malawi is still a desperately poor country with no strategically critical resources and, as events turned out, the president was already so closely identified with the strategy of accommodation that his support had become inconsequential.

Epilogue

The 1970s have not dealt kindly with Dr. Banda's reputation for foresight. The most distinctive feature of Malawi's policy in the five years following independence was its pursuit of detente with the Republic of South Africa and with other states in southern Africa still ruled by European minorities, a policy that reflected Dr. Banda's judgment—or so he was wont to insist—that the military power of these states would continue, for the foreseeable future, to be the dominant influence in the southern part of the continent.

It is still too early to discount the fighting capacity of the Republic, but the transformation of former Portuguese territories to radical and at least potentially powerful independent states has produced a fundamental change in the balance of power and an accompanying realignment of policy options. When the Republic was seen to be bargaining from a position of strength, it needed only to provide evidence that it could deal on amicable terms with independent, black-ruled states; the weaker they were, the more impressive the evidence of Boer magnaminity. It is no longer sufficient for the Republic to engage in dialogue; the Republic now needs the support, or at least the acquiescence, of states that carry weight with their African neighbors.

The possibility of confrontation between more equally matched forces than had seemed possible in the 1960s may have induced a lively awareness among the prospective combatants of the virtues of negotiation, but such negotiation would be on terms very different from those envisaged by Dr. Banda. The impetus would come, not from a growing understanding of the essential desirability of cooperation, but from mutual

fear of the alternative. In these circumstances Malawi has little
to offer. She is too weak to be a redoubtable foe or formidable
ally, and the role of go-between for which she might have been
qualified as a consequence of that very weakness is not open,
precisely because of Dr. Banda's earlier overtures to the Republic and his repeatedly expressed scorn for the OAU.

That Dr. Banda appears, in the course of events, to have
backed a loser should not lead one to conclude that his judgment was any worse than that of his rivals. His calculations
went astray because of events that neither he nor his critics had
anticipated. Few protagonists of confrontation had expected
during the 1960s that revolution was imminent in Portugal,
and no more than a handful would have contemplated the
possibility that Cuban troops would play a decisive role in the
ensuing Angolan civil war

Surprised as he may have been at the turn of events, Dr.
Banda might still have felt that his South African strategy had
already given him a good return. It offered him domestic protection at a time when he might otherwise have been vulnerable
to a shrewd blow from his opponents, and although he was not,
as it happened, obliged to call upon his ally for assistance, the
knowledge that he could do so may have proved a powerful
deterrent to all except the most deeply committed of those who
wanted to see him overthrown. By the time that it had become
either impossible or impracticable to call upon Portuguese or
South African military help, the president had developed so
tight a control upon the economy, politics, and society of Malawi that he had little to fear save his own physical decline and
the rather slender possibility of a palace revolution.

Dr. Banda's successor, whoever he might be, should not find
it too difficult to disassociate himself from Dr. Banda's policy
toward South Africa. Even should he have offered it his enthusiastic support in the past, everyone will know that the exigencies of life in Malawi make it more than usually expedient for
the president's subordinates to temper principle with pragmatism. The country does not have the economic resources or
military potential to stimulate an appetite for continental
leadership or to rouse fear among its neighbors, but an astute
successor to Dr. Banda may have an opportunity to play the

role of diplomatic broker on the continent, particularly if—as seems not at all unlikely—the anticipated end of white rule in Rhodesia is followed by a sharpening of differences among the groups and countries presently allied against the Ian Smith regime.

Bitterness between the president and the supporters of the former Cabinet ministers has not diminished with the passing of time, but it is possible that Dr. Banda's successor will seek some form of reconciliation with the former ministers, or at least with their followers, acknowledging what many people in the country feel—that this is a rift which is better bridged. Controversy over matters of policy has long since been subordinate to personal animosity, and with the departure from the scene of the president and perhaps one or two other members of the MCP, it may be possible to arrive at an understanding that would remove, or at least diminish, one potent source of domestic conflict. An understanding of this nature might also ease the new government's task in improving relations with its African neighbors.

Ending an old quarrel may, however, prove easier than preventing the emergence of new ones. A small but prosperous and potentially articulate entrepreneurial class has been fostered by government patronage. Its members, whether or not they prove to be efficient businessmen, will scarcely be willing to relinquish their privileges; there will be no shortage of rivals for government favor, and there will be others who disapprove of both incumbents and contenders, casting doubt upon the wisdom and propriety of devoting so large a proportion of development funds to programs that directly benefit so small a proportion of the population. If the new government maintains present policy and practice, it will give offense to unsuccessful candidates for privilege who are convinced that their claim is every bit as good as that of those who succeed, it will risk the resentment of the less articulate majority who find themselves excluded from government patronage and may provide a rallying ground for ideological opposition; if it changes the system, it will risk the loss of economic benefits associated with the system and may provoke bitter hostility among those who are presently enjoying government patronage.

The growth of urban areas and the development of modern manufacturing are likely to be accompanied by pressure to raise industrial wages and to devote a larger proportion of infrastructure expenditure to the urban areas. Meanwhile, the living standards of the majority of small farmers are unlikely to rise substantially, even if there is a move toward more broadly based rural development schemes. Many of the poorest rural areas will suffer, at least in the short run, from the diminution of opportunities for temporary migration to Rhodesia and the Republic of South Africa, and from mounting pressure on the land resources required to provide adequate subsistence by traditional methods.

Malawi's very backwardness has, thus far, protected her from the problem of urban drift, which has been so marked a feature in more prosperous states of Africa, with migrants pouring into towns and cities in search of higher wages and producing dangerously high levels of unemployment. It is possible that the combination of urban growth, surplus labor, and shortage of land could prove to be a catalyst for dynamic change—both demanding radical improvement in productivity and providing the incentives to bring it forth—but it is more likely to be the cause of a heavy and unrewarding drain on the country's precariously limited resources.

The most critical, and as yet unanswerable, question about the future of the Malawian economy is whether or not it will continue to be largely dependent on a continual net inflow of foreign capital. It may prove necessary to put much more severe constraints on the consumption of the relatively well-to-do in order both to raise the level of investment provided from domestic sources and to reduce the deficit on the balance of payments current account. If this is so, the government will have to choose between a sharp fall in the rate of economic growth and the risk of severe disaffection among some of its closest supporters.

The economic record, if not as spectacular as Dr. Banda would have us believe, has been a creditable one, but the next twenty years will most likely prove to be more testing. The country has been shielded from many of the more difficult problems of choosing among rather disagreeable alternatives;

protected by a combination of its own poverty and the availability of credit, it has been passing through an age of economic
innocence, in which there has been adequate land for agricultural expansion, availability of "bargain sector" industrial investment, ample foreign credit, and few effective domestic
pressure groups. If the country's present efforts to achieve economic development meet with some success, as seems probable,
its leaders may learn rather painfully that a widening range of
options brings greater danger as well as greater opportunity.

It would be optimistic to expect a new government to relinquish voluntarily any significant part of the domestic powers
acquired and developed by Dr. Banda. Men and women with
an appetite for power are not easily persuaded that the public
interest is best served by limiting their functions, and there will
be sufficient geniune points of contention in the country to
provide not entirely implausible support for the belief that free
debate would degenerate into anarchy. There may be some
period of relaxation, while present feuds are settled and before
others rise to the surface, but in the longer run the expectation
must be for strong rather than open government.

It is not impossible that economic and political circumstance
will improve significantly during the next twenty years; Malawians are subtle and adaptable people with a prodigious capacity,
at their best, for hard work, self-discipline, and endurance. But
the odds against such an outcome are formidable.

Bibliographical Essay

The most valuable single work on the history of Malawi is still *Independent African: John Chilembwe and the Origins, Setting and Significance of the Nyasaland Native Rising of 1915* by George Shepperson and Thomas Price (Edinburgh: The University Press, 1958). The authors set out to examine the causes and consequences of the Chilembwe Rising in 1915, but in setting these events in their proper context the authors develop a rich and subtle portrayal of the economic, social, and political characteristics of the far-from-uniform colonial society in Nyasaland and of the ways in which Africans sought to come to terms with the changing environment. *Independent African* can be re-read with profit and pleasure as one learns more about its subject. One may disagree with many of the authors' judgments without losing one's appreciation of the authors' instinct for asking important questions or the skill with which they marshall their evidence.

Shepperson's continuing contribution to the study of Malawi's history is reflected not only by the profusion of articles he has produced but in the stimulus he has given to graduate students working with him at the University of Edinburgh. Among a number of very useful doctoral theses, that of Andrew Ross, "The Origins and Development of the Church of Scotland Mission, Blantyre, Nyasaland, 1875–1926" (Ph.D. 1968), is especially worthy of note. The mission's leaders included some remarkable men, and Ross has a keen eye for the delineation of character and situation; he has an interesting story to tell, and he tells it well, but the element that raises Ross's work well above the usual history, to say nothing of the usual Ph.D. thesis, is his capacity to find the kernel of great themes in seemingly trivial events, ambitions, jealousies, and aspirations.

H. W. Macmillan's University of Edinburgh thesis (Ph.D. 1970), "The Origins and Development of the African Lakes Company, 1878–1908," tells us a great deal about Nyasaland in the period preceding colonial rule as well as about the affairs of the company. Roger Tangri's thesis (Ph.D. 1970), "The Development of Modern African Politics and the Emergence of a Nationalist Movement in Colonial Malawi, 1891–1958," provides us with a wide-ranging and judicious survey of organized African political and social movements, of protest or adaptation, during the colonial period.

A good general introduction to the history of Malawi is to be found in Bridglal Pachai, *Malawi: The History of the Nation* (London: Longman, 1973). Its value lies in the information it presents rather than in any sustained attempt at analysis and, although it takes the story through the period of independence, it is weak on events since the mid-1950s. Griff Jones's *Britain and Nyasaland* (London: George Allen and Unwin, 1964) is an interesting, rather idiosyncratic, commentary on the country's history by a former colonial administrator, seeking to balance concern for justice with the need to maintain an inevitably arbitrary authority.

Pachai, who has been professor of history at the University of Malawi, has edited a very interesting collection of essays, *The Early History of Malawi* (London: Longman, 1972), which includes contributions from several of the most notable chroniclers of the pre-colonial and early period: Schoffeleers, Alpers, Vail, and Channock.

Other important collections are Eric Stokes and Richard Brown, eds., *The Zambesian Past* (Manchester: Manchester University Press, 1966)—especially the chapter by J. K. Rennie—and the Proceedings of a Conference at the University of Malawi in 1968, edited by Pachai, Smith, and Tangri, *Malawi, Past and Present*—especially the chapter by Langworthy and Omer Cooper.

The complexity and ambiguity of missionary attitudes and of the African response to them are illuminated by the life of David Livingstone and the experience of the missions most directly inspired by his experience. Tim Jeal's *Livingstone* (New York: Dell, 1973) provides a lively account, which clearly brings out the many-sided nature of the man—the harshness and disingenuousness of which he was capable, as well as the nobility of his vision, his courage and endurance—and illustrates the heterogenous and often conflicting motives of those who supported him. George Martelli's briefer and earlier book, *Livingstone's River: The Story of the Zambezi Expedition* (London: Chatto and Windus, 1970), had dealt perceptively with the less sympathetic aspects of Livingstone's character, and the detailed *David Livingstone: His Life and Letters* (London: Lutterworth Press, 1957) by George Seaver, while putting much greater emphasis on the more admirable features of Livingstone's behavior, did not seek to disguise the fact that he was often a difficult man to deal with.

The experience of the Church of Scotland Mission at Blantyre is best described in the thesis by Andrew Ross, which has already been described; the aspirations and impact of the Free Church Mission at Livingstonia have been studied by K. J. McCracken: his most accessible works include papers in W. Montgomery Watt, ed., *Religion in Africa* (Centre of African Studies, University of Edinburgh, 1964), and in Terence O. Ranger, *Aspects of Central African History* (London: Heinemann, 1968). A less analytical but more wide-ranging, and often perceptive, discussion of early mission history in Nyasaland—and a good deal else besides—can be found in Michael Gelfand, *Lakeside Pioneers,* (Oxford: Basil Blackwell, 1966).

The *Society of Malawi Journal* contains a wide variety of articles, some of which are important contributions to the study of the nation's history—as, for example, Ian Linden's paper "Some Oral Traditions from the Maseko Ngoni" in the issue of July 1971.

The fortunes of the export economy have been relatively easy to chronicle and, in the early days of the colonial period, exports probably accounted for a large part of all increases in the country's output. Information about the rest of the country was, however, sparse. One has to rely on impressionistic accounts about the effects of migration, the gradual development of cash-crop production for the local market, the expansion and improvement of local markets, and the varying fortunes of different economic, social, and tribal groups.

The annual *Colonial Report for Nyasaland* (London: H.M.S.O.) contains a great deal of information about the performance and problems of European producers and traders in Nyasaland, about colonial government revenue and expenditure, and about exports and imports. For the early period there is a very useful compilation of statistics provided in S. S. Murray, *A Handbook of Nyasaland* (London: Crown Agents for the Colony, 1922). One important consequence of colonial economic policy was the flow of migrant workers from Nyasaland to Rhodesia and South Africa. B. S. Krishnamurty, who takes a view very different from that of the Nyasaland authorities, has written well on this subject. See, for example, his paper "Economic Policy: Land and Labour" in Pachai, ed., *Malawi*. The equally important history of the complex and contentious issue of land tenure in colonial Nyasaland is reviewed clearly in the *Land Commission Report, 1946* (Zomba: Government of Nyasaland) to the governor of Nyasaland by S. S. Abrahams.

Phyllis Deane's pioneering classic on the estimation and interpretation of national income data, *Colonial Social Accounting* (Cambridge: Cambridge University Press, 1953), provides an interesting impressionistic account of economic conditions just before and just after World War II, although one cannot relate her estimates of national income to those later calculated, on a quite different basis, by the Central Statistical Office in Salisbury. Much useful information is given in A. G. Irvine's *The Balance of Payments of Rhodesia and Nyasaland 1945–1954* (London: Oxford University Press, 1959), although it is, in some respects, a less ambitious undertaking than that of Deane.

William J. Barber's *The Economy of British Central Africa: A Case Study of Economic Development in a Dualistic Society* (London: Oxford University Press, 1961) is about Rhodesia, but contains some information about the Nyasaland economy. Arthur Hazlewood and P. D. Henderson, in *Nyasaland, the Economics of Federation* (Oxford: Basil Blackwell, 1960), demolish most of the economic arguments that were so frequently asserted to establish the case for federation, but they agree that Nyasaland gained some (small) benefit from the arrangements. Hazlewood returns to the subject in "The Economics of Federation and Dissolution in Central Africa," which appears in A. Hazlewood, ed., *African Intergration and Disintegration* (London: Oxford University Press, 1967). A different view was taken by the authors of the *Report on an Economic Survey of Nyasaland, 1958–1959* ("The Jack Report") (Salisbury, Southern Rhodesia: Government Printer, 1959).

A considerable amount of information about the economy has been provided in the postindependence period but it tends, not surprisingly, to be concerned with the conventional categories of national income analysis and doesn't tell us much about the distribution of income and expenditure among social or economic groups. There have, moreover, been a number of changes in the method and practice of estimating the value of important economic variables so that great care has to be exercised in comparing the figures given in one year with those given in another.

The most useful summaries of data for the sixties are given in the annual *Compendium of Statistics for Malawi,* (Zomba: Government Printer), which was followed by the *Statistical Yearbook* (Zomba: Government Printer), the annual *Economic Report* (Zomba: Government Printer), and the publications of the Reserve Bank of Malawi—the quarterly *Financial and Economic Review* and the *Annual Report*. More detailed figures on specific issues are given in publications such as the annual report on *Earnings and Employment,* the annual report on *Balance of Payments,* and *The Annual Statement of External Trade.* There was a population census in 1966, and both the provisional and final reports make interesting reading.

There are two very good books on the political economy of Dr. Banda's presidency: Philip Short, *Banda* (London: Routledge & Kegan Paul, 1974), and Carolyn McMaster, *Malawi Foreign Policy and Development* (London: Julian Friedmann Publishers, 1974).

Philip Short's book is a well-written and informative life of the president, a sympathetic but far from uncritical account. The author is, I feel, rather inclined to take Dr. Banda's own explanation of events at face value, in spite of evidence that Dr. Banda is given to revising his interpretation of what has taken place to meet changing circumstances. Compared with my own estimate of Dr. Banda's character, Short's Banda is rather more benevolent, considerably less intelligent, and much more prone to inexplicable behavior. Short does not, however, seek to force his views on the reader or tailor his account to fit any preconceived pattern; the reader is given a great deal of information and should be able to make up his own mind on these issues.

Carolyn McMaster offers a perceptive account of the main features of Malawian policy since independence. Her conclusion (though hedged with qualifications) is a more conventional one than the probing analysis of some of the earlier chapters had led one to expect, but the principal value of the book is in the skillful way in which the author has brought together and presented much of the relevant evidence.

In 1975, M. W. Kanyama Chiume presented his account of Dr. Banda's return and the eventual split between the prime minister (as he then was) in *Kwacha: An Autobiography* (Nairobi: East African Publishing House). The questions most intelligent people will want to ask about these events and, in particular, about Chiume's role in them, will not be answered by this book, but some fresh questions may be raised. Chiume denies that Banda ever had great popular personal support and portrays him as an inept and corrupt megalomaniac; the book doesn't help us understand why, if that was true, Dr. Banda so completely dominated the Cabinet, nor why Chiume himself could not, or would not, develop an argument along these lines during the September debate. The paradox of Chiume's book is that, in the attempt to ruin Dr. Banda's reputation as a leader, he presents an account of events which becomes comprehensible only if one believes that Dr. Banda was a man of the most formidable force of character.

Index